KU-239-821

WHITHER SCOTLAND?

WHITHER SCOTLAND?

*A prejudiced look
at the future of a nation*

Edited by Duncan Glen

LONDON
VICTOR GOLLANCZ LTD
1971

© Duncan Glen 1971
© Andrew Hargrave 1971
© Michael Grieve 1971
© T. R. Bone 1971
© Norman Buchan 1971
© Esmond Wright 1971
© John Herdman 1971
© Anthony Ross 1971
© Derick S. Thomson 1971
© George Mackay Brown 1971
© David Murison 1971
© Alexander Scott 1971
© Cordelia Oliver 1971
© Hugh MacDiarmid 1971

ISBN 0 575 01323 0

MADE AND PRINTED IN GREAT BRITAIN BY
THE GARDEN CITY PRESS LIMITED
LETCHWORTH, HERTFORDSHIRE
SG6 1JS

CONTENTS

FOREWORD

ALL THE ESSAYS in this book have been specially written for it. With the Conservatives returned to power at the general election of 1970 and Mr Heath leading a newish government which may take the United Kingdom and Northern Ireland into Europe, this would seem a particularly appropriate time for the voices of Scotsmen to be heard discussing the future of their country.

In a very real sense this is a book without a "policy" or a common viewpoint. I myself belong to no political party and indeed a recent reviewer of my latest book of poems suggested I might be apolitical. I doubt if an apolitical person would have wished to edit this book, but equally strongly do I doubt if a person committed to one party—Conservative, Labour, Liberal, Scottish Nationalist or Communist—would have given the book the collectively independent position which I believe it to have. The contributors are variously present as political spokesmen and as specialists, although some of them obviously belong in both categories. Biographical notes on each of them appear on pages 253-256. They disagree over many matters but where, perhaps, they would agree is in believing that Scotland (whether as independent nation or as region of the United Kingdom) needs a revival and a renewal, whether economic or cultural or political or all three. One of the essentials of this revived Scotland, I believe, will be a non-conformity which is the very antithesis of much of present-day, safety-first Scotland. There is a need for a great outpouring of ideas from many different intellectual stances to give new purpose to the nation and to resist the challenge of stand-still secular and religious authoritarian forces. These will be the twins of suppressive conformity —secular as well as religious bigotry—whose challenge will almost certainly be made whatever the political future of Scotland.

I have edited this book and written my contribution to it

with the hope that its publication will be another step towards such an intellectually open outlook and that the variety of opinion—the disagreements—revealed in it will be seen as a sign of growing or improving intellectual and cultural health. The contributors, as I have said, do not represent any one point of view and, indeed, were in some cases selected in the hope that they would give varying insights into where Scotland may perhaps be going. I hope that the debate will continue with passion as well as with intellection and that the insights of poets will be thought to be as important as those of politicians, academics or economists—perhaps even more important!

DUNCAN GLEN

JANUARY 1971

NATION OR REGION?

Duncan Glen

In this introductory essay I shall attempt briefly to give something of the historical background necessary to an understanding of the problems facing Scotland as we move into the last quarter of the twentieth century, but having asked the question "Whither Scotland?" I shall also attempt to give my own answer to this question which is asked as a continuation of the debate which has been proceeding since at least the end of the 1914-18 war, although no doubt some would see it as proceeding from the Union of the Scottish and English parliaments in 1707—if not from the Union of Crowns in 1603. Perhaps through lacking the full status of an independent nation, we Scots are over-fond of looking back, but such have been the traumatic experiences suffered by Scotland the nation that I have no doubt that ignorance of this past would make it very difficult to understand the many contorted positions of today.

Aggressively patriotic Scots have been known to claim Scotland as the oldest surviving nation in Christendom; other Scots have suggested that the idea of Scotland as a nation belongs to the past and that Scotland is now simply a region of the United Kingdom. A hundred years ago the second statement might have sounded plausible, with Scotland often referred to as North Britain; today, with a hundred years of increasing national consciousness, the idea of Scotland as North Britain no longer exists and Scotland is obviously, in the Scots consciousness of a separate national identity, less of a region of England than it was in the eighteenth and nineteenth centuries. In the wider context of true independent nationhood Scotland, of course, is still ruled from London by the English. There will be protests at that statement but it is strictly accurate in that all final decisions relating to Scotland are made by the Westminster parliament which is controlled by English votes and, indeed, by English ideas. The idea of a selective employment tax is not an idea that could have originated, whatever its merits or demerits for England, in Scotland. As Professor H. J. Hanham, an independent New Zealander, said in his excellent book *Scottish Nationalism*: "Both the selective employment tax and the Transport Act, 1968, drawn up with English conditions in mind, have had to be adapted for Scottish purposes painfully and inadequately."[1] No doubt the Conservative government elected in 1970 could play party politics with these examples but, whatever party is in power at Westminster, it remains true that the basic thinking is done with English conditions in mind and adjustments are then sometimes made for Scotland. For good government of Scotland, the thinking should obviously start from conditions in Scotland.

Today the country does not govern itself through an independent parliament but a case can be made for the independence of the three institutions of Church, Education and Law. For hundreds of years the Church of Scotland has been a powerful influence on Scottish thinking and the Scottish way of life; it could be said to have moulded the modern Scottish character, but its influence is most definitely in decline and in recent years the evidence of the decline of Scottish presbyterianism, with its emphasis on the logic and law of Calvinism and on an apparently democratic—but in local practice authoritarian—church government is to be seen not only in dwindling membership but also in the fact that talks have taken place on the possibility of union with the Church of England. That does not look like a realisable union but the talks alone would have been unthinkable when the Church was a real and vigorous cultural power in the land. What does remain, however, as one of the few occasions of the Scottish year is the meeting of the General Assembly of the Church in Edinburgh each spring. The General Assembly remains, with the Scottish Trades Union Congress almost the only other, one of the few forums for semi-national debate, although, obviously, it (like the Congress) is too short-lived and too narrowly based to be of truly national importance. Its importance reflects, indeed, on the lack of a national forum.

The Scottish legal system is well protected not only by the Act of Union, which has often been disregarded by new Westminster Acts, but by the pride and independence of the Scots lawyers. It could be argued that the Edinburgh lawyers are the only truly culturally confident group of Scots in Scotland. They are involved in an activity the centre of which can still be regarded as being in Edinburgh despite the general tendency of the Westminster government to think English first, last and almost all the time. They have, since the Union, claimed direct political involvement as well as a legal one, and were a very powerful political force in Scottish life at least until this century. The English governments have looked to the Edinburgh lawyers for advice and ideas. Most other Scottish activities have lost this sense of final Scottish involvement in decision-making although, of course, the lawyers have never had the full reality of *final* power.

The educational system in Scotland is something of a national pride-piece. I cannot say show-piece since that would suggest approval of a system which I personally believe to be only beginning to drag itself into the second half of the twentieth century out of a drill type of learning and absorption of facts, rather than an education of the mind to think and to appreciate life and art. Nevertheless it is a distinctive and administratively independent institution, although when we turn to look at the Scottishness of the actual syllabuses we find that it is only now beginning to reflect the revival of Scottishness which this century has seen. The neglect of Scottish literature and Scottish history (from a Scottish standpoint) is a real pointer to the two hundred years of neglect and betrayal of Scottish standards that followed the Union of 1707.

We have two languages distinct from English—Gaelic which is spoken in the Highlands and Western Islands, and Lowlands Scots or Lallans spoken, naturally enough, in the Lowlands—and a speech related to English but not a dialect of it as some assume. Scots is, however, being anglicised and the speakers of Gaelic are a declining minority although this century has seen a remarkable revival of writing in Gaelic, as in Scots, with Sorley Maclean an undoubtedly major poet in Gaelic and Hugh MacDiarmid of equal stature in Scots. For centuries, however, English has been the language of education throughout the whole country and its position in Scotland has been similar to that which it held in the old English Empire—an imperialistic language. The difference between Scotland and, say, Nigeria was that in Scotland English was imposed by Scots (anglicised Scots albeit) on Scots and by Scots who believed that it was for the good of the nation. English is now well-established as the socially superior language of Scotland although few Scots educated in Scotland can in fact achieve in speech a pure English-English vocabulary, far less an English pronunciation.

I have already hinted at what I regard as a conservatism in Scottish education and personally I would put this down to the need for a vocational training from the earliest days of schooling. The keystone of this bias towards "training" even in the primary schools is the instant need to teach the socially acceptable English and so eradicate Lowland Scots which has been seen (and largely continues to be seen) as a handicap to advancement, not only in England but also in the Scottish education system and in Scottish business and commerce. The Scottish Department of Education now acknowledges the revival of the national consciousness and the Scottish literary renaissance which has put Scots back into use as a language of major poetry by advocating the retention of Scots forms within the English language; but snobbery is not easily overcome and many of the teachers still regard the Scots language as a barbarism and many of the older ones are, thanks to an anglicised Scottish education, illiterate in Scots literature apart from parts of Burns, Walter Scott and a few ballads. But changes are taking place and the last seventy years have seen a new status given to Scots and to Gaelic in the schools and universities. The literary renaissance has also led to the study of Scottish literature in foreign universities, particularly in the United States and Canada, and this can only help to give the culturally insecure Scots an increased confidence in their native Scottish traditions—which brings me to the great tragedy of Scotland : the selling out of Scottishness by the Scots.

No doubt there will be loud protests from Scots and surprised gasps from the English at the idea of the Scots selling out their Scottishness, but despite a pride in the non-essentials of Scottishness—such as the success of individual Scots in London or abroad, or in the success of a football team such as Glasgow Celtic—there can be no denying the evidence of history that the Scots have, as a nation, sold Scotland to a superior, richer power—to England. I do not here think particularly of the Act of Union, although that was pushed through by a few self-interested leaders against the wishes of the Scottish people. It was a Union bought with English gold and with the promise, or thought, of gold and power to come. Both have come richly, it should be said, to many Scots who have taken the famous high road to London and who have accepted the

English culture. It is this selling-out of Scotland the nation by abandoning it for self-interest that I primarily refer to.

But Scotland has also been sold out by those who remain in Scotland who have tended also to serve not the idea of Scotland but rather the idea of England. They would no doubt deny this but how else can the anglicisation of Scotland by Scots be otherwise seen than as an implementation, in Scotland, of the idea of England. This Idea of England I personally admire very much, as I admire an Idea of Scotland, but when the Idea of England is imposed (whether imposed from within or externally) then it becomes Imperialism and a destructive force. It creates a second-class people and so prevents the full development of these people and of their way of life—of their national culture. And it is a virile culture which gives life and purpose to a people; life and purpose are what Scotland has long lacked and continues to lack despite the stirrings of a new demand for a new life for the nation. For at least 270 years Scotland's leaders have attempted to give the country that life and purpose through an absorption of the English way of life, by the acceptance and the encouragement of anglicisation. With England a great and rich power this would seem a practical or sensible or eye-on-the-main-chance plan of action, but with Scotland always lagging behind England and the rest of Europe, materially, socially, and almost always culturally, I would have thought that this facile waiting upon England had been proved to be a disastrous and senseless policy for the majority of Scots, whatever it may have done for the anglicised ruling minority. But this waiting upon England still seems to be taken by the masses of the Scottish people as inevitable; they see the good material things of life gradually being given to the English people and then—more slowly—being passed on to themselves. Of course the ambitious today, as in the past, will not be content to live twenty years, or ten years for that matter, behind the English (or thirty behind the Americans) and they will be off across the border or across the Atlantic leaving Scotland to rot and further decline into a tenth-rate nation—or a second-rate region of England.

Of course, as I have said, the Scots still proudly call themselves Scots and, indeed, retain their individual Scottishness, but it has to be recognised that this is a provincial pride and a provincial culture and, until the emergence of the modern Scottish literary renaissance, the world knew nothing of modern Scotland. And as a political or economic power, the Germans or French or others are obviously interested in England and not in Scotland as a potential partner in Europe. By working through England for their so-called successes the Scots have, as any European will say when speaking honestly, turned themselves into a northern region of England, economically and politically less important than the Midlands far less the South of England. That is a realistic truth and yet the potential of the Scottish people is surely an asset that could make a vital contribution to Europe. As yet it remains an unrealised and dormant European asset and its worth has to be proved. Indeed, its very existence has to be proved. But of course these are not truths most Scots are willing to accept and so gradually we have had the rise of Scottish nationalism, both as a result of misgovernment or lack of government from Whitehall and as part of the nationalist movement which is sweeping the globe and so giving a new richness to the cultures of the world. The ignorant often fail to distinguish between nationalism—which is an essential for internationalism—and imperialism, which may arise from nationalism (as in Germany or Italy; or France or England or Russia or America for that matter) but which is a destructive force in that personal freedom of development is denied to the overruled people. This is what has happened to the Scots even if they have acquiesced in their own loss of national cultural independence.

One of the tragedies for Scotland the nation, although it may be a compliment to the essential and moral pride which has remained in the Scottish people, has been the failure of the Scots to appreciate that they are, finally, a suppressed people, and so they have never felt hatred for their English overlords, to whose Imperial Empire they have belonged even if they were given a superior or "trusty" position in that Empire and were even able to assume such positions in England itself. Of course, the Scots may know deep down that they have been politically absorbed into the English Empire and they may be simply protecting their pride by not admitting it. And yet I feel that there is a genuine simple innocent pride in the Scots' refusal to allow themselves to hate the English : we are as good as them and are voluntary—even if junior and dominated—partners. Without this feeling the Scots would, like the Irish, have fought for their independence with cold steel and guns rather than with poetry and intellectual debate although, of course, the Irish waged both the violent and the cultural battle.

Still, Fyfe Robertson would seem to be expressing a truth when recently he wrote in *Punch* : "If independence can't come peacefully it will never come violently. You could say we are too cautious. But you could say, more truly, that we're too civilised."[2]

Certainly a less generous part of this "civilisation" is a belief by the Scots that they could (and can) use the Union to their own personal advantage and even to the advantage of Scotland. But even the personal successes, achieved through an acceptance of English ways, can with hindsight be seen as being a failure of potential. J. M. Barrie, or Harry Lauder the music-hall star, may have thought they were highly successful in making rich careers for themselves by giving the English (innocents, of course, in the mythology of the shrewd Scot) what they wanted from Scotsmen, but in corrupting his own culture and in playing the wild Celt Barrie most certainly also destroyed himself as a potentially great dramatist. There are countless examples of this in Anglo-Scottish literature, but what about Ramsay MacDonald, the only true Scot to become a Prime Minister? Did he not just sell himself to London and then to the English aristocratic Establishment? And the so-called Clydeside Red rebels—did they not finally individually sell themselves short by playing the wild Scot who was in fact firmly caged by the soft iron glove of the English Establishment? Kirkwood, with his peerage, obviously fell for this and even Maxton was pacified and made into a tame rebel from wild and romantic Scotland. They were not, finally, taken seriously by the English who would, and did, give short shrift to Northern working-class rebels. Scotland, and the Scots, are largely a fantasy world to the Southern English Establishment, indeed to Englishmen generally and, sadly, the Scots have done much to make this fantasy real. They have become great imitators and compromisers. This is the tragedy of the second-rate Scot.

If the Union of 1707 was pushed through against popular opposition from the masses of Scots, the instigators of the Union had their eyes firmly fixed on the golden advantages of joining England, the rich trading nation, and after the Union was a reality the ruling classes generally were not slow to realise on which side of the border their bread could be buttered—and jammed. The Scots began (or continued) their long tradition of showing short-term practical—and economic—common sense. The Scottish rulers began (as they have continued) to sacrifice their Scottishness, and their fellow-Scots in Scotland, who have suffered from living in a country which has now suffered from hundreds of years of both ruling-class-drain and brain-drain, to achieve personal power, influence and wealth alongside the English ruling classes who, with the Union, were now also the true rulers of Scotland though they used Scots as advisers and front men. Not that they had any more interest in Scotland than today's Russians have in Czechoslovakia except as a safe frontier, or as part of an Empire, although the Scots have been very privileged members of that English Empire since they were allowed in on the Empire success game (who could stop such aggressive wolves?) and allowed to achieve positions of power and spacious rooms at the top in almost all departments at home and abroad.

The general and popular eighteenth-century hatred of the Scots (as personified, to the Scots, in the reasonably mild Dr Johnson) arose not only from a natural enough dislike of the fawning yet aggressive way of the Scots on the make but also from the fact that over-many of these greedy persons, with their strange customs and "uncouth dialect", actually made it. But of course we still suffer, as a nation, from the indignities which we went looking for and duly suffered after the Union. We are both aggressively Scottish and defensively unsure of our native cultural traditions. We suffer from the guilt complex of a people who have sold their country short, and continue to sell it short for personal ambitions.

I believe the cultural sell-out to be very important, but the failure to retain a government and parliament within the Union was surely the biggest sell-out. As Professor Hanham said, "It is at least arguable that Texas got better terms when it joined the United States than Scotland got when it joined Great Britain." But of course this was not the first sell-out. The Reformers, led by John Knox, sold out their culture for political ends by having English translations of the Bible introduced into Scotland, as they attempted to unite Scotland with protestant England against the old ally catholic France. But James VI perhaps really set the example when he trooped off to London to claim the English crown. Historians always seem to regard this as a natural journey, but it was a selling-out of his Scottish subjects to personal ambition, and even more so in that he returned only once to Scotland and ruled Scotland from Whitehall, boasting, "This I would say for Scotland, here I sit and govern it with my pen. I write and it is done, and by a Clark of the Council I govern Scotland now, which others could not do by the sword." But the sword was used effectively enough also and particularly against the Gaels of the Highlands, although that was a pacification not fully pursued until the butcheries of Cumberland and his Scottish and English soldiers after Culloden in 1746. The Redcoats in popular Scottish mythology are English, but in fact many eighteenth-century Lowland Scots hated the Highlanders more than did the English.

But if James VI or I governed by the pen from Whitehall then so also did the Scottish rulers of the eighteenth and nineteenth centuries. It is a time largely ignored from the Scottish standpoint in Scottish schools today but it is largely a time of misgovernment or bad government. Scotland was basically governed by the eighteenth-century equivalents of Huey Long except that they wished largely for inertia and peace and quiet. Two Dukes of Argyll ran Scotland for the Whigs and for decades the mighty Henry Dundas, first Viscount Melville, ruled Scotland for the Tories, then he passed his power to his son, the second Viscount Melville. This was the time of the lawyers' rule of Scotland and gave the Edinburgh lawyers the political involvement, as Whigs and Tories, which survives to this day. I cannot resist suggesting that the Lord Advocate was king of Scotland, unlike the real kings who had each been King of Scots—of the people, not the state. But it was very much a *laissez-faire* government (or lack of government) as indeed can be seen from the modern comment by J. D. Mackie, one-time professor of Scottish History and Literature at Glasgow University and so a respectable establishment writer : "After Bute's fall (1763) remote control was exercised from England, often by the Secretary of the Northern Department; but the management of Scotland tended to fall into the hands of the Lord Advocate."[3]

This "falling-into" government continued until 1885 when a Secretary for Scotland was appointed to run the new Scottish Office but for long after this Scotland failed to produce an alternative policy to that of English rule on the advice of Edinburgh lawyers and, indeed, one wonders if it is any different today. The lawyers were generally happy with London rule and apparently had no fears of the anglicisation of their country that went hand in glove with it. But dissatisfaction was growing and this can be linked to the growth of political power amongst the working classes

who had, of course, less to be conservative about than the anglicised upper or middle classes. The Scottish Labour Party was
founded in 1888 and Home Rule for Scotland was one of its
policies. The first Home Rule Association was founded in 1886
and the first parliamentary resolution for Home Rule for Scotland
was moved in the House of Commons by G. B. Clark in 1889.
There followed a succession of Home Rule Motions until the
1914-18 war put a halt to them, although that war, supposedly
fought in defence of small nations, proved to be a stimulant to
nationalism in Scotland as elsewhere in Europe. Indeed, the
second Home Rule Association was formed in 1917 and other
Home Rule Associations were formed during the twenties; they
mostly came together in 1928 to form the National Party of Scotland.

In 1932 this party merged with the Scottish Party as the Scottish National Party, which survives to this day and indeed is the
party which has made such a startling impact in recent years. But
London had responded to the nationalist movement long before
the present upsurge of the S.N.P. In 1926 the Scottish Secretary
became a Secretary of State with a seat in the Cabinet and with
some new powers. In 1939 his "headquarters" were moved from
London to St Andrew's House in Edinburgh and there were
Departments for Home Affairs, Health, Agriculture and Education. The power, of course, remained in London, and the management of Scotland continues with the Secretary of State, the new
name for the Lord Advocate. To bring this management tale,
up-to-date, the Secretary of State for Scotland has a Minister of
State as deputy and provision has been made for three Under-
Secretaries of State for Scotland. This may have greatly improved the administrative management of Scotland but obviously
this is no sort of responsible government for a people who believe
that they live in a nation and not an administrative area or a
region of England.

Scotland may be poorly governed but, even more important, it
continues to lack a political involvement in its own affairs. British
government remains primarily orientated towards the government
of England, to the disadvantage of Scotland, Wales and Ireland
where conditions are markedly different. But if administratively
Scotland is treated as a sort of idiosyncratic provincial region of
England there is no question but that the Scottish people, although

they put up with this unsatisfactory situation, continue to believe that they are the people of the oldest surviving nation in Europe, and even if this is a compensatory attitude it does give a hope that one day the Scottish people will again achieve political maturity and play a part in the affairs of the world directly as Scots.

And yet, despite this belief which has always existed, the acceptance of English paternalism and of English standards has been challenged effectively only in this century. This can perhaps be seen best in the Lowland Scot's attitude to the Scots language. The Scots lords and M.P.s who went to Westminster in 1707 soon assumed English ways and became the elite, followed by the Scottish ruling classes who were soon sending their sons to English public schools to acquire an English accent and an English education to facilitate entry to Oxford and Cambridge, which were to become the supreme heights of a non-Scottish Scottish education.

This cultural sell-out of Scottish standards, I believe, as have all writers (historians as well as poets, novelists and dramatists) of the Scottish literary renaissance movement, to be the crux of Scotland's present-day troubles. Its failure to be itself and the failure of its political and cultural leaders to be their Scottish selves has created the intellectual and cultural void which is at the centre of Scottish affairs. The deliberate process of the acquisition of the spoken English language highlights the lengths the upper-class Scots of the eighteenth century went to in order to achieve an English acceptance and so places in the ranks of the successful in England. Scots remained the natural speech of all classes of Lowland Scots until at least the middle of the eighteenth century but immediately after Union the upper classes moved towards an acceptance of English as a superior tongue. The judges in Parliament House were issuing their harsh sentences in Scots but the House of Lords was now at the top of the Scottish legal system and Scots did not go down well there. Of course, as always, the Scots accommodated the English and we soon find Lord Kames considering himself too old to unlearn Scots but wishing "the rising generation to speak English with grace and propriety".[4]

The Scots began to compile a list of Scots words and phrases which they considered contaminated their speech. Fanatical in this direction was James Beattie who, by 1771, was writing of Scots: "for more than half a century it has even by the Scots been considered as the dialect of the vulgar".[5] Literary justice was

19

administered to Beattie in that the only decent poem he wrote is in Scots. Of course, the Edinburgh anglicisers advised Robert Burns to drop his "uncouth" Scots (the one-time speech of kings and judges and Scottish ladies, as well as peasants) and write in the politically and socially advantageous Addisonian English. Of course again the poet had the last laugh as he is remembered round the world, and the anglicised *literati* who attempted poetry in English are a joke. But this sad sight of the Scots learning English ways is worth pursuing a little further as it is a failure of national confidence which still afflicts the Scottish nation today. Beattie issued a collection of Scotticisms in 1779 "designed to correct Improprieties of Speech and Writing" but as early as 1761 Thomas Sheridan (father of the dramatist) was giving English elocution lessons to polite Edinburgh society and Beattie was followed into publication by John Sinclair, who got to the core of the reason for the new popularity of English when he wrote in *Observations on the Scottish Dialect* in 1782 : "such as wish to mix with the world, and particularly those whose object it is to have some share in the administration of national affairs, are under the necessity of conforming to the taste, the manners, and the language of the Public. Old things must then be done away with—new manners assumed, and a new language adopted."

The extent of this neurotic concern not to be thought provincial or "uncouth" and which had the very opposite result in that the abandonment of the independent Scottish culture inevitably made the Anglo-Scots provincialists, is well and truly laid bare by Sinclair in a final note : "Nor is the capital (London) itself exempted, though in general accounted the standard of good language. And although it is proper for the Scots to acquire the real and genuine English words and phrases, yet such as are either provincial, vulgar or cockney, ought to be carefully avoided."

But these hard-headed eighteenth-century Scots saw both the advantages and disadvantages of an assumption of English ways and of an English education. They asked the right questions but although in accepting anglicisation as inevitable they may have furthered the careers of their relatives, they also continued the cultural selling-out of Scotland which began with one or other of the Unions. David Hume asked the right questions at a personal level in 1767 but his questions should be asked at a national level and we should give the opposite answers to those of the great philosopher who failed to rise above the attitudes of his time. Since then, however, we have had 200 years of Scottish waste of the potential of the Scottish people and we should surely have learned the correct answers by now. It was in a letter to his brother, John Home of Ninewells, that Hume wrote: "The Question is, whether he (Home's son) had better continue his Education in Scotland or in England. There are several Advantages of a Scots Education; but the Question is whether that of the Language does not counterbalance them, and determine the Preference to the English. He is now of an Age to learn it perfectly; but if a few Years elapse, he may acquire such an Accent, as he will never be able to cure of. It is not yet determin'd what Profession he shall be of; especially, if it shou'd prove, as we have reason to hope, that his good Parts will open him the Road of Ambition. The only Inconvenience is, that few Scotsmen, that have had an English education, have ever settled cordially in their own Country, and they have been commonly lost ever after to their friends."[6] And lost for ever after to Scotland, which is more important to the life of the nation. It has created a break between rulers and ruled and despite the myths of a democratic Scottish education which are obviously exposed by the realities of the class-conscious schools of Edinburgh and Glasgow, Scotland has an as well-defined class system as England —perhaps an even more rigid one. A Frenchman visiting Scotland and England can see no differences between class assumptions in the two countries. Whereas he undoubtedly can in the United States where the petrol-pump attendant feels naturally the equal of his customers, whereas the Scots or English "workers" "know their place"—and indeed seem to like knowing their place.

The drain of Scottish resources continues but it leaves more than a void created by an educated brain-drain; it leaves the Scots looking outwards for their final authorities in educational and cultural matters as well as in governmental ones. There is a void in the nation and, as a nation suffering from a sense of inferiority and from a withdrawal from involvement in its affairs, Scotland becomes a parochial region of the United Kingdom and its people second-class citizens whose birthright of Scottishness is a handicap to be overcome rather than an asset to be put to the creation of a virile, active culture contributing works and ideas to the greater culture of Great Britain and Europe.

This was the vision of the writers of the Scottish renaissance who

emerged after the 1914-18 war, but the idea of a Scottish
Scotland, after the centuries of acceptance and encouragement of
English cultural dominance, is not easily accepted by the powerful
minority of Scots who have themselves, of course, been "educated"
out of their Scottishness and so are isolated in the no-man's-land
between the polite English and the popular Scottish cultures. They
fight back and attack those who believe in a Scottish Scotland. So,
for example, we have spokesmen for the Anglo-Scots like Edwin
Muir taking the pessimistic stance that the process of anglicisation
has proceeded so far that we can do nothing but curse our luck for
being caught between two cultures and attempt to be absorbed
into the superior dominant one—the English one—even although
we recognise (as did Muir) that the Scots are unlikely to be able to
make a major contribution to this culture which we have to
attempt to accept as our own. We have, say the Anglo-Scots, no
choice but to be second-class cultural citizens.

In other words, the answer of Muir and his anglicised like to the
question "Whither Scotland?" would be that we are going, as
Scots, nowhere since we are to become English and achieve what
success we can through England. That, as I have said, has long
been the attitude of the Scottish rulers (and they have got their
jam); the ordinary Scots have also looked for English progress and
some later licking at the jam. Of course, if all the Scots want is a
higher standard of living with more cars and holidays on the Costa
Brava, then they can lie back and let the English or the European
Community do the thinking and the creating for them and therefore be at least a decade behind the English in getting the new con-
sumer luxuries. The Scots can be nonentified finally, fed and
housed and entertained by others even if they do the routine and
non-creative work, whether it be lawyers' or car-builders' or
teachers' work. They must also expect the brain-drain to persist
and foreign executives and managers to continue to flood in to
take the top jobs. Quite an electronics industry, for example, has
grown up in Glenrothes in Fife, but it is intelligent and hard-
working cheap female labour that attracts the American companies: very few Scottish graduates are working in Glenrothes.

The solution is obviously not simply political independence—
that will only change the seat of government—but the difficult
assumption of a cultural independence which will give a new
dynamic to the country. It may be that political independence is

essential to cultural independence, but the vision of Hugh
MacDiarmid and those other cultural leaders who have fought for
the idea of a Scottish Scotland is not a plan to have the same
Scotland under new and better (economic) management but of a
new Scotland which will be the intellectual, cultural and social
equal of the best in Europe. And despite the continuing betrayals
by the anglicised, the conservative and the timid, the last fifty
years of literary renaissance suggest that an educational and
cultural revolution has begun in Scotland and that the country is
at long last moving towards achieving the unity, common purpose and maturity to be fully itself again—a Scottish Scotland
with a European outlook. That is a vision seen by the renaissance
poets of the last fifty years and seen most clearly in the poetry of
Hugh MacDiarmid whose work alone, without the other fine
poets who give him support, gives the lie to those who believe
that Scotland is culturally and nationally dead.

A great poet, such as Scotland has in MacDiarmid, expresses in
his poetry the true life of the nation and exposes the false and the
superficial. The poet has to be true to himself to achieve great
poetry, and in being true to himself he reveals the realities of his
culture—in his poetry. What MacDiarmid reveals is that Scotland
remains Scottish and that a hope for a mature culture, and so a
mature nation, is reliant upon a recognition of this fact of Scottishness. As in the past, an easy escape into the arms of anglicisation
can result only in a falseness and a betrayal not only of one's own
potential but of the potential of the whole Scottish community.
For too long the Scots have been afraid to fail; they have relied
upon practical common-sense whereas what is required is a new
creativeness—although, as MacDiarmid has said, there can be no
creation without the risk of destruction. For such a new creative
spirit in Scotland, a seat at the United Nations between Saudi
Arabia and Senegal may not be an essential, but the revival of a
feeling of continuous involvement in the essentials of nationhood
most certainly is—as is a non-neurotic national and natural (taken
for granted) pride. There we can most certainly learn from the
English.

NOTES

1. London, Faber and Faber, 1969, pp. 198-9.
2. *Punch*, 21 July 1970, p. 86.
3. *A History of Scotland*, Penguin, 1964.
4. John Ramsay of Ochtertyre. *Scotland and Scotsmen in the Eighteenth Century*, ed. Alexander Allardyce, 1888, vol. 1, p. 212.
5. See H. G. Graham. *Scottish Men of Letters*, 1908, p. 382.
6. *The Letters of David Hume*, ed. J. Y. T. Greig, 1932, vol. 2, pp. 154-5.

2

ECONOMY AND INDUSTRY
Andrew Hargrave

W HEN THE 1 9 6 0 ' S began, I was industrial correspondent of the *Scottish Daily Express*. I was writing for basically
optimistic paper which often meant toning down the bad things
and magnifying the good ones and generally making tentative,
exploratory and even vague plans appear more as solid prospects.
But if I was frequently guilty of what has since been dubbed
"sunshine journalism", it was not altogether because I was writing for the *Express*, but because after a decade of stagnation
many of us felt we were on the eve of a new, exciting advance.

Some of those plans and prospects did incidentally solidify into
firm policies and plants. The "growth point" philosophy with its
implied regional development aid was codified in the Toothill
Report and eventually accepted by the Tory Government in its
last years of office. The subsequent Labour Government not only
accepted the building grants, training grants and other fixed cash
incentives but added investment grants and the regional employment premium. It also broadened the development area to
embrace all Scotland but for the Edinburgh district.

B.M.C. (now British Leyland) and Rootes (now Chrysler)
hailed as the forerunners of the industrial transformation of Scotland, are still with us, albeit with serious problems. The newest of
new industries, for which Scottish representative bodies, local
authorities (large and small) had all been eagerly casting
around—electronics—grew five-fold in terms of employment
during the 1960's. In all, there had been a shift of 200,000 jobs
from contracting industries and services into expanding ones by
the end of the decade.

This shift in jobs, however, disguises another shift—that in the
composition of the labour force. Although the figures quoted in
the *Digest of Scottish Statistics* are not strictly comparable

because of changes in computation, the distinct rise in the number of working women compared with a corresponding fall in the number of men shows an unmistakable trend :

	1959	1969
Total in civil employment	2,145,000	2,162,000
Of these: Men	1,393,000	1,331,000
Women	752,000	831,000

In other words the jobs for coal miners, shipyard workers, railwaymen, farm workers were replaced by jobs for women in, for instance, electronics. Jobs for women were, of course, badly needed in the districts such as mining; the fact remains that as the new decade begins, the main and vital need is for male jobs for two reasons. Unemployment among men stood at 5.9 per cent in October 1970, compared with 4.5 per cent for the working population as a whole (itself a very high figure); and, according to an unpublished Scottish Office paper, a very high proportion of emigrants are young, skilled men.

Emigration, a major headache for Governments, prospective employers and the numerous bodies engaged in attracting new industries to Scotland was running at very high levels throughout the 1960's, averaging 35,300—fully 10,000 more than the net average during the previous decade.

Towards the end of the 1960's, the trend of emigration was downward, dropping to a net 21,000 in 1969-70. The Registrar-General's projection is now a net figure of 15,000 by the end of the decade which would allow a modest rise in the population of 5.2 million.

Another major change in the 1960's was the disappearance of many proud independent companies through mergers and takeovers. Scotland's native manufacturing industry has all but gone. Those which survived have done so by themselves absorbing others (such as the Weir group or Coats Patons), or coming together like the Upper and Lower Clyde shipbuilders forming their respective groups.

The upshot—of which more later—has been a gradual loss of control over the economy. It is arguable, as we shall see, whether this is altogether detrimental : but the fact has to be recorded that to a very large extent the fate of individual enterprises is now determined from outside Scotland—indeed, in many cases out-side Britain. On the last count just over 10 per cent of the total Scottish manufacturing labour force was employed by companies owned by or associated with U.S. corporations.

One more lesson to be learned from events in the last decade. Industries hailed as "new" or "science-based" ones when it began have themselves proved the accelerated rate of change which brought them into existence. The closure of newly-equipped plastics and fibreglass plants in Glasgow and a cutback of 450 in the electronics labour force at Glenrothes has shown that the revolutionary products of the early 1960's have become the rejects of the 1970's.

Is Scotland's new industrial structure geared to absorb such shocks and setbacks? Can it once again renew itself when the new industries of the 1960's become the old ones of the 1970's—a not unlikely event as the pace of change accelerates? Are Central Government policies, once again modified by a new Government, conducive to renewal and is the economic climate in Scotland receptive to change?

Forecasting is a standard business practice, particularly in the United States. It is to the U.S. that the Scottish Council (Development and Industry) has turned, as so often in the past, for a guide to its own study on the effects of centralisation. In February 1969, the Council prepared a long memorandum on the subject, following it up with a study based on the "Delphi" technique first applied in the U.S. by the Rand Corporation. Six-teen distinguished Scots in as many walks of life were invited to hazard views, guesses, comments on the impact on Scotland of the continuing trend of business centralisation in London, over three rounds of questions and answers. Their summarised conclu-sions were presented to the Council's first International Forum, on the same theme, in November 1970.

These indicated that centralisation would go on throughout the decade, though the effect was not likely to be as disastrous as feared in the Council's memorandum. There would, the pundits thought, be an increasing need to delegate authority from the centre, just because of the growth of industrial giants. Moreover, they felt, the whole process would go into reverse beyond 1980, "because of the growing size and immobility of London".

The necessity for improving management training,

communications and housing, and also the supply of "people of sufficiently high calibre" was emphasised. A "unanimous expression of the need for a regeneration of spirit" was coupled with the hope that "an effort of will could go a long way to obtaining an improvement".

In an explanatory note the Council admits that this sort of inquiry was not likely to produce "simple, clear-cut solutions". Unfortunately it did not produce many signposts either, nor did the subsequent forum. Even that centralisation existed as a problem had not been "unanimously conceded".

This is not altogether surprising. The panel had been selected not only for its assumed impartiality but also, even though unintentionally, as broadly representative of the Scottish establishment. Politicians (except for a couple appearing under a different guise), people of strong and perhaps extreme views, trade unions (except for one elderly representative) were omitted. It was never on the cards that such an assortment would come up with new ideas—ideas that were not merely extensions of present trends, ideas that would be in fundamental conflict with the existing order of things.

I fear *The Influence of Centralisation on the Future,* as the study was called, was no great help in charting the course for Scotland, except in a negative way. It did warn of the danger of assuming that the 1970's will be no more than an improved version of the 1960's; that established patterns will change only on the fringes; that Britain's—and Scotland's—role in or out of the European Economic Community may be as crucial to economic development as any other factor in the first half of the decade.

But there is no reason to believe that centralisation and the resulting congestion of people, ideas, cash, influence and technology in single centres will reach an ultimate saturation point whereafter frustrated manufacturing and business enterprises will of necessity take to wide open spaces of remote regions such as the Highlands or the Solway Firth. There is no evidence of Paris, Tokyo, Buenos Aires, New York, Los Angeles or Moscow, all growing at a faster pace than London, showing signs of dispersal except within a relatively narrow radius.

Apart from the social menace of congestion and unequal distribution of wealth, the economic disadvantage of "backward" regions holding back growth, there is an obvious political danger in having disaffected groups within a single nation state. This is particularly true of Scotland and Wales which happen to have their own histories, national identities and sub-cultures.

There is also the political danger. Centralisation has meant large international companies straddling the globe which have carved themselves extra-territorial rights; and have not always set their objectives to meet the needs of local communities. It would not be fair to assume that they have never paid any attention to these and have at all times been guided by motives of profit and self-interest. In the long term, however, it is invariably the requirements of the corporation that must come first, no matter what the effect is on the community in which it operates. No code of behaviour such as the Canadian Government has hopefully set to U.S. corporations operating in that country can change the ultimate goal of profitability and the interests of shareholders.

The corollary is that the objectives of the community must on occasion clash with those of foreign-based corporations to an even larger extent than with the home based ones. Even the closest scrutiny of intentions prior to starting, by rigorous "vetting" of incentives, of planning applications, etc. cannot prevent changes in company policy, reaction to market trends or simple inability to settle in the new surroundings. So the ultimate sanction of political control must be held in reserve to safeguard the interests of the community. As this essay is not directly concerned with political control, suffice it to say that Scotland (except as part of Great Britain) possesses little control of this kind.

In economic terms, centralisation is neutral. Examples may be cited where it was advantageous to Scotland; others where it proved to be disastrous. What it does show, however, beyond any doubt is that the offshoots of large international corporations, usually a specialised component of the parent organisations, are particularly sensitive to world market changes. For example, the U.S. recession has led to the loss of 1,000 jobs at the Singer sewing machine factory, at Clydebank, and 400 jobs at Ranco Motors' Tannochside works. Fall in tractor sales has led to a cut of 550 in British Leyland's Bathgate labour force. Another way in which over-reliance on branch factories may hit the local economy is rationalisation as a result of mergers, takeovers, overall recession or a setback in a company's fortunes.

In the Glasgow area alone five factories were closed in the

second half of 1970 under the heading of rationalisation. A sixth one was closed, indirectly, on the same grounds, as the "goodwill" was acquired by a competitor, but not the plant or the labour force.

Examples can, of course, be cited where rationalisation worked in Scotland's favour. After the giant merger of G.E.C. and A.E.I.-English Electric, it paid the new board to concentrate production of certain articles in Scotland where labour was cheaper, incentives better and factories more modern. For the same reason, Beckman Instruments decided to bring a London subsidiary to Glenrothes where it already had a plant and concentrate its U.K. efforts there.

On balance, however, rationalisation tends to work against a subsidiary or branch factory, particularly when orders shrink or profits are on the slide. The impact may be mitigated to some extent by the desire to protect investment—the heavier the investment, the greater the reluctance to abandon it or trim it. But in the final analysis, no company can carry a "loser". The heavy losses being sustained by British Leyland and Chrysler—or for that matter, Upper Clyde Shipbuilders—must fill the observer with foreboding.

The case of U.C.S. (which more recently decided to go for the mass market rather than the small "sophisticated" segment of it) points to the vulnerability of companies depending on the state of world markets, no matter whether home or overseas-based.

Indeed from here one could argue the larger, the more diverse, the geographically more extended the organisation is the more capable it is of absorbing shocks and responding to market fluctuations. At the same time who can deny that a board, State or private, will react more readily to local pressures if it is based in the locality than the local boss or the director arriving with the morning plane to announce the bad news and flying back home the same evening?

The Scottish Council's panel of oracles may, of course, be right in suggesting that merger mania could burn itself out eventually, that ill-fitting oligopolies will fall apart and constituent pieces will assert their independence. (The prospect of the Society of Graphic and Allied Trades splitting into its original constituent parts may be a straw in the wind; or just an example of a clash of personalities leading to divorce). But for the foreseeable future there is no evidence to substantiate the panel's view of the trend changing. Companies are bought and sold, expanded or closed down—but these transactions very rarely lead to independence. They usually end in groups getting bigger and more powerful.

The Council's memorandum on centralisation is only the last of many warnings about the loss of talent as the power of decision-making slips away from a community. The Pitlochry metallurgist R. H. S. Robertson analysed this in a historical context[1] fully ten years ago. The Toothill Report referred to it in 1961 and I attempted to relate it to Scotland's economic future in a Fabian pamphlet[2] in 1964.

Indeed, at the risk of venturing into other authors' preserves in this book, the low standard of political debate and the indifferent quality of the bulk of politicians at both parliamentary and local government level may well be the result of many decades of losses of creative and executive talent.

Centralisation of Government must, of course, itself lead to such talent gravitating towards the centre—i.e. London. There are hopeful signs of the process of centralisation being reversed in this sphere, and the Tory idea of a Scottish Convention is only one of these. But in the economic field where there is a certain amount of political spin-off while industrial entrepreneurs, leading trade unionists and creative rebels operate in the area, the prospects are not so good. The gradual and accelerating shift of economic decision-making away from Scotland has led to a further impoverishment of Scottish politics and consequently to an erosion of Scottish influence on U.K. and world affairs.

Improved communication with the outside world, from air, rail and sea links to telecommunications, would not by itself redress the balance. At the same time it could help in opening up Scotland to the world and also eliminate some of the inward-looking parochialism one notes with sadness in contemporary Scotland. According to the Scottish Council, this would also serve as a powerful additional incentive both to outsiders to invest in Scotland and to existing organisations to broaden their vision. But while the Tory Government has shown signs of supporting export and investment promotion through the Council and other agencies, it seems unlikely that it would subsidise the State and private airlines to maintain, for instance, unprofitable flights to the Continent.

Political devolution apart, the Government can itself play a role in reversing the centralising process by dispersing its own activities. A recent paper by Ian C. Freeman, published under the auspices of Strathclyde University, argues in favour of steering specialised public offices to selected regional centres such as Edinburgh, supporting the scheme with improvements in the infrastructure, by training as well as a publicity campaign. (He mentions the National Computing Centre, set up in Manchester, as an example; another is the Inland Revenue office in Edinburgh).

During the past decade, Scotland has gained the Post Office Savings Bank and lost the Forestry Commission. Such decentralisation of administration as carried out by successive Governments has usually been kept within a fifty-mile radius of London.

It is worth noting that among manufacturing enterprises, it is the U.K. ones that generally show more reluctance to moving some distance from headquarters. The comparative performance of offshoots of U.K. and U.S. enterprises may have some relevance in this respect, as the table below based on a Scottish Council survey indicates:

% Growth 1964–66	Employment	Investment	Turnover	Exports
U.S. Companies	30	53	50	57
U.K. companies	6	17	13	−3

The Council's basic argument for attracting more overseas companies to Scotland, particularly from the U.S.A., rests partly on the success of their performance as well as on their stake in major growth industries, such as electronics, office machinery, earth-moving equipment, etc.

Yet in the memorandum on centralisation, and elsewhere, the Council has increasingly shown reservations and even a certain amount of unease about the low research and development content of some of these "science-based" companies. A more recent Strathclyde University survey on U.S. companies in Scotland indicates that between them they took on only 250 graduates in the years 1965 to 1969—half a graduate per company per year. In the memorandum, the Council urged that more of the "creative" sections of these enterprises should be sited in Scotland and that Government policy should aim at encouraging this.

So far there has been little indication of an extra premium on quality in Government incentive packages.

The tide of foreign enterprise to Scotland, so evident in the late 1940's and mid-1960's, has now slowed down to a trickle. The new towns, particularly East Kilbride, are among the few areas in Scotland still attracting new investment, albeit on a small scale. The credit squeeze in the U.K. as well as in the U.S. has put a brake on expansion : and relocation is usually an overspill of expansion, more so than the negative force of industrial development certificates.

There is already evidence, too, that the Government's new development area incentive package may no longer be as attractive an incentive as it was under the Labour Government's 1966 package or, indeed, the one before introduced by the previous Tory Government in 1963. Calculations as to the relative merits of investment grants and tax allowances (100 per cent depreciation in Development Areas, 60 per cent in the first year elsewhere, the rest spread over the next four years) vary; but it is generally recognised that, even allowing for high profits, the cash value of the allowance will be considerably less than the investment grant's.

This is tacitly admitted by the Government when it estimated the differential value of the allowance in Scotland at £30 million a year compared with the £40 million yielded by the 20 per cent differential in investment grants.

In an article on 8th November 1970, the *Sunday Times* estimated that the reduction in cost on plant and machinery under the new system of free depreciation will be 11.4 per cent compared with 25.5 per cent under the 1966 system and the 33.3 per cent maximum achievable under Chancellor Maudling's 1963 package which was based on a tax rate of $56\frac{1}{4}$ per cent.

Incidentally, it is also understood that the 10 per cent discretionary investment grant available in the Maudling package will not be revived, leaving the 10 per cent rise in building grants and other smaller incentives provided under the 1960 Local Employment Act as the only "carrots" to offset the loss of investment grants and Regional Employment Premium to some extent.

Apart from the relative cash values of the two types of investment incentives, the new system will hurt the new enterprises,

33

both starting from scratch and coming from overseas, which for some years cannot expect any profits to depreciate against. It will further damage the liquidity of some companies struggling to regain profitability—the shipbuilding industry in general and U.C.S. in particular is a case in point. R.E.P., attacked by the Tories in opposition as well as others as a sop to the inefficient, to labour hoarders and as an incentive to unjustified pay rises, is to be phased out in 1974 with no alternative inducement proposed when it expires. So there cannot be any sanguine hopes of a revival in the invasion by overseas companies or U.K. companies elsewhere. The question is : will existing industry fill the gaps left by contraction in the older ones, considering that even at the high tide of new enterprise in the mid-1960's, more jobs were lost than gained.

When the Labour Government was voted out of office in June 1970, some 55,000 new jobs were believed to be in the pipeline, over an indefinite period. However, already in the last year of that Government, the projects for which industrial development certificates were issued showed a drop of fully one-third in job potential over the previous year. Experience indicates that only about three-quarters of the potential is ever converted into real jobs, which means that it could barely balance two years' job loss at the current rate. Note also that the "pipeline" may contain proportionately fewer jobs for men than those leaking out at the other end.

On the face of it, taking a static view, the picture for the next few years is a depressing one. Action is necessary on several fronts to avoid an economic decline of the kind experienced in 1958-63 or—a more remote possibility but by no means ruled out—in the years midway between two world wars, of truly catastrophic dimensions. The lessons and remedies of those two periods would however be of little use in an age of conglomerates, a fact insufficiently appreciated by all too many politicians, employers and trade unionists. Action to be taken must be on the basis of forward planning, with all the uncertainties and risks this entails. Action is particularly essential in the exploitation of natural assets by exploration and increased investment; in people by training at all levels; by improved communications and intensified promotional activities, both within the U.K. and overseas; and by—an admittedly vague notion—improving the economic climate.

There are, of course, other vital fields of action, though not within the scope of this essay. There must be a concerted attack on poverty, on social inequality, on poor housing; on improvement of educational opportunities, again at all levels; an energetic implementation of the Wheatley Report to reform local government; and a major reform of U.K. Government, allowing for a devolution of administrative, political and financial powers away from the centre.

Natural assets include the mineral deposits in the Northern Highlands as well as coal in the Central Belt and the oil "gusher" just discovered by British Petroleum in the North Sea off Aberdeen. Several exploration companies have taken options on the mineral deposits and B.P. is hopeful that the oil strike may yield as much as 12 million tons of crude oil a year, which is equivalent to one-eighth of Britain's oil consumption in 1970.

Another set of natural assets consists of the deep-water facilities of the Clyde and the Moray Firth. Chevron Oil and Murco, two U.S. companies, have sought (the latter so far unsuccessfully) to establish oil refineries in the Clyde Estuary. The British Steel Corporation, too, has provisional plans for a major iron ore terminal at the Hunterston peninsula, near the proposed Chevron site. At the time of writing the Secretary of State's decision on both projects—and on an associated "green field" steelworks tentatively proposed—is still pending.

At Invergordon, in the Moray Firth, British Aluminium's £37 million aluminium smelter, is sited there partly because of the deep-water harbour, though it is unlikely that the bauxite carriers would ever be much larger than 40,000 tons deadweight. Grampian Chemicals, too, has bought a site near the harbour to build a £100 million petrochemical complex. The project is still hanging fire because of the company's inability to raise that sort of finance—but, again at the time of writing, the Highlands and Islands Development Board is hopeful of other applicants in the same field.

It is said that these projects carry the seeds of the destruction of amenity in the Highlands and on the Clyde. Protagonists on either side argue in black-and-white terms; hampering any of these projects, even burdening them with extra costs to minimise pollution, would lead to economic atrophy, says one lot. Allowing

35

any of them, even with safeguards, would spoil the countryside for ever, says the other.

The decision is clearly political as expressed by the Secretary of State, but the final choice is with the people. The destruction or reduction of amenity must be weighed against economic benefits and also the degree to which the beneficiaries are willing to keep pollution and destruction to the minimum. The nature and amenity lovers must take into account the possible dereliction and deterioration that would result from barring major new industrial development altogether.

For example, the Oceanspan concept of a Clyde deep-water terminal as an entrance point from the North Atlantic being linked to a European exit on the Forth by a "land bridge" would no doubt lead to *some* loss of amenity at each point and along the route. But if we want a mini-Rotterdam on the Clyde and Forth, this must be accepted. If we do not, let us not beat about the bush but say so and take the consequences.

There is no sign yet of private investors, apart from the British Steel Corporation and the U.S. oil companies, rushing to exploit the deep-water potential of the Clyde, or finance a land-bridge to Europe. The Government's West-Central Scotland planning steering group will no doubt take account of possible developments and the need for road and rail links, land provision, etc. as a back-up to Oceanspan.

But one suspects that a Government dedicated to non-intervention in the economy will avoid any direct investment, be it a massive infusion of cash and expertise in the Clyde Port Authority, special incentives to shippers and to ancillary industries or a major publicity drive to alert them to the advantages of the Clyde. A Scottish Council-led promotion or the one planned by Glasgow Chamber of Commerce and local authorities in the West of Scotland cannot be substitutes for a campaign publicising an Oceanspan-type project.

Man-power training has three facets. Needs have to be defined some years ahead and provision has to be made to meet them. Finally, the working population, both young and not so young, has to be made aware of both the opportunities and the consequences of failure to respond : the opportunities in growth industries and services and the danger of skills no longer required.

On all three counts, Scotland's effort has been on far too small a scale. Less than one-half per cent of the working population is involved each year in re-training, in Government training centres and on factory premises. Apprentices, by and large, are trained by methods largely copied from Europe instead of being geared to future needs. The acceleration of industrial change is being talked about but not fully accepted or even understood by managements and unions. This is not unique to Scotland, but not less destructive because it happens to be true elsewhere in Britain.

Higher education at both university and technical college level presents a more hopeful picture. With its eight universities (three of them technological) and numerous technical colleges, with its embryonic tripartite business school, Scotland is as well equipped as any small country to produce able managers, scientists and technicians. (It is a pity, as the Strathclyde University survey indicates, that 50 per cent of all engineering and science graduates still have to leave Scotland to find a suitable job).

Liaison units at three of the universities provide help to innovators. Although, Scotland's share of U.K. research institutes is not much greater than its population share, the case for having more would be stronger if those already there had wider local support.

Finally, the economic climate! This is one for subjective judgement, difficult to quantify. For the climate is created by a vast variety of factors, from the quality of opinion-makers to the awareness of conflict within the community, from Government attitudes to the response of institutions to change.

In an over-centralised country like Britain it is difficult to segregate the economic climate of any particular component part from the whole. It is becoming increasingly evident that the trade winds blow across the Channel and the North Sea, the Atlantic and even the Pacific. Scotland, on the northern fringe of Britain as well as Europe, cannot create its own climate in isolation.

Then there is less and less scope for the individual merchant adventurer (he would soon be bought up or wiped out). The tentacles of the giants in industry, commerce and finance are reaching into the small crevices of the economy, snapping up many of the remaining home-based companies.

Scotland still has sizeable companies or groups. But the top "native" company in terms of assets (Distillers) is only just among the Top Ten in Britain. Only a fraction of the wage bill of the largest employer of labour (Coats Patons) is spent in Scotland. In some individual industries or services such as whisky distilling and brewing, in jute and in investment trusts and in insurance (one large company) Scotland is among the market leaders; but in most others, the control lies elsewhere. So the Scottish climate, is influenced by boards in London and New York, Birmingham or Detroit. It is a hazy picture, making any meaningful forecast hazardous, to say the least, particularly with the Common Market entry still undecided.

So where do we go from here?

We could, as Mr Peter Balfour, chairman of Scottish and Newcastle Breweries, suggested at the International Forum already mentioned, "pull ourselves up by our own bootstraps". This would mean cutting across political party lines, employer-employee relations, conflict between old and young. A "Dunkirk spirit", if you like. But one is bound to ask : to what end should all these hatchets be buried? Do we see Scotland of the future as a paradise for paternalistic enterprise where each individual knows his station and sticks to it? Or do we see it as the battle-ground with an eternal chase for an elusive parity with workers in the South? Or as one where the social evils of our age are progressively reduced and where Scotland once again opens its gates and eyes widely to the world outside. This again is a political decision. As democrats, we can only hope that the majority of Scots will recognise where their future lies.

NOTES

1. *Scotland's Scientific Heritage*, Oliver & Boyd, 1961.
2. *A Nation of Labourers*, Glasgow Fabian Society.

3

THE LOWLANDS
Michael Grieve

N ARROW AND UGLY, slum-cluttered, Scotland's industrial belt stretches tight across the 24 miles from the
estuary of the Clyde to the Firth of Forth. On the east coast, the
belt expands to include Dundee—yet it is on this strip of development that one measures the size and importance of the Lowlands—and gauges the present strength of Scotland. Black from
the toil of yesterday and today—with islands of bright,
cardboard-like factories on special estates—this industry-studded
belt secures the flapping underpants of Scotland's south, and pins
the spectacular but moth-eaten blouse of the Highlands.

The Lowlands is a vague, geographic term, meaningless unless
clearly defined away from the confusion of county boundaries.
From Gourock in the west, in a line above Stirling—soon to be
by-passed as Scotland's roads tortoise their way along—and including Fife, Dundee, Angus, Aberdeen and Caithness *is* Lowland
Scotland—"the Highlands have only one coast : the west. Scotland's northern and eastern seaboards are lowland." There are
other definitions, and in any catalogue it is obvious that the counties of Wigtown, Kirkcudbright, Dumfries, Roxburgh, Berwick,
Selkirk, Peebles, East, West and Mid Lothian, Fife and Clack-
mannan would be included; plus parts of Ayrshire, Lanarkshire,
Renfrewshire and Stirlingshire. But for practical purposes I
intend largely to ignore the isolation of Galloway, the frontier
lands and the rough vigour and individuality of the Borders—for
it is that deeply engrained scar across Scotland's pinched middle,
with Dundee and Aberdeen as northern outposts, that commands
priority.

More than three-quarters of Scotland's 5 million population
are herded in this strip of development, as though for a ritual
slaughter. Indeed, 40 per cent of Scots live in Glasgow and the

Clydeside conurbation—many in tumbling slums, or viciously
mean streets, or bloated housing estates that are a striking testi-
mony to the combined ignorance, lack of initiative and confused
priorities of planners and politicians. Glasgow is the mechanical
heart of Scotland, the trip-hammer pulse of industrialism that
beats out its flagging message day and night. A transplant is long
overdue. Once, it was the Second City of an Empire on which
the sun never set. But now Glasgow wallows behind, desperately
trying to cut its population below the million mark by overspill
agreements; and at the same time is so debt-ridden that it can
only be a matter of time before large-scale government intervention is required.

Hope-in-poverty can, perhaps, be maintained in the country
areas where people are acknowledged as humans, recognised as
neighbours, where a spontaneous community spirit exists—but in
the thrusting city shadows made blacker by the neon-lit pools of
prosperity, it is much more difficult. Hopes unrealised or frustrated
do not necessarily fade and die: they can become the food
for much more savage appetites. Yet there seems an almost compulsive desire to continue, even to expand, the mistakes of the
past. In housing, the skyscraper slums of the future disrupt the
skyline, monuments to the folly of treating people and houses as
bloodless statistics, and not as families and homes. Even the lifts
cannot take a stretcher—or a coffin. Scotland's five new towns—
East Kilbride, Glenrothes, world-award winning Cumbernauld,
Livingston and Irvine—have all been carefully planned and sited
to add to the density of the industrial belt. There has been no
effort to spread Scotland's population north or south; no serious
attempt made to expand industry, to involve the nation as a
whole, to demonstrate that opportunities can be created and
sustained not as a colonizing charity but as a deliberate decision
to widen the horizons beyond the annual holiday escape. The
geography of industry, the geology of people are being foolishly
neglected as Scotland's central belt—on a much more moderate
and less disastrous and corrupting scale—oozes out like Greater
London. It was Professor Ritchie Calder, scientific populariser and
defender of environment long before it became fashionable, who
once pleaded for the drift south to stop, saying: "This is not the
lament of a Scot bewailing 'Lochaber No More' in sympathy
with the Welsh sobbing 'Land of My Fathers'. This is sense not

sentiment. In the last century William Cobbett, the courageous radical, called London the Great Wen. The wart he was talking about has become ulcerous and cancerous. It is disfiguring the landscape and eroding the body-politic." The same is true of Scotland's industrial belt—pressure of business, facilities available, and basic government policies have combined to denude the rest of the country of its population; at the same time destroying the close-knit individuality of people who contrive to be more than a conveyor-belt society struggling to exist, even to flourish, in debasing housing schemes such as Glasgow's Drumchapel or Castlemilk, the biggest in Europe.

Events in history, like symptoms of an illness, need to be recognised and understood if what is wrong is to be accurately diagnosed and put right. Scotland has never been short of politicians who, in *opposition*, will talk common-sense. Unfortunately, ideas and ideals rarely survive the journey to London : they become self-aborting, especially if the trip is to the Scottish Office's headquarters at Dover House, with its engraved frieze of slaves for ever captive in the stonework.

A nation's population is its first asset—and movements in the population trend have a vital bearing on the future social and industrial fabric. It is self-evident. And any policy which does not take into the fullest consideration the probable future size and composition of the population is more than usually futile—even if the policy is churned out to aid vote-hungry politicians. Yet it is a curiously disturbing fact that though hundreds of thousands of Scots have been effectively outlawed through unemployment or forced emigration, no action and no serious sustained thinking has been evoked by their plight. Scotland has been a great training ground for talent, one of the most fertile in the world. But a poor employer of it.

In 1801, when the first census was held, the northern counties contained 45 per cent of the population. Today they barely hold 18 per cent. In 1801 the counties of Dunbarton, Renfrew, Ayr and Lanark was where 20.5 per cent lived. Now they have 48 per cent and the pressure is still growing. Scots can be excused if they laugh, or merely look bewildered, at the frightening statistics produced by those experts who are charting the world's population explosion, and the social effects it will have from sterilisation to famine. For Scotland is a wonderfully spacious country, averaging a distant 174 to the square mile compared to the 900-plus who shoulder their way through life in England.

On 30 June 1969, Scotland's population was estimated at 5,194,700. The Clydeside conurbation—the only area so designated—accounted for almost exactly one-third with 1,746,313; and the four "counties of cities"—Glasgow, Edinburgh, Aberdeen and Dundee—housed another third. However, despite the world's galloping population, and a predicted rise in England and Wales of some 20 million by the turn of the century, Scotland today has fewer people than five years ago—the result of heavy and consistent emigration.

At a massive investment cost (Australia values an average unskilled emigrant at £11,000 when he steps ashore), and apart from the much more crucial loss in terms of people, the Scots have been voting decisively against the present political-economic situation. With their feet. And Scotland's population, 15.2 per cent of England and Wales' in 1801, is now just over 9 per cent, and rapidly getting less. In 1921, for instance, there were 4,882,497 people despite the murderous slaughter of the first world war—but in the ten years to 1931 more than 391,000 Scots emigrated. Over-all population, as in recent years, went down. But in Great Britain as a whole it increased by 2,000,000, or 4.8 per cent.

In a repeat performance, the same trend is with us again. In the ten years up to 1968, 355,000 more people have left Scotland than have come in. Net emigration, in 1969, was said to have fallen to 25,000, and this was hailed as an epic achievement by the Labour Government. An extensive and fully-documented report on Scottish emigration, however, prepared by the working group on population of the Scottish Economic Planning Board, and which former Scottish Secretary Mr William Ross made an unsuccessful attempt to keep secret, shows clearly that there has been no marked improvement when *gross* emigration figures are considered in context. International comparisons of net migration from 1961–66, for instance, also demonstrate the unique and sorry position Scotland has among the industrialised nations of Western Europe.

Over that five-year period net migration from Scotland averaged 7.4 per 1,000 population compared to a ratio of 0.7 per cent in Finland, 0.3 in Norway and 0.1 in Austria. Denmark, the

Netherlands, England and Wales, Sweden, Belgium, Luxemburg, West Germany, France and Switzerland gained through migration; and even the poorer, agricultural countries on the periphery of Europe—such as Spain, Greece, Portugal and Eire—fared better than Scotland. It is not surprising, therefore, that the over-all quality, intelligence and enterprise of the Scot should be substantially less than it was. A moderate amount of blood-letting may be necessary in certain situations—but uncontrolled haemorrhages are not merely dangerous and undesirable : they can reduce the patient to an insensitive and barely knowing lump for whom, merely to be alive, is sufficient.

Allied to the compound evils of emigration has been widespread and heavy unemployment, with a drastic reduction in opportunity. The five-year plan for the Scottish economy (1965–70), heralded with a blast of eager trumpets by the Labour Government, was "designed to create more employment opportunities so as to take up, in the widest national interest, the available resources of labour, and to reduce emigration." This worthy hope was a total failure. Labour planned to provide—through the mythical "pipeline" with which Scots have become so familiar—an extra 45,000 jobs for men by 1970. Instead, there are now 65,000 fewer jobs for men than in 1964—a shortfall of 110,000 jobs. So much for government planning measured against performance.

The harmful and depressing effect of heavy unemployment has obviously held back the whole economic growth of Scotland. From 1954 to 1964, under a Tory Government, Scotland's unemployment averaged 3.4 per cent compared to 1.5 per cent in England and Wales. Scotland was, therefore, $2\frac{1}{4}$ times as badly off as England. In the last few years, under a Labour Government until June 1970, Scotland's situation has remained equally bad, though in comparison to England and Wales—where unemployment has crept up slightly—it appears to be relatively better. But the blunt fact is that for the last three winters at least one out of every twenty working Scotsmen has been on the dole.

It has been argued that the older, more poorly-paid jobs are being run down in favour of new, highly paid ones. Like a belch after dinner, this is yet another empty boast, no more appreciated because it is so familiar. For if, as the Scottish Office has claimed, the wage gap between payment for the same job is diminishing, then the only explanation for the sharp increase in the over-all wage gap (as revealed by P.A.Y.E. statistics) is that the quality of jobs in Scotland is declining *vis-à-vis* England. It is also claimed officially, as another side of the same misleading argument, that the fall in the number of Scotland's male employees has been unavoidable due to the rundown of labour requirements in certain industries, such as coal mining or ship building—traditional industries of the Lowlands. There is no evidence, however, to show that the situation with regard to Scotland's lost jobs is of unique magnitude. Indeed, the international evidence is the reverse.

Many of the so-called older industries which have been decaying, or compelled towards industrial suicide in Scotland, are booming elsewhere. World shipbuilding tonnage more than doubled between 1960 and 1968, rising substantially in every country except France and Scotland. Spain and Yugoslavia built more ships than Scotland, where the tonnage launched in 1968 was only 43 per cent of the 1960 figure—or the same as that for the Depression year of 1932. Put another way, Scotland's share of world shipbuilding declined from 12 per cent in 1850–54 to a sinking 1.3 per cent in 1968. This downward trend can be observed and charted in many more of Scotland's industries as the over-all population slumps and Scottish accents grow louder and more confident in Canada, Australia and New Zealand, not to mention England.

As Glasgow, belatedly, tries to dispense with her legacy of slums, a hangover from the first Industrial Revolution, and New Towns earnestly seek to develop a heart and spirit of their own, it is worth noting that Scotland is not geared for change. And that's official. Of course, there are new industries, such as electronics started by Ferranti in Edinburgh after the second world war; and new skills marching with the substantial influx of American-controlled firms, such as Honeywell with its magnificent growth record. But the lack of emphasis on retraining has effectively sabotaged much advancement in Scotland.

According to St Andrew's House there are 1,500 training places in Scotland, with an annual capacity of 2,500—or just over *one-tenth of one per cent* of the Scottish labour force. This turnover in skills is not a matter for a press release. It is abject. A recent survey by the Organisation for Economic Co-operation and Development states that experience of retraining facilities in advanced countries (perhaps Scotland is not reckoned to be one) "suggests that the capacity of such schemes would need to be extended by about 1 per cent of the labour force per year if identifiable advantages are to be gained."

On this realistic basis, the retraining facilities in Scotland will remain insignificant until annual capacity reaches 22,000—or 1 per cent of the working population. Sweden, however, already retrains more than 2 per cent of its working force every year—and retraining has become a major component of Sweden's pacesetting manpower policies. Meanwhile, in Scotland where old skills are becoming redundant and new skills are in demand, retraining opportunities remain a farce. Not enough people can be retrained for the normal conditions of change, let alone enough to aid Scotland meet the deep-rooted crisis of today.

The vicious circle which dominates thinking and action in Scotland—unemployment, emigration, low wages and the worst housing in Europe—must be decisively broken if Scotland is to have any recognisable future, as Scotland. Let alone a worthwhile and prosperous one. Or is it the intention of a Westminster government to finally announce several hundred-million pound projects—"in Scotland's interests"—and ship up large numbers of English families as the population explosion really begins to hurt in England?

As the New Towns, spread like mines through Scotland's land bridge of industry, grow in population, and many people have a first-ever chance to move into good housing, it is worth firmly stating that the housing position in Scotland today remains a threat to the health and happiness of hundreds of thousands. Even with the so-called "record" figure of 42,629 completions in 1969, the Labour Government never came anywhere near to achieving their promised increase in the housebuilding rate to a—still—pitifully inadequate 50,000 per year. Instead, the position is deteriorating—for existing properties are becoming slums at roughly twice the rate of slum demolitions.

Many generations of Scots have been born and brought up needlessly in slum conditions. The shock finding of the Cullingworth Report in 1967 was that "one in three persons in Scotland lives in a house considered either sub-standard or unfit for human habitation". Finding conditions so bad, this government-

appointed committee led by university lecturer Barry Cullingworth stated in forthright condemnation :

We have found ourselves forced to use strong and emotional
language. Some may feel that this is inappropriate for an
official committee of inquiry; but we have no hesitation in
expressing ourselves thus. The situation in the country generally and in Glasgow particularly, constitutes an indictment of
Government policy. We place the blame squarely on the shoulders of the central government, for though local authorities by
no means come through our examination unscathed, the problem, especially in Glasgow, is of such huge dimensions as to
place it beyond the resources of any single authority, even
though it be the biggest authority in the country. The central
government have failed to provide the necessary leadership
and the resources to encourage, assist and (in places) to compel
local authorities to tackle the problem with the drive which it
requires.

Since those words were printed and published in 1967, the
house-building programme in Glasgow, and throughout Scotland, has slumped; and Glasgow's interest repayment debt—let
alone the capital debt—has grown ever more impossible to manage. Few cities in Britain (perhaps Birmingham was the *only* one)
have gone bankrupt. Glasgow may well be the next.

In Sweden, the situation is slightly different. More than 14 per
cent of all families now own a second home. In Scotland,
however, the public sector has dominated house building—and
still does. From 1945 to 1968, 85 per cent of all houses completed
in Scotland were in the public sector, while the corresponding
proportion in England was only 54 per cent.

The number of major economic or social aspects which have a
direct bearing on the progress of a nation, or the spreadout of its
wealth, are many—embracing everything from education and
transport, to job opportunity and that vague but effective phrase,
"the quality of life". One that cannot be glossed over, and which
has been specially and effectively spotlighted by the Scottish
Council (Development and Industry)—so often compelled to take
over certain aspects of government in Scotland and point the
way—is centralisation.

In its report—*Centralisation*—the Scottish Council stated :

46

"One influence now dominates the industrial scene of Scotland as it is, and as it will develop in the years ahead. This is the rapid acceleration of the amalgamation of industries and of commercial organisations, both in private and in public ownership, together with the stampeding centralisation into London of the real decision-makers which accompanies the process of amalgamation. This is the influence which now pervades the majority of important decisions and policies with which we have to deal. It is not a new phenomenon—but the rate at which it is spreading gives it a new significance."

The effects of centralisation, when carried forward without regard for its regional consequences, is an affliction which is not new to Scotland. An early example of the results of such action by government was the establishment in the early part of this century of virtually all governmental research and development laboratories, and of government research expenditure within industry—both for Defence and civil purposes—in the south of Britain. This was the main cause of that distortion of the geographical pattern of growth of new technological industries which left Scotland bereft of new enterprises in the 1920's and 1930's.

It is hard to realise that for a short time after the first world war Glasgow, among other Scottish centres, was expanding in new fields such as the manufacture of automobiles—the Argyll plant at Alexandria was the second in the world to produce more than 1,000 cars a year—aircraft, radio and cinematography. Then came the sell-out, and many new industries of world-wide potential were closed down and sold-out to competitors in the south. The government exercised no responsibility, and Scotland was abandoned. A write-off.

It is worth recalling that the Scottish Development Council—forerunner of the Scottish Council—was set up by Sir James Lithgow and other magnates as a result of the 1931 slump and terrible unemployment in Scotland—as well as in response to the insistent demand for new light industries to offset the over-concentration on heavy industries. But in the ten previous years Sir James, the bowler-hatted Glasgow shipyard man, had become the uncrowned king of Scotland. With his associates he controlled nearly all of Scotland's main industries—coal, iron, steel and shipbuilding.

How, then, did the Development Council tackle the job of

creating new industries and new employment? From being 26 per cent worse in 1932, Scotland's unemployment became 101 per cent worse than England's by February 1937, and yearly more Scots factories were shut than opened. On 14 November 1937, the Commons was told that the following new factories had been opened in Great Britain and the distressed Areas of Scotland (under Lithgow's sway) in recent years :

	1933	1934	1935	1936
Great Britain	467	520	514	551
Distressed Areas of Scotland	3	5	2	6

Even by 1941 Scotland had only 4,500,000 square feet of factory accommodation allocated for the storage of armaments, and less than 500 square feet for production—one square foot for production to nine square feet for storage. In England, the figures were one square foot for production to two for storage. And Scots were conscripted to work in England. The foregoing illustration could be matched by many others. It is no wonder, then, that Scotland is in grave difficulties—with friends like some Scots, there is no need for enemies. And, inevitably, the situation has grown worse.

The Scottish Council's *Centralisation* report states : "In some ways the situation is more serious than on the surface it might seem to be. Scotland has something over one-tenth of the U.K's population and about the same proportion of its industry. But if we add together the decision-makers who determine the course of future events, their proportion in Scotland—taking private industry, nationalised industry, trade and industrial organisations, and the machinery of government dealing with industry—is likely to be much nearer one man in 50 than one man in 10."

In the publicly-owned sector the headquarters of all the large industries—such as the Coal Board, Steel Board, B.E.A., B.O.A.C., as well as the Forces and Civil Service structure—are in London. In private industry, it is much the same, even though the companies may have large interests in Scotland; may, indeed, be "Scottish" companies.

The Scottish Council's report also pointed out: "centralisation exercises a great effect upon the service industries which support manufacturing industries. This became apparent many years ago, when the formation of the Coal and Hospital Boards led to the rationalisation of such services as printing and medical supplies; these greatly reduced the business of a number of Scottish companies . . ." Equally to the point is this comment: "As the positions of authority within industry diminish in number, as opportunities for employment in Scotland at the top of the tree diminish—whether for people in general management or in finance or in marketing or in research—so also does the vigour and the drive of the whole public life of the community run down. The public activities of the community in large part depend upon the qualities of the men who have got to the top of industrial or commercial organisations, because the same qualities are required for enterprise and success in public affairs . . . Scotland knows only too well the excessive demands made upon the time and energy of people able to give leadership . . ."

It was geography, in conjunction with thrusting and inventive men, which helped us to build our iron, coal and manpower resources into a world-beating combination during the Industrial Revolution—a time when Glasgow's population surged from 12,000 to more than a million in less than 100 years. Now, once again, geography can give Scotland the base she requires to mount firmly a steady advance towards continued prosperity—a prosperity that will seap throughout Scotland from the Solway to the Shetlands.

In another report—*Oceanspan*—the Scottish Council again summarily pre-empts any pretentions the Scottish Office has to authority or leadership, and states: "We may think of Scotland as being an inherently poor nation. But nature has endowed Scotland with a wonderfully varied environment which is the envy of the world. By enlightened planning and enterprise, this can undoubtedly be the setting for the development of a prosperous community."

A reasonable, even conservative statement. But who is going to supply the "enlightened planning and enterprise"? The deep-water facilities of the Clyde estuary are the finest in Europe. The Scottish Office, however, has never produced a blueprint for the area—much of which is of high amenity value—to show how they would like to see it developed.

Sir William Lithgow, son of the old industrial "king", has calculated that the "theoretical cost of bringing iron-ore from Australia to the Clyde in a 200,000-ton ship is the same as the present cost of bringing it from Norway in a 10,000-ton ship". And Tom Craig, once chairman and managing director of Colvilles, and now a board member of the British Steel Corporation, with special responsibility for Scotland, has said that "economies of around 20 per cent would be obtainable if we took full advantage of the Clyde Estuary". If we don't, he warned, steel in Scotland will be "condemned to become a second-rate industry".

In Scotland, it is an unfortunate fact that any of the key industries can be examined, and it can be clearly and objectively observed that short-sighted, hand-to-mouth legislation is useless. Equally observable, and even more unfortunate, is that no government seems able to single out, or even recognise priorities and objectives. The fabric of Scottish life is neglected on a wholesale basis. Three times the size of Holland or Belgium, nearly twice the area of Denmark or Switzerland, Scotland (30,411 square miles) is three-fifths the size of England. But there has been no chance to exploit the many obvious advantages in the interests of the Scots, let alone those that are hidden, because there is no independent Scottish economic planning. It was on 16 December 1882 that Lord Rosebery, who had been made an Under-secretary at the Home Office with responsibility for Scotland, wrote to his friend Gladstone, complaining: "I serve a country which is the backbone of our party, but which is never recognised."

At least Lord Rosebery had the guts to complain—and the honesty to recognise and resent his lack of power. Former Scottish Secretary Mr William Ross, answering questions on television after Labour's 1970 election débâcle, was asked whether he did not think that some measure of devolution would be a good thing, considering that once again Scotland had voted overwhelmingly for Labour—yet were to be ruled by a Tory Government from Westminster. Mr Ross, a self-confessed Scot who proclaims that he yields not an inch in patriotism to anyone —had no doubts: he was against any kind of devolution. Yet when the Tory Government abandoned the comprehensive school scheme, it was Mr Ross who eagerly pointed out in the Commons that they had no right to take a step in Scotland "where you have no mandate..."

This kind of political, or economic schizophrenia is widespread, manifesting itself in all aspects of Scottish life from trade unionism to tourism. It has a debilitating and erosive effect, combined with a painful lack of coherent thinking followed by constructive action. Much, for instance, has been made of major industrial projects which have been directed by the government to come to Scotland for political, rather than sound economic, reasons. The Invergordon aluminium smelter will cost public funds some £35,000,000 and will provide only 160 jobs. Used as risk capital for the setting up of small companies, the money could easily have provided 7,000 to 10,000 jobs. And what of ancilliary industries? Is the smelter to operate in the costly isolation of Rootes, another Government-directed venture? Or is it, and other ventures, to be fully backed up so that the industry is integrated? The whole direction, or attraction, of industry needs to be thoroughly examined—for if major projects are to be established they must be very much more than mere manufacturing units, ready to shut down at the first blink of a Chancellor's eye.

In the *Scots Law Times* of 3 July 1970, Glasgow University Professor David M. Walker produces evidence to show that there is a large body of discontent in Scotland; and the nationalists, who seek independence, "are only the most vociferous". The discontent, Professor Walker believes, is:

because Scotland, so different from England in many ways, is not permitted to have control of its own affairs. The Parliament which sits in Westminster is predominantly the English Parliament, and thinks and acts as such, and Scotland is dragged at the heels of England. Legislation and administration from London is not only distant and remote, but frequently ignorant of and neglectful of peculiarities and differences attaching to Scottish conditions. A large majority of M.P.s have no reason to know or care about how their decisions affect Scotland, and even among lawyers in England there is the most profound ignorance about Scotland and Scottish things. People in England know no more about Scottish affairs than they do about life among the Bushmen, and frequently speak and act as if Scots were equally primitive.

In a different context, the shame of Scotland's position is equally forcibly examined by Andrew Sykes, Professor of Sociology at Strathclyde University. Writing in the *Glasgow Herald Review*—a mid-year survey of the Scottish scene published in June 1970—Professor Sykes states:

> there is no systematic planning of industry in the Scottish interest. Occasional spectacular projects are supported for their publicity value; for their effect on the trade unions, and as a morale booster for local M.P.s with marginal seats. The overall expenditure is not great, when it comes to real government spending Scotland is, to use a Forces expression, "sucking on a hind tit".

Admirably put—and worth a thousand apologetic and self-excusing Scottish Office reports, instantly recognisable for their lack of initiative and dullness of language, reports deformed at birth.

Instead of sprinting whenever the division bell in the Commons demands they toe the line, Scottish M.P.s should be put in touch with the depressing reality of what is *really* happening in Scotland behind the white propaganda shrouds. Probing the social consequences of stale and ineffective economic measures, Professor Sykes observes:

> The man who stays in Scotland faces a long hard struggle to reach a top post that in London terms is no more than a middle-range job readily available to mediocrity. The result is a drain of the able and ambitious to the south. This acts as a depressant on the whole of the national life and on that of industry in particular. The top jobs and salary levels in Scotland are already very much lower than those in the south and these in turn depress all other salary levels. To stay in management in Scotland means few opportunities of promotion, a lower salary, and a lower ultimate ceiling of salary and status. The general result is a loss of interest and incentive, those who stay have little to work for, those who are determined to get on get out.

Professor Sykes adds :

With a combination of English and foreign control much of Scottish industry is being rapidly reduced to the level of battery hens with much the same degree of initiative and control over their future : they are hand fed, they produce, when they cease to be sufficiently productive they can be disposed of as broilers. The comparison is not exaggerated for, as the managerial, engineering and other skills leave Scotland, so also does the ability to build new industry of her own and the future becomes completely dependent on the goodwill of others and on decisions made elsewhere. While we spend money to develop backward countries Scotland herself becomes a pensioner nation.

All credit to the Scottish Council—but what an indictment of the Scottish Office—when Professor Sykes can state (as I have said previously in the *Daily Record*) that the Council :

has done more for the industrial development of the country [Scotland] than any government or combination of governments. The Scottish M.P.s themselves are ineffectual as a pressure group ... Certainly no M.P., would further his political career in a national party by becoming identified too closely with Scottish interests. The same problem exists with the trade unions ... power and promotion within them lies in the south.

If the Lowlands of Scotland cannot be made to work effectively, if the work-load cannot be spread so all Scotland becomes involved—then the future is bleakly desperate for the emptying Highlands and Islands, the forgotten South-West and the Border counties. The present situation is already an indictment of those with power but no will.

In 1964–65 the Labour Government set up ten economic planning divisions for Great Britain, of which Scotland was one. This move was followed by the ill-fated and discredited five-year plan for the Scottish economy, issued in January 1966. In it, Scotland was sub-divided into five areas—the Highlands and Islands, the North-East, Central Scotland, the Borders and the

South West—all of which were to be studied separately. A sixth area—Tayside—with Dundee as its focal point was added later.

On 20 July 1970 the government-sponsored Tayside study was published, the result of a two-year planning and economic investigation. The hurry was because Tayside was one of three parts of the United Kingdom—the other are Humberside and Severnside—which the Government then wanted studied for long-term population needs. Scotland's?—or as an overspill area for England? The study is primarily concerned with the region's prospects over a 30-year period—the potential is outlined for increasing Tayside's population from 450,000 to up to 750,000 by the year 2001—but it also considers immediate problems and puts forward a first-phase plan covering the next 10 years. This would involve a population increase of 56,000 (meaning at least 10,000 new manufacturing jobs) with the bulk of this initial development concentrated in the Perth-Dundee-Arbroath axis— which the planners see as a "spine" for the long-term city region expansion which they recommend. In other words, it would not only be a first move to develop a 3,000-square-mile area covering Angus, most of Perthshire, North Fife and Dundee : it would also consolidate the power and drawing strength of the narrow industrial belt.

The estimated cost of the plan is put at £1,800 million, and if the full regional plan is achieved Dundee's population would rise by 110,000 to 325,000, Perth's by 50,000 to 109,000, and Arbroath's by 27,000 to 52,000. Big increases are also expected in towns like Forfar, Montrose, Blairgowrie, St Andrews and Cupar. At present, as the Study notes, the major economic problem on Tayside (and most other places in Scotland) "is its slow growth, the main indications of which are falling employment, sluggish growth of incomes from employment and relatively high net emigration from key age groups". A further matter of particular concern is the Study's forecast shortage of jobs for men in the area.

Meanwhile, the Central Borders study, which envisaged expanding the population in its area from about 25,000 to 100,000 by 1980, has ground to a halt in controversy and court orders, plus two public inquiries with perhaps more to come. At the same time, the Border railway has been closed, demonstrating how little the Transport Minister in London cared about subregional policy, and how little power former Scottish Secretary Mr Ross had, or could use.

While the argument continues, it is worth noting that the Highlands and Islands Development Board, discussing government control at regional level, told a sitting of the Crowther Commission on the Constitution in Glasgow: "We have never been in doubt that this close control was imposed with the very best of intentions"—what else *could* the Board say? "But it is our view that it blurs the concept of responsible management and accountability. We think there is a wide field where decision-making could be carried out nearer the cutting edge."

Pointing out that there was a lack of flexibility, and that policies on industrial development incentives appeared to be framed to meet the generality of problems found in development areas in Great Britain, the Board added: "But these policies do not necessarily meet the extraordinary requirements for the effective development of a region such as ours . . . we suspect that too little regard may be paid to the consequences, for regions such as ours, of national fiscal policies." Behind the words, bland as a trout rising at sunset, is the bite of helpless bitterness. For the whole economic running of England and Scotland should be operated on distinct levels, let alone meeting the special requirements of the Highlands with its heritage of betrayal, neglect, despair and blossoming landlordism.

The Selective Employment Tax, which the present Tory Government is pledged to abolish—is not only an unpopular and blunt instrument of fiscal policy: it does great harm to many areas of Scotland which have a low proportion of manufacturing industry relative to services.

Talk about Scotland—its problems and its potential—has been endless in the past few years. Little has been done compared to what could so easily have been achieved by any interested and constructive government. The impact of the Scottish Economic Planning Council has been derisory—an occasional claptrap echo has signalled a rare sitting, an event which even responsible and news-hungry journalists largely ignore. Part-time officials spend some 15 hours a year planning for a nation.

In the Lowlands there is magnificent scenery—though it may lack the historic grandeur of the North-West; and the people, from those in Ayrshire mining villages to the shepherds and gamekeepers of Langholm up to Carter Bar, or the farmers and fishermen on the Solway, and those up the east coast from Berwick, or who live in such Border towns as Hawick, retain an individualism which is almost a philosophy.

It was the late Tom Johnston, thought by many to be the only Scottish Secretary of State worthy of the post, who wrote in the foreword of G. S. Fraser's *A Vision of Scotland* :

I come of a breed of men who for centuries were the wardens of the Scottish marches, and who, as Camden the English historian records, bore the brunt of the resistance to the English invasions. Upon occasions we would be decimated to some five hundred "proper and sufficient men", but aye somehow we survived. And in my own person I represented in Parliament for over twenty years the field of Bannockburn and the Wallace Monument on the Abbey Craig. So that alike by pedigree and personal contact my affinities lie in the soil north of the Cheviots, and with the people who dwell there . . .

Few Scots, indeed, have passed New England Bay and explored the Mull of Galloway where, from the lighthouse on a clear day, you can "see the Isle of Man, the Mountains of Mourne, and Kintyre to the Paps of Jura away over in the Western Isles". Nor do all that many know the lonely hills between Selkirk and Moffat, or the fishing villages, sprayed by the North Sea on the wild coast from the lost town of Berwick to Dunbar.

Dr Malcolm Slesser, 43, lecturer in chemical engineering at the University of Strathclyde, and a mountaineer and explorer of international repute, does not want his children to grow up as second-class citizens in an industrial colony :

I am qualified to assess Scotland's assets for I have travelled the world and lived abroad. I can see that Scotland has every national asset necessary for her to become a modern prosperous state. Even as it is, through past endeavours, Scotland is the fourteenth richest country in the world (average income per head) yet its most talented sons and daughters are obliged to leave their homeland year by year to seek elsewhere the opportunities they cannot find at home. Why? Because Scotland is like a ship without a rudder. It is without a controlling force to manage its present and plan its future . . .

There are enough guide books on Scotland to satisfy the most indulgent of armchair travellers. But the survival and future of Scotland depends on the narrow strip between the Clyde and the Forth—a cartridge belt of industry. But the powder has long been damp, and the "promises" and the "plans" are all at the muzzle-loading stage. Yet despite the continuing crisis—and there are many fields such as education and transport which I have omitted—and despite the protestations from politicians, it is significant that the total floor area for industrial development approved in Scotland for 1969 was 9.1 million square feet—2.7 million square feet less than in 1968. The total floor area approved in Great Britain, however, increased from 110.3 million square feet to 115.9 million square feet. Scotland, therefore, so obviously needing to thrust forward and achieve a break-through, received only 7.9 per cent of the total floor area of indus-trial development certificates approved in Great Britain in 1969. A seemingly unexciting statistic—but one which demonstrates that on the vital front of industrial expansion Scotland, far from getting an extra boost, is lagging further behind.

With the Wheatley Report on the restructuring of local government still to be implemented in some way; and negotiations still continuing to achieve entry to the Common Market, though Scotland has not even the pretence of effective representation, it is obvious that unless power of decision is achieved we will con-tinue to suck the "hind tit" until Scotland, officially, has "shire" added on. It is up to the Scots. If they fail to recognise the situa-tion, if they find they cannot act together with resolve, then I can echo the comment made by Lord Kames, when he paid his last visit to the Court of Session in his eighty-seventh year : "Fare ye a' weel, ye bitches!"

4

EDUCATION

T. R. Bone

S OCIAL CHANGE IS inevitably reflected in educational change, and Scottish education by 1981 will be different from what it is in 1971 if for no other reason than that life in Scotland in 1981 will be different from what it is today. If fewer unskilled workers can be employed in the community, the period of general education will be longer and more of our young people will reach a level of attainment which will take them into skilled jobs. If people have more leisure, more time will be spent in schools helping them to learn how to achieve personal satisfaction through leisure pursuits. If social attitudes become more permissive, authoritarianism will be less evident in the schools. If society becomes more egalitarian, our school system will put less emphasis on differences of ability among young people; if in local government power moves from the smaller to the larger units, there will be a similar movement in education; if our society comes to depend more and more heavily on technology, there will be greater use of technological aids in our schools, colleges, and universities. Or if for some reason, in any one of these instances—permissiveness, perhaps, or the egalitarian movement—the direction of social change is suddenly reversed, our educational system will respond accordingly.

Looking back over any lengthy period, this correspondence between educational and social change is so clearly marked that one comes to take it for granted, to assume that it will always happen anyhow, but the particular form that the changes take, as distinct from the general direction, always depends on specific pressures operating at the time. In 1960 17,175 young Scots were presented for the Leaving Certificate at the end of their secondary education; in 1968 there were 87,448 who were presented for the Scottish Certificate of Education.[1] The expan-

sion in certificate work may have indeed been historically inevitable, but the actual shape that that expansion took was determined largely by the deliberations of a small Working Party
which reported in 1959.[2]

Thus an attempt to forecast what lies ahead for Scottish
education in the 1970's must be based on an examination of the
particular pressures operating within the system just now, looking back first at what happened in the 1960's to see how much
further particular movements still have to go, and to identify
the origins of the forces which are likely to shape the changes of
the near future.

In primary education, the period of the 1960's was one of
transformation and even upheaval, largely because of the
appearance and reception given to the Scottish Education
Department's memorandum *Primary Education in Scotland*.
This document, published in 1965 and containing little that
would have been regarded as novel by many English junior
school teachers of the 1950's, marked an important change in
official thinking in Scotland, for it shifted the emphasis away
from teachers teaching and on to children learning. Whereas
such previous S.E.D. publications as the 1950 *The Primary
School in Scotland*, had stressed the teacher's responsibilities to
society, saying for instance:

The time available for instruction is all too short, and the
teacher should consider carefully whether that time is being
used to the best advantage.[3]

In 1965 official concern now concentrated on the needs of the
pupils:

It is now recognised that learning occurs most effectively
when the learner is personally involved in purposeful activity
which captures his interest or arises from it. Consequently the
emphasis in primary education is now more on learning by
the pupil than on instruction by the teacher ... The teacher's
role is changing as teacher-dominated methods and subject-
centred curricula give way to methods and curricula based on
the needs and interests of the child.[4]

It can be argued[5] that such documents as the 1965 *Primary Education in Scotland* are never attempts to persuade the whole teaching profession to alter their established practices, but rather endeavour to accelerate changes which are already taking place, and it must be admitted that in 1965 there were Scottish primary schools which were already moving along lines approaching a child-centred view of education, but such schools were very much in the minority, and it would be wrong to underestimate the importance of the part played by the committee of inspectors and teachers who produced the memorandum. Indeed the long-founded Scottish emphasis on instruction—what James Scotland[6] refers to when, in summing up the Scottish traditions in education, he says that the most important person in the classroom has always been the teacher, whatever the theorists may say—was so strong that the 1965 document would probably have had little effect if it had not been for the unusually powerful nature of the follow-up it received.

Three separate factors contributed to this. The Department now had a team of inspectors[7] who had been largely freed from divisional responsibilities to be concerned with the development of primary education, and they mounted a prolonged campaign in support of the memorandum, arranging meetings of teachers all over the country, calling on the experience of those who had successfully experimented with projects, centres of interest, activity methods, etc., and generally doing all that they could to encourage teachers in hitherto traditional schools to adopt the new approaches.

The second factor was the work of the colleges of education, which, with occasional reservations, quickly began to use the memorandum as prescribed reading for their students, and to advocate the adoption of its views. The colleges, of course, had long been more progressive than the schools, and they found the appearance of *Primary Education in Scotland* an encouragement to fresh efforts in the direction of a more pupil-centred curriculum. Soon all were also heavily involved in the provision of in-service courses on which the new methods were explained and demonstrated to practising teachers. This was particularly the case with the three new colleges which opened in the mid 60's, Craigie, Callendar Park and Hamilton, for their freedom from the distractions of providing courses for secondary teachers, and from the development of the B.Ed. degree, allowed them to throw themselves into the battle on behalf of child-centred education with admirable enthusiasm.

The third development which lent support to the 1965 memorandum was the decision of some of the largest of the education authorities to appoint their own local advisers.[8] This decision was partly taken for administrative reasons, since the directors of education and their deputies were finding it increasingly difficult to spend much time in the schools they controlled, but its general effect was to send into the schools a new group of men and women whose function, in part at least, was to promote development and professional growth, and these advisers, as far as their work lay in the primary schools, found in the 1965 memorandum a natural guide for their efforts. Some of them, indeed, had been the very teachers whose success with the new methods had provided a slipway for the launching of that document.

The result of all this has been a period of considerable change in the primary schools of Scotland.[9] Few have remained entirely untouched by the new movements, and many have been transformed—so much so that parents have often been puzzled by the differences between the practices of the schools they themselves attended in the late 1930's or early 1940's and those of the schools attended by their children in the late 1960's. Some schools even found it necessary to hold evening meetings and open days so that new methods might be explained to parents and the results they could achieve demonstrated.

Partly the changes were curricular; partly they were methodological. The curriculum was broadened by the introduction of new subjects like French, and Mathematics and Science of a kind hitherto unknown in Scottish primary schools made their appearance. Older subjects like Music and Painting were accorded a much more prominent place; Drama in some schools became a regular rather than an end-of-term activity; and Physical Education was revolutionised by a shift towards free movement instead of carefully predetermined exercises.

Most important was the emphasis put on combining what had previously been quite separate subjects, so that they might together contribute to the better understanding of some problem or topic of interest. The *Primary* memorandum had stated that it was "quite impossible to treat the subjects of the curriculum in isolation from one another if education is to be meaningful to the child"[10], and "integration" became the watchword of the day. History, Geography, Science and Arithmetic were linked together in what was called "environmental studies", an attempt to harness the characteristic methods and skills involved in these disciplines to enable the child to achieve a fuller understanding of the world around him.

The methodological changes were even more significant than the curricular, however. Whereas Scottish schoolchildren in the past had been, by and large, expected to spend most of their time sitting quietly at their desks, listening, watching, or carrying out specific tasks under instruction, now a much larger proportion of the school day is spent by children in what the memorandum called "purposeful activity".[11] Instead of sitting in straight rows facing the front (clearly the best position for an audience), children in very many Scottish primary schools now sit in groups, facing one another (the best position for shared activity).

The teacher's role is now less that of the instructor, and more that of the promoter of learning, the difference being that the instructor knows in advance what skills she wants her pupils to master, and has planned the children's activities so that they do master them, whereas the promoter of learning is much less systematic in her approach, and tends rather to take advantage of situations or interests that arise naturally in the classroom, exploring the educational potentialities of experience, being willing to allow pupils to follow up their own suggestions and letting them "discover" (a key word in the new movement) ways of solving the problems which they meet. Oversimplifying, one can say that when a child asks a question, the instructor tends to supply the answer, and the promoter of learning tends to ask the child another question which will lead him to find the answer for himself. The instructor employs regular tests, tends to encourage competition among pupils, and normally invokes sanctions of some kind if things begin to go wrong. The promoter of learning tends to encourage work of a kind that cannot easily be assessed by tests, depends quite heavily on co-operation among pupils, and hopes that she can rely on the interest of the children in what they are doing to prevent difficulties of the kind that would necessitate punishment.

While it would be unfair to suggest that the vast majority of Scottish primary teachers were in the past no more than instructors in the sense described above, they tended to conform more closely to that model than to the other, and the recent shift of emphasis has not come easily to them. While the promoter of learning, if successful, can achieve work of a standard beyond that of the normal expectation of any instructor,[12] her type of teaching can easily fail, and when it does the failure tends to be spectacular. The lack of well-defined objectives, the lack of direction, and the lack of sanctions can lead to an almost complete breakdown in the classroom—and a breakdown of a kind completely foreign to the Scottish tradition, since it is one in which the teacher is seen to have lost control of the situation. The instructor may be failing and no one—headmaster, other members of staff, or the instructor herself—may realise it; when the promoter of learning, as described above, fails, everyone is soon aware of it. The fear of this kind of failure, or sometimes the actual experience of it (often while still unsure of herself in the classroom), has made it specially difficult for the Scottish teacher to adopt this role.

Thus the primary changes, both in curriculum and in methods, have not endeared themselves to all Scottish teachers, and it would almost certainly be a mistake to regard the 1970's as a period in which the new style of teaching will come to replace the old completely. Resistance has come, and will continue to come, partly because the changes create difficulties for teachers, and partly also because some at least of those changes are open to logical dispute. *Primary Education in Scotland* did not argue a detailed case for all of its suggestions, but, perhaps for greater impact, contained a large number of short chapters, in which some of its key concepts, like "activity", "discovery", "integration" and "needs" were advanced in a way that made it all too easy for them to become slogans to be brandished rather than understood. Some of the work done by teachers in the name of "discovery" or "integration" has been alarmingly naive.

It would be blatantly wrong, however, to judge educational reforms by the abuses performed in their name, and most Scottish teachers would not be guilty of such unfairness. Much more powerful objections could be made to some of the proposals of the memorandum. For instance, the suggestion that arithmetic could be embraced by "environmental studies" has been scorned by the teachers, who may have accepted opportunities to relate numerical skills to the exploration of the environment, but who have insisted on the continuation of a systematic, if old-fashioned, coverage when teaching the skills in the first place.

More serious still have been the criticisms of some of the attempts to modernise the primary curriculum. Parts of the "new mathematics" may have merely replaced old "lumber" with new; and the attempt to introduce a foreign language has now been officially admitted to have been almost wholly a failure.[13]

Thus if one has to forecast what will happen in primary education in Scotland in the 1970's, one should probably say that we shall see a quite lengthy continuation of a process that has already begun—the process of assimilating the most durable of the 1965 memorandum's suggestions into the existing Scottish tradition. There will be some movement back towards the regular practising of skills; there will be a little less emphasis on work arising from the spontaneous interests of the children, and slightly more on the encouragement by teachers of such interests as seem to them worthy of the expenditure of time and effort in the classroom. But many of the recent changes will never be reversed : the formal rows of the past will not return to schools that have managed to relinquish them; children will never be required to play as passive a role as they too often played before.

Perhaps this is a pessimistic forecast, perhaps more radical reforms are needed, but it does not seem likely that they will occur. Change in education very rarely comes from within, and in the 1970's in primary education there may well be an absence of the kind of pressure from without which would be needed to effect it.

Pressure came in the mid 60's from several directions; from a memorandum which was felt by the Scottish Education Department, for some years before it appeared, to be needed because the official Scottish position on primary education looked so backward when compared with that of England and elsewhere; from a newly created team of inspectors who gave that memorandum the support it needed; from the new colleges which found in the memorandum a gospel to propagate; and from local advisers who threw themselves into a new job with natural enthusiasm and drive.

It does not seem at present likely that the S.E.D. will issue a major new primary document in the 70's, and the coming diffi-culties in secondary education, with the addition of important changes in local administration, will almost certainly keep the Department preoccupied for most of the decade ahead. The inspectors will find the task of consolidating the gains of the late 60's in the primary schools sufficient for at least several years ahead, and may even have to fight hard at times to combat reactionary moves, but by the end of the 70's the most import-ant of the 1965 changes will have been assimilated. The col-leges of education will be concentrating most of their efforts on producing secondary teachers, and the three new colleges will either be drawn into this work or drift into a backwater as far as higher education is concerned. And the local primary advisers could perhaps run out of steam, as their own classroom achievements recede, or alternatively they may come to assume a more administrative role and spend less of their time in schools.

The main reason for this forecast of assimilation rather than further change in the primary schools is, however, a very simple one. The area of greatest concern in the decade ahead is bound to be that of the secondary schools, for it is there that the growth of population and of educational expectations, backed by the raising of the leaving age, will create the greatest need, and the difficulties of meeting that need are likely to be so enormous, both in the matter of the supply of teachers and in that of devising appropriate curricula, that the attention of educational planners and administrators, both at national and local levels, is bound to be concentrated on that area. The problems of the primary schools will seem relatively unimportant.

There is one area, nevertheless, where there is likely to be further changes in the primary schools. This is the area of relation-ships between parents and teachers, of contact and communica-tion between the home and the school. The importance of such contact, and of parental interest in and support for the work of teachers, has been clearly demonstrated by a number of research studies,[14] and especially by the national survey

65

commissioned by the Plowden Committee of 1967,[15] which showed that a pupil's performance in school work is more likely to be affected by the level of interest taken by his parents than by either the locality of his home and the living conditions it provides or the quality of the school he attends.

As more and more parents come to have a good education themselves, and to realise the importance of education in their children's lives, there is likely to be an increased parental willingness to show interest in schools and to support the teachers in their work. Indeed, the 1960's have already supplied abundant evidence of this growing concern on the part of parents in the form of attendances at parent-teacher meetings and the emergence of bodies like the Confederation for the Advancement of State Education. With a little more encouragement from the schools, parents could come to play a very useful part in the educative process.

But British teachers are very cautious about giving that encouragement. Not only have they tended to underestimate the interest that parents take in the education of their children, as was shown in Catherine Lindsay's study of relationships in Easterhouse;[16] they also have been reluctant to involve themselves in regular meetings with parents or in the kind of reciprocal contact that could be so beneficial to the children. Young and McGeeney's work in a difficult London area demonstrated this very clearly.[17] The teacher's reasons are of course understandable. They fear that their cherished autonomy in the classroom may be destroyed if parents are allowed to play too prominent a part. The teacher, as a professionally qualified person, naturally would resent having her opinion on matters of curriculum or methods challenged by laymen. If society is not willing to pay teachers the salaries they feel entitled to for what they do already, society can hardly expect them to give up more of their time in undertaking further responsibilities in the evenings. And if the teacher is asked to carry too many extra burdens of this kind, there is a danger that the work which she is best qualified to do, the actual teaching of the children, may suffer.

Yet one cannot but feel that once the process of involving parents in closer contact with the schools begins, it is not likely to be reversed, and every year we are seeing more headmasters and school staffs proving willing to advance towards greater co-operation. In the 1970's, with more parents who themselves have had an education which did not stop at the minimum leaving age, and with television and newspapers continuing to excite widespread interest in education, the probable forecast is that parental involvement in school affairs will considerably increase.

If it is to happen smoothly, and to be profitable for all concerned—parents, teachers, and especially children—it will be best if it is initiated by the schools, and such measures as are taken cause parents to appreciate the teachers' professional skills and insights into children's learning processes. One example would be improved school reports of the type used by Lawrence Green,[18] in which parents are given a full assessment of their child's abilities and needs, instead of the almost meaningless list of marks which has been too often all that schools have passed on to parents as an indication of their offsprings' progress, and, perhaps significantly, efforts to institute much more meaningful reports have recently been made in Scotland.[19]

If this does happen, and schools receive much greater support from parents, one other forecast can confidently be made. The more parents are involved with the schools, the less will be the need for corporal punishment, and the less will teachers be inclined to have recourse to sanctions of that kind. Scottish education was for many centuries noted for the use of severe punishments, and it is unfortunate that even today, when the majority of advanced educational systems have abandoned it, the belt is still regularly used in many Scottish schools. To relinquish it will not be easy, but there may be a very significant change in the position within the coming decade, thanks to the easing of the teacher shortage for primary schools, the appearance of more men teachers, and the closer contact between teachers and parents.

Attention in the 1970's will not be concentrated on primary schools, however, but rather on their secondary counterparts, for it is there that the heaviest pressures are bound to be felt. Because of the population explosion, and the growth in general expectations about education, it is expected that the number of pupils in secondary schools will rise from about 230,000 in 1956 to about 410,000 in 1986, as against the much more modest increase from about 620,000 to 670,000 in the primary school population over the same period.[20] It is this vast increase in the demand for secondary education, to be compounded by the raising of the minimum school leaving age to sixteen in 1972, which may well create conditions of crisis in our secondary schools.

The greatest problem, of course, concerns the supply of teachers needed to cope with this coming wave of secondary pupils. In Scotland only university graduates are qualified, after training, to teach the academic subjects in secondary schools, and therefore the Scottish position may be worse than the English, where college trained diploma students can teach in the lower forms. What makes the position specially serious is that though the universities have greatly increased the output of graduates, the proportion entering teaching has not in recent years been sufficient to meet the needs of the schools. The Robbins Committee estimated that the number of graduates teaching in Scotland would rise from 17,400 in 1961 to 21,000 in 1970, and to 35,000 in 1980.[21] But in 1969 there were only 16,800 graduates teaching in Scotland—600 fewer than in 1961—so that we are over 4,000 short of the Robbins prediction for 1970. It is no wonder that we are talking of a crisis ahead.[22]

The teachers' associations hope that a larger proportion of university graduates can be attracted into teaching, perhaps by higher salaries, but one cannot but doubt the likelihood of this happening on the necessary scale. It would appear that some new source of supply will have to be found.

The most effective new contribution to the supply of secondary teachers made in the 1960's was the establishment of the B.Ed. degree, awarded by the four ancient universities in conjunction with the colleges of education at Jordanhill, Moray House, Aberdeen and Dundee, where most of the four year courses are actually provided, and those who have had contact with them generally agree that the B.Ed. graduates are in many ways being better prepared for their work in the schools than are those who add a one year course of teacher training to an ordinary degree from a university. But there are simply not enough. B.Ed. students to meet the urgent need of the early 1970's, and though the numbers taking this degree will undoubtedly grow, the restrictions originally imposed by the universities, coupled with the caution displayed by the colleges themselves, have prevented rapid development of a kind which might otherwise have been achieved. If those students who performed very well in the first year of the ordinary college diploma courses could transfer to the B.Ed. course, and so become qualified for secondary teaching, it might do much to alleviate the shortage in that area, but only in the smallest college, Dundee, have arrangements with the university made this possible. The 1970's should see some rationalisation and improvement in this situation.

Another important suggestion to alleviate the secondary teacher shortage has been that of the institution of an associateship course in the colleges, which would lead, after four years, to a qualification for secondary work. This suggestion was made by the college principals as long ago as February 1965, but it has been steadfastly opposed by the teachers' associations, who view it as blatant dilution of the entry requirements for teaching, and the General Teaching Council rejected the idea in 1968. Obviously what matters most is the standard reached by a person at the end of a course, rather than the level of his qualifications at the beginning of it, but the teachers' associations have committed themselves so clearly to opposition to this associateship that it is no longer a political possibility. If some other way could be found of achieving the same ends, but saving the faces of all parties concerned, it might be accepted however, especially in the grave situation in which the secondary schools will soon find themselves.

It is also possible, of course, that the crisis may be delayed by a reversal of the decision to raise the school leaving age in 1972. This would have been highly unlikely if the Labour Party had won the General Election of June 1970, since the Labour Government aroused a storm of resentment among its own followers when it was forced to decide against raising the leaving age in January 1968, and would obviously have been extremely reluctant to break its promises on this matter again. After the Conservative victory, it is still unlikely that the decision will be reversed, since the Conservative Election Manifesto committed that party to raising the leaving age, even if the extension of secondary education for all is more a Labour policy than a Conservative one. Since the population curve dips slightly for fifteen year olds in 1972, that is the best time to raise the age, and we must assume that it is going to happen.

69

In that case, one must recognise that the most serious educational problem of the decade will be the matter of providing courses suitable to the needs of those pupils who would otherwise have left at fifteen.

Revision of syllabuses has been one of the marked features of secondary education in the 1960's, and far-reaching changes have been introduced in many subjects, especially Physics, Chemistry, Biology, and Mathematics. To compare the Consultative Committee on the Curriculum's Paper No. 7, *Science for General Education*[23] with anything produced in Britain before 1960, for instance, is to see how far thinking about syllabus revision moved in a relatively short time. But while curriculum revision has been fairly successful as far as certificate pupils have been concerned, the revision of courses for non-certificate pupils has proved a more difficult problem.

When the leaving age is raised, undoubtedly there will be some pupils who will go on successfully to "O" grade certificate courses who would otherwise have left school, but there will also be large numbers uninterested in, and unsuited for, certificate work as we know it at present at least, and many teachers will admit to being extremely worried as to what to do with them. The S.E.D. laid down general guide-lines in its 1966 document *Raising the Leaving Age : Suggestions for Courses*,[24] urging that three elements should be stressed—social and moral education, preparation for leisure, and vocation-based activities—but these admirable ideas need to be worked out in much greater detail if many teachers are to be convinced that they will succeed, and the "yellow peril", as the teachers referred to that 1966 document because of the colour of its jacket, has been largely disregarded.

Some useful work has been done by individual departments in colleges of education to prepare students for work with this 15 to 16 non-certificate group, but one is forced to admit that preparations have so far been inadequate. The basic trouble is that even now so many people do not really believe that the leaving age will be raised; this step has been postponed so often that they feel it will be postponed again.

In this situation, there are many who consider that we are wrong to be thinking of raising the leaving age, as it was first thought of in 1918, in terms of schools and schoolteachers alone. They have noticed how many pupils have left schools at fifteen because there was something about the discipline, or the general atmosphere, that irked them, perhaps because they had reached a stage where they objected to being treated as school pupils any more, and some of these young people have gone happily to further education colleges where they felt that a more adult atmosphere prevailed. The "educators" most successful with adolescents of this type have sometimes not been schoolteachers, or even further education lecturers, but youth leaders and social workers. Thus there are many who consider that a variety of educational agencies should be deployed to tackle this problem, so that the schoolteachers could be assisted by trained youth leaders, and that the fifteen-year-old non-certificate pupils could spend a good part of their time in further education courses.

The danger here is that general education will be neglected in favour of apparently more relevant training in specific skills, when of course the main argument for raising the leaving age at all is the need to extend general education in an age when specific skills can quickly become obsolete. Presumably it is this which caused Mr William Ross, as Secretary of State, to declare himself unequivocably against the transfer of any pupils on a full-time basis to colleges of further education for their final year of compulsory schooling.[25] Yet if general education must not be forgotten, the case for drawing on the resources of the further education colleges, and the youth leaders, is a strong one, and if it is the schools which must bear the main burden in the coming crisis, it will be surprising, and perhaps disastrous, if they are in the end left to bear it alone.

In spite of the 1970 Election results, these schools will mostly be comprehensive. After the appearance of S.E.D. Circular 600 in 1965, urging local authorities to reorganise their secondary schools on comprehensive lines,[26] plans for a comprehensive system were developed in most areas, and these were related to building programmes in such a way that any attempt at reversal would put many authorities back more seriously than they would be prepared to accept. Thus though Mr Gordon Campbell has now withdrawn Circular 600,[27] and has made it clear that the Conservative Government does not wish to impose any particular form of secondary education, the local authorities, being free to proceed as they wish, are likely to continue with their existing plans—and these are comprehensive in most cases.

What has been effectively stopped by the 1970 Election result has been the attempt by the Labour Secretary of State, Mr Ross, to end the position of the fee-paying and selective local authority schools in Edinburgh and Glasgow. Indeed the Conservative victory proved a triumphant justification for the delaying tactics employed by the education committees of those two cities, which even exploited loopholes in the law to keep fee-paying and selection alive in local authority schools after the Education (Scotland) Act of 1969 had been passed with the specific intention of ending them. Now these few schools appear safe for at least a few years longer.

Within the comprehensive schools, the problem of teaching mixed ability groups at present attracts most attention, but it is likely to be solved in one way or another before the end of the 1970's. The Secretary of State, in Circular 614 of 1966, advised local authorities that pupils should not be allocated to certificate or non-certificate courses on the basis of their primary school record or on a transfer test taken at 11 or 12, and he urged that a decision on a pupil's course should not be taken till there had been time for a careful assessment of his interests and aptitudes in the initial stages of secondary schooling.[28] This implied a "common course" with mixed ability groups in at least the first year of the secondary schools, and by 1969 most local authority secondaries were making some attempt to provide this. But the results have been in many ways unsatisfactory, partly because of the genuine difficulties of teaching subjects like Mathematics and French to pupils of widely varying ability, and partly because most Scottish secondary teachers have been predisposed against the attempt. Group methods, which help primary teachers to deal with a comparable situation, have not been widely used. By and large, one can say that the sooner most secondary teachers have been able to divide their pupils up into reasonably homogeneous ability groups, the happier they have been.

This situation gives cause for concern, since it means that the reasonably accurate and objective system of selection which prevailed in the days of the transfer tests has been replaced by streaming or setting (which is streaming within subjects) based on the inevitably subjective and less accurate judgements of individual teachers. Unfortunately, when this happens teachers are likely to discriminate unconsciously against working class pupils rather than middle class, against "difficult" pupils rather than those who are quiet and well-behaved, and even perhaps against boys rather than girls. Clearly this is far from what the Secretary of State was hoping for when he issued Circular 614.

The problem is so serious that it is improbable that the decade of the 70's will pass without some further attempt to deal with it on the part of the Scottish Education Department and the local authorities. There will be a temptation to return to standardised tests, taken of course at the age of thirteen or fourteen rather than eleven or twelve, and this may seem particularly suitable in areas where a two-tier system of comprehensive schools has been instituted, with a move for certificate pupils from a junior high school at fourteen. A Conservative Secretary of State would probably allow authorities to employ such tests if they wished. A quite different idea, however, more in keeping with Circular 614's suggestions of the need for flexibility in the "period of orientation", would be to experiment with the French belief that children of different abilities should be allowed different lengths of time to reach the same stage—that some children, for instance, may take three years instead of two to attain sufficient mastery of basic skills for them to be allowed to go on to certificate work. Our greatest difficulty at present, especially in "sequential" subjects like Mathematics and French, is that we try to carry pupils of different abilities along at the same pace, and find this impossible.

One should like to think that the 1970's would see some weakening of the stranglehold which examinations exert on the secondary curriculum in Scotland, following the highly attractive recommendations of the Ruthven Report of 1967.[29] The pressures of parents for certificate success for their children, however, backed by the demands of principal teachers for more time to teach their rapidly expanding syllabuses, will make it hard for headmasters to ensure that all pupils receive a properly balanced course, catering for the total development of their personalities as well as for their academic needs.

One development that may help will be the gradual realisation that the S.C.E. certificate examinations are already, and soon will more obviously be, little more than a standardising check on the teachers' own estimates of their pupils' abilities. The sheer impossibility of providing a completely reliable grading of so many thousands of young people in so many different subjects has forced the S.C.E. Examination Board to rely heavily on the teachers' estimates in the 1960's, and as the number of pupils taking the examinations climb steadily in the 1970's, this process will continue. Quite certainly, the S.C.E. examinations will move rapidly towards the employment of objective tests, capable of being quickly scored by a computer, but since these can only test certain aspects of important subjects like English, the S.C.E. examination will have to be seen as a standardising procedure which ensures that the schools' own assessments of their pupils' worth are scaled to a national pattern.

If this happens, the schools will have more freedom to develop their own syllabuses, and this could be highly advantageous to teachers of imagination and enterprise. But the S.C.E. objective test will pose a threat nevertheless, for the schools will doubtless devise their own objective tests to prepare their pupils, and a long series of examinations of this kind could lead to the destruction of creative work.

The new comprehensive schools will tend to be larger than those we have known in the past, and inevitably will create problems. The bureaucratic nature of large institutions tends to cause the territorial barons within them, in this case the heads of the subject departments, to guard their own interests jealously and to resist plans for integrated endeavour towards goals which pertain to the whole institution rather than the subject department itself. The baron does not like to see some of his knights going off from time to time to fight under another banner. Yet integrated action of this kind is certainly needed in our secondary schools.

Another weakness of the large institution is that its very size creates problems for its chief administrators, who have to be highly skilled in management if they are not to become submerged by matters of a routine nature. As more and more pupils have to be catered for, more and more teachers communicated with, and more and more complex arrangements made, it will be an exceptional headmaster who will be able to afford sufficient time for planning improvements in his school's provision, rather than just coping with problems as they arise.

But it will not be good enough for the educational managers to be running very hard simply to keep themselves in the same place; education must move ahead, to keep up with the rapid pace of development in society.

Fortunately the headmasters will be assisted by a growing band of housemasters, who will take over some of the administrative and pastoral duties with regard to particular groups of pupils. This should give headmasters more opportunity for long-term planning, and it should also help to link the schools more closely to the other social services in the community. As Catherine Lindsay's Easterhouse survey showed,[30] at present the welfare officers, health visitors, probation officers, family case workers and police, etc., are frequently possessed of information about boys and girls which would help the schools they attend to deal more adequately with their problems, but the schools have no system for making use of all this information. One hopes that the housemasters will be the levers by which schools will gradually be shifted a little nearer to the other social services.

If one looks beyond the local authority for a moment, one must forecast that the fully independent schools, like Fettes, Glenalmond, and Gordonstoun, are likely to remain untouched in the 1970's. The Labour Government's conscience was troubled by their survival, but even if Labour had remained in power it was improbable that there would have been either sufficient determination to overcome the resistance that the independent schools, especially in England, could put up, or sufficient money available to provide an adequate state-controlled system to meet the need for boarding school provision as indicated by the Public Schools Commission Report of 1968.[31] Such money as is available for education will be fully required to meet the growth in provision consequent on the increase in the numbers of secondary pupils. The Conservative victory, however, put these schools beyond immediate danger.

The position of the grant-aided schools, such as the Merchant Company schools in Edinburgh or the Hutchesons' schools in Glasgow, depended quite seriously on the election. The re-election of Labour would almost certainly have brought about some change. As the Second Report of the Public Schools Commission said, "Under a nationally agreed policy of comprehensive education, it is no longer possible in principle to justify the payment of public funds to support schools whose role is not only inconsistent with, but an impediment to, the full development of that national policy",[32] and since the financial cost of change in this sphere would have been comparatively small,[33] it is unlikely that a government determined to press on with its policy of comprehensive education would have allowed these schools to survive as they are. Almost certainly the consequences would have been that some of these schools, like George Watson's perhaps, would have chosen to become fully independent, thus becoming too expensive for some of the pupils who now attend them, while those which agreed to participate in the national comprehensive system would have been altered almost beyond recognition. Once again, the Conservative victory will mean the preservation of these schools, for a time anyway, in either their existing form or a form acceptable to their supporters. One could not have viewed their destruction without great regret, and one cannot view the continuation in education of social class divisions, which these schools aggravate in a city like Edinburgh, without regret either; such are the dilemmas of educational provision today.

Expansion will also be the characteristic feature of higher education in the 1970's. The Robbins Report of 1963 laid down the guiding principle that "all young persons qualified by ability and attainment to pursue a full-time course in higher education should have the opportunity to do so",[34] and quite clearly the growth in the number of pupils completing a full course of secondary education, and gaining appropriate certificates at the end of it, will create a demand for university places on a scale that even the Robbins Committee did not envisage. The most recent projections of the planning staff in the Department of Education and Science suggest that the number of university students in Britain will have to rise from about 220,000 in 1969 to 450,000 in 1980.[35] The required Scottish increase will be from 35,000 to 68,000.

These increases need not mean the acceptance of students of lower quality than the universities have been accustomed to in the past. As the Robbins Report showed, expansion after the second world war was achieved without any lowering of standards,[36] and the increase in numbers was not accompanied by

76

any increase in wastage.[37] There was much talk in the late 1950's of a limited pool of ability, which should be fully drained but could not be expanded, but the Robbins Committee suggested that any such pool must be one "which surpasses the widow's cruse in the Old Testament, in that when more is taken for higher education in one generation more will tend to be available in the next".[38] We are going to witness a vast increase in the numbers of students taking degrees in the 1970's, and they will fully deserve to be doing so.

The existing universities, however, may not be able to cope with such a flood of entrants. They certainly will not be able to do so unless the country is prepared to face enormous financial expenditure (the universities at present cost the nation nearly £240 million per year), and no government, Labour or Conservative, will find it easy to provide support on the scale that will be needed. Yet if they do not do so, there will be a major social and political crisis, since people have now become accustomed to the idea that there should be places for all who have the necessary ability.

If any serious restriction of entry does become necessary, one wonders on what basis it should be imposed. A number of studies, including a recent one conducted by Nisbet and Napier in the University of Glasgow,[39] have shown that the level of a student's entrance qualifications offers only a moderate prediction of his success in a degree course. Motivation and personality factors are highly important, and as yet we have no very appropriate means of testing these at the entry stage.

The universities have proved themselves adaptable in the past, and, if the necessary money is available, may manage somehow to accommodate the coming multitudes. They could do so, perhaps, by re-arranging their academic year, or by working a shift-system of some kind, but this would be undesirable for many reasons, and it would cost so much in the provision of extra staff that it would not in fact be attractive to any government. Moreover, if the universities become mass institutions, like some of those on the Continent and in the United States, their character will be fundamentally altered for the worse, with a weakening of ties between staff and students, a disappearance of the sense of shared commitment to the disciplined cultivation of the intellect, and perhaps a reduction of the university experience to little more than the passing of examinations. In Britain we have seen many signs of this process beginning, with resulting disillusionment of students and staff alike.

The older Scottish universities have now grown into very large institutions, but they have done so gradually over a long period, and in general have been successful in accommodating their increased numbers to their traditions of disciplined study. They have so far been little affected by serious troubles of the kind that have become common in the student world in recent years, and one hopes that in the 1970's such a situation will continue. That will only be likely, however, if their growth rate can be kept within reasonable bounds, and one feels that they could not double their numbers in ten years without serious self-injury.

Quite clearly it will be the newer universities, like Stirling or Heriot-Watt, which will grow fastest in the decade ahead, but though they have a need to strengthen themselves for the sake of efficiency, they too could suffer from over-rapid expansion. Where the great bulk of the students are not only the first generation of their families to go to university, but also the first to have stayed on at school past the minimum leaving age, and where very few of even the senior staff have had previous experience of university administration, an institution can be very vulnerable to changing pressures from outside. Traditions can be formed, and broken, overnight, in a way quite impossible in a university like St Andrews or Edinburgh.

There is no necessity, however, for degree work to be confined to the existing universities. Others may be established, or, more likely perhaps because of the cost, degree-granting powers may in various ways be conferred on existing institutions of a different kind. This process has begun already, with the institution of the B.Ed. degree in four colleges of education, where nearly all the teaching is done in the colleges themselves though the degrees are conferred by neighbouring universities, and it would now seem not unlikely that through time these colleges should come to award their own degrees. Jordanhill, for example, which is already larger than one in three of the universities in Britain, presents an obvious case for developments of this kind. In the same way also degree-granting powers may well

come by the mid 70's to the schools of Art, the colleges of
Music and Drama, and the Domestic Science colleges, either
acting independently or, as is in some ways more desirable, by a
federation process which would link up several of these specialised institutions, along with a large college of education, to
form a new city university.

Thus the extension of the power to award degrees may well
be the crucial issue of the 1970's as far as higher education is
concerned. The 1960's saw first an increase in the number of
institutions able to confer degrees independently, with an expansion from 23 to 44 British universities in a decade, and then the
introduction of new avenues to degree work, through the
appearance of the National Council for Academic Awards and
the establishment of the Open University. The 1970's will inevitably continue the process. Further education will become
more closely merged with higher, since many F.E. colleges will
be doing C.N.A.A. degree work with their best students. New
polytechnics will spring up in the cities. One hopes that it will
still be difficult to obtain a degree in the sense that one will
have to reach a high standard in the courses one follows, but it
will not be nearly as difficult as it was only ten years ago to
obtain access to a degree course, and the variety of such courses
will have widened considerably.

Possibly the most sweeping of all the educational changes in
the next decade will be those in the sphere of administration,
since the implementation of the Wheatley Report's proposals on
local government reform[40] will bring about a transformation as
complete as that accomplished in 1918, when the old school
boards were superseded by county education authorities. Local
government reform is now overdue in Scotland, and the case for
a movement towards large regional authorities, as argued by
Wheatley, is very difficult to refute. It is based most firmly on
the need to make planning possible on a broad scale, and to
strengthen the local authorities and make them less dependent
on the central government, but there is a strong case for reform
of this kind from the view-point of education alone.

It is obvious that some of the existing authorities are too
weak in terms of financial resources, and too small in terms of
numbers of schools and pupils, for the full development of a
personal service like education in today's conditions. (Glasgow

has about 180,000 pupils in its schools, but nearly half of the other authorities have fewer than 10,000). This weakness has already been exposed in the fields of further and special education, and is being seen once more in the inability of some authorities to provide the facilities and highly qualified staff necessary for curriculum development at the local level. And as education becomes more closely linked with the social work services the need for larger units of control will become still more apparent. Even from the standpoint of the educational administrators themselves there is need for change, since in the small authorities the directors of education have to fill general roles, and the specialisation of function required by conditions of constantly increasing complexity is only possible in cities like Glasgow. There is a very strong case for the education service to be administered over areas such that each deals with a population of at least 200,000 people.

In making their recommendations, however, the Wheatley Commission could regard education as only one of the functions of local government, and the new administrative structure it proposed could not be determined solely on the basis of what was best for education. In fact priority had to be given to the requirements of long-term planning, for the conduct of local government in the future will be dominated by such considerations as the siting of major industries, and the building of motorways and new towns, and provision of services like education will be dependent on these factors. The concept of planning is the key to the thinking behind the Wheatley Report.

The pattern of local government proposed on this basis by Wheatley was therefore not the one which might have been suggested if education alone had been under consideration. Four of the seven regional authorities would probably be considered by most knowledgeable people to be right for education—the North East, East, Central, and South East—but the South West is still too small, the Highlands and Islands is too extensive in terms of territory, and the West region, with half the population of Scotland, is probably too large for manageable administration. It is on the West region, indeed, that most of the educational complaint has been focused, since it merges a number of large existing authorities which have a record of highly efficient administration. Few of the criticisms of the present system could be levelled at Renfrewshire, for instance, and it is only natural that there should be objection to its being submerged in the vast West region; yet from the considerations of planning the problems of Renfrewshire, like those of Lanarkshire and Dunbartonshire, cannot be separated from those of Glasgow.

The Conservative Party, while in opposition, criticised the Wheatley pattern, and seemed to favour the establishment of about twelve regional authorities, so that one must now assume that is what is likely to come about in the mid 1970's. These authorities may practise varying degrees of delegation of power, of course, and in any very large region there could be sub-division of a kind that left a number of directors of education in charge of units of about 200,000 population, but there would still have to be some kind of director general over the whole region, with powers to enforce co-ordination of services.

For education the consequences of this reorganisation will mainly be beneficial. Each region will be powerful enough to provide the full range of educational services, linked effectively to social work, health, etc, and with the facilities and personnel available to initiate developments in curriculum, methods, and school organisation. Local advisers will spread all over the country to an extent hitherto seen only in Glasgow and Edinburgh. There will be greater mobility among teachers, as the possibility of promotion opens up over a wider area, and this will help to spread new ideas and to strengthen schools by giving them staff with more varied experience. And there may well be a movement into the sphere of higher education, with the emergence of regional polytechnic colleges, teaching for degrees of the National Council for Academic Awards. Provided there is some effective kind of sub-division of responsibility so that the authorities are not too remote from the schools, regionalisation can probably be made to work to the advantage of the whole system.

One cannot avoid wondering, however, what will be the role of the central authority once this regional system of local government has been instituted. It will help to co-ordinate the various plans, of course, but inevitably the balance of power will have been considerably affected. The Wheatley Committee intended to make the local authorities less dependent on central government, but their proposals for the mammoth West region could have created an authority so potentially powerful that it could almost have been independent of central control (within Scotland at least). After all, in any dispute between them, the chairman of the authority for the West region could have said he was speaking for half the population of Scotland. Who would the Secretary of State have been speaking for—the other half? The Conservatives are not likely to go so far as Wheatley wished, but even so we may find that within the 1970's the importance of St Andrews House diminishes with the Secretary of State's role becoming more that of an intermediary between the Government in London and the Scottish regions.

Paradoxically, the Conservative Government may prevent the emergence of super regions like Wheatley's west, and yet, by stressing the freedom of the local authorities and being more reluctant to impose central direction, do more to weaken the position of the Scottish Office.

In Education, this could mean either that distinctive differences arose among the various Scottish regions, or, perhaps more likely, that they were all subjected to influences that brought them gradually closer to the position in England. Very many people would deplore it if Scottish education were to lose its distinctive features and be gradually assimilated into the quite different pattern of England, but it could well happen.

Regret for any loss, or danger of loss, of the local differences which are a natural response to varying local needs should not blind us to the need for a strong central authority in education, however. Over many centuries, the development of Scottish education has received its impulse almost always from the centre, first from the Church, then from the Church operating through the power of the State, and finally from the State itself. In the last hundred years or so, the Scottish Education Department has striven continuously for improvements in the organisation of schools, in curriculum and methods, and in the raising of standards both among pupils and teachers. Though it has been prepared to delegate powers in recent years, to bodies like the Scottish Certificate of Education Examination Board, or the General Teaching Council, the leadership and guidance it has provided has continued to be the main determining factor for growth in the system. Few would like to see that leadership removed.

Yet if change in education comes almost invariably as a result of pressure from outside, one hopes that in the years ahead the pattern of response to external pressure will more frequently be determined by those within the local authorities, the schools, and the colleges, themselves. Leadership of too strong a kind can produce a drying up of initiative, where people wait simply to be told what changes to make next, and then, since they have not felt involved in the decision-making process, adopt the new system without the enthusiasm or conviction necessary to make it effective. We have seen something of that in Scottish education at various times. But the local authorities are going to become stronger, the colleges are becoming stronger, and, above all, the teachers in the schools are being given opportunities to play a stronger part in the shaping of educational development. The coming decade should see many more people involved in working out the means by which we adapt our system to the inevitable pressures of a changing society, and wider involvement could bring wider commitment. The problems which lie ahead will be so serious that a co-ordinated effort from all concerned will certainly be needed.

Notes

1. S.E.D. *Education in Scotland in 1960*, HMSO., 1961, table 6; and *Education in Scotland 1968,* H.M.S.O., 1969, p. 24.
2. S.E.D. *Report of the Working Party on the Curriculum of the Senior Secondary School,* H.M.S.O., 1969.
3. S.E.D. *The Primary School in Scotland,* H.M.S.O., 1950, p. 11.
4. S.E.D. *Primary Education in Scotland*, H.M.S.O., 1965, p. 60.
5. Osborne, G. S. *Change in Scottish Education*, Longmans, 1968, p. 134.
6. Scotland, J. *The History of Scottish Education*, University of London Press, 1970, volume 2, p. 275.
7. Bone, T. R. *School Inspection in Scotland*, University of London Press, 1969, p. 229–31.
8. S.E.D. *Education in Scotland in 1968*, H.M.S.O., 1969, p. 12.

9. Low, J. M. "Primary Schools", a chapter in *Scottish Education Looks Ahead*, edited by J. Nisbet and published by Chambers, 1969.
10. S.E.D. *Primary Education in Scotland*, H.M.S.O., 1965, p. 37.
11. Ibid p. 60.
12. Stenhouse, L. A. *Culture and Education*, Nelson 1967, Chapter 7.
13. S.E.D. *French in the Primary School*, H.M.S.O., 1969.
14. Fraser, E. *Home Environment and the School*, U.L.P., 1959; Douglas, J. W. B. *The Home and the School*, MacGibbon and Kee, 1964.
15. Department of Education and Science : *Children and their Primary Schools*, H.M.S.O., 1967, Chapter 3.
16. Lindsay, C : *School and Community*, Pergamon 1970, Chapters 3, 4, 5.
17. Young, M., and McGeeney, P. : *Learning Begins at Home*, Routledge, 1968.
18. Green, L. : *Parents and Teachers, Partners or Rivals*, Allen & Unwin, 1968.
19. S.E.D. *Pupils' Progress Records*, H.M.S.O., 1969.
20. S.E.D. *Scottish Educational Statistics 1967*, H.M.S.O., 1968, Chart 2.
21. *Report of the Committee on Higher Education*, H.M.S.O., 1963, Appendix I, Annex B.B.Table BB3.
22. Elliot, J. : *A Study of Graduate Teachers in Scotland*, unpublished Ph.D. thesis, Glasgow University, 1970.
23. S.E.D. *Science for General Education*, H.M.S.O. 1969.
24. S.E.D. *Raising the Leaving Age : Suggestions for Courses*, H.M.S.O. 1966.
25. S.E.D. Circular 740 : *Raising of the School Leaving Age : The Schools and Further Education*, October 1969.
26. S.E.D. Circular 600 : *Reorganisation of Secondary Education on Comprehensive Lines*, October 1965.
27. S.E.D. Circular 760: *Organisation of Secondary Education*, July 1970.
28. S.E.D. Circular 614 : *Transfer of Pupils from Primary to Secondary Education*, June 1966.
29. S.E.D. *Organisation of Courses leading to the Scottish Certificate of Education*, H.M.S.O. 1967.

30. Lindsay, C. *School and Community*, Pergamon, 1970, p. 97.
31. The Public Schools Commissions : *First Report*, H.M.S.O., 1968.
32. Public Schools Commission : *Second Report*, Volume III, Scotland, H.M.S.O., 1970, p. 90.
33. Ibid, Chapter 13.
34. Committee on Higher Education: *Higher Education*, Report, H.M.S.O., 1963, p. 49.
35. Figures quoted by Sir Charles Wilson, Principal of the University of Glasgow, at a Conference in Jordanhill College, 13 April 1970.
36. Committee on Higher Education: *Higher Education*, Report, H.M.S.O. 1963, p. 12.
37. Ibid, p. 53.
38. Ibid, p. 54.
39. Nisbet, S. and Napier, B. L.: *Promise and Progress*, University of Glasgow Publications NS 136, 1970, pp. 18, 19.
40. Royal Commission on Local Government in Scotland: *Report*, H.M.S.O. 1969.

5

POLITICS

I

Norman Buchan

I F STANSTEAD HAD been in Scotland the bureaucratic errors committed there three times over would have been attributed to one simple fault; remote Government. It would have been called Westminster Government or London Government, and seen as a failure of English dominated Governments to understand or even see the problems of Scotland 400 miles away. Furthermore, the storm it created would not have been restricted to its own area but would have embraced the whole of Scotland. It would have been a national cause, a national issue. And therein lies both the strength and weakness of much of the political controversy in Scotland in the last few years.

Because of course Stanstead was only half an hour car run from Whitehall. The problem was not *horizontal* remoteness, a geographical problem. It was *vertical* remoteness, between governors and the governed. Precisely, it was a problem of democracy. But in Scottish terms at any time during 1968 and 1969 it would have been seen as a problem of nationhood. Geographical proximity, however, does not prevent bureaucracy, nor does it always prevent bad government. On the contrary, as local authorities demonstrate daily, it can often exacerbate it.

The Scottish Nationalist movement eventually foundered on the simplistic nature of their diagnosis and of their panacea. This was their final weakness as for a short period it had been their very strength.

For the argument of course had real strength too. Scotland is a nation; fact one. That neither requires demonstration nor proof. It is not only its separate and historic institutions—its own legal system, education, and (largely) political structure. It neither does, nor needs to, abide question in this way. A sense of nationhood cannot be argued. If people feel they are a nation then they are. We Scots certainly do. But the simple conclusion by Scottish Nationalists that "therefore" we must demand a separate state does not, of course, follow at all. But it was this that was their Ark of the Covenant. Thus we had Mrs Ewing making an embarrassing attack on multi-national states, calling for their dismemberment, during the emergency debate in the House of Commons on the Czechoslovakian crisis. The fact of Soviet aggression was seen as *because* it was a multi-national state. The fact that the victim was also multi-national could not be encompassed. As the victim it could not be "evil"; ergo could not be multi-national. This was not just insensitivity as many people listening thought. It stemmed from an article of faith that went beyond facts. Like the man who saw an elephant for the first time and said "I don't believe it".

Their basic deduction was a false one. But the sense of nationhood remains. It is right that an issue such as our "Scottish Stanstead" example should become a national issue. It expresses a healthy sense of identity on which much can be built. But that requires two things more. One, a recognition that the double malaise of Scotland, shared with many other areas of Britain, was not, firstly, a problem of nationhood, but a problem of democracy. And secondly that the real social and economic problems were not a problem of national suppression but of the uneven development of capitalism.

Scotland since the war has suffered from exactly the same kind of problem as the North East of England for example, or Wales. It suffered from its very success in the First Industrial Revolution. It was built on coal and iron and shipbuilding. Growth in recent years therefore was slower than in the snowball areas of the Midlands or the South East. And the decline of the old industries when it came, came sharp and concentrated.

For example, in the decade between 1957 and 1967, after massive investment, both public and private, in plant, machinery and in infrastructure, and pushed and cajoled, bribed and persuaded by Government intervention, the motor vehicle industry in Scotland was built up to a force of around 19,000 men. In the same period, in two traditional industries alone, coal and shipbuilding, there was a loss of around 76,000 men. In other words a loss by the traditional industries in the ratio of four to one.

This speed of decline, and the colossal investment needed to offset it, was the size of the problem facing Scotland as we entered the sixties. It is still, despite massive structural change, the nature of the economic problem facing us in Scotland in the seventies.

Clearly these two problems, the democratic and the economic, are interlinked. The trouble is that we have muddled and confused them, often seeing a solution to the one, say by independence, as being a necessary and sufficient answer to the problem of the second, say low wages and slow growth. This was especially true of the economic spokesman for the Scottish National Party, Dr Simpson, both in his pamphlet *Scottish Independence; An Economic Analysis* and in his essay in *The Scottish Debate*. Of this Professor Alexander commented, "It is not Dr Simpson's economics that are 'separatist' but his psychology."

The discussion over the last few years, therefore, was almost a classic "Basis—superstructure" argument. The slogans used, the banners under which the issues were being fought, were different from, often at variance with, the situation giving rise to the heat. The *feeling* was "Scotland is getting a raw deal", based on social and economic realities, but it was given *expression* in the form of votes for constitutional change. Paradoxically, therefore, but not surprisingly, every analysis of Scottish Nationalist voters showed only a small fraction who actually wanted a separate Scotland. In the same way, when Donald Dewar, then M.P. for South Aberdeen, wrote in 1969, "I believe that the structure of government in Scotland will be a major issue in the 1970 election"[1] he seemed to be manifestly correct. In fact it played virtually no part *as such* in that election. Curiously it was the very heat of the "raw deal" feeling itself that largely prevented any real debate on the constitutional or democratic issue from being properly joined.

Apart from one pamphlet from David Steel, *Out of Control*, and John P. Mackintosh's *The Devolution of Power*, the issues largely disappeared at a political level in fierce but arid polemics. A great opportunity was lost, because of course it really does matter. If Mr Dewar was wrong, along with many of us, in saying that the structure of government would be a major issue in the election, he was right in adding : "More importantly, I believe it ought to be."

And it matters above all in Scotland. Because while I believe that the problem is basically one of democracy and not one of nationhood (above all nothing to do with any national suppression) nevertheless the primary element of democracy, its solvent, is a necessary sense of identity, of belonging. And this we have in Scotland *in excelsis*, if not, indeed, *in extremis*. And therefore when the whole nature of our democracy is under consideration, often subsumed within the "in" word, participation, we can have an added strength in Scotland. Because the mainspring in the drive towards participation in society is first and foremost the need to belong. Only then comes its political articulation in the demand for a full and meaningful share in decision-making whether within the social and political organisation of our society or within industry. I believe that much of the feeling in Scotland was closer to the demands for worker-control in industry than to the classic nationalism of the nineteenth century. And it is this that we have to come to grips with.

In this context the election of June 1970 was a tragedy for Scotland. It is tragic not only because Scotland voted Labour and is ruled by Tories, but because in a very real sense this is the first ideologically committed Government for half a century, and it is committed to the Right. Since the war there had been a general consensus on two points : one, on the welfare state, and two on the need for government involvement to a greater or lesser extent in industry. It was, for example, under the Tories and by Government stimulus that the motor car industry came to Scotland. Admittedly under intense political pressure. But the pressure was effective largely because the consensus was there. But Butskellism is now dead. And therefore the centre of political discussion has moved to the Right. We are forced into the position of fighting defensive battles, battles indeed that all had thought were fought and won from the Beveridge Plan onwards. And Scotland above all needs policies from the Left. Not only because of our powerful radical tradition but because the economic and democratic needs of Scotland demand it.

The danger we have to face is that in waging these defensive battles we may fail to map out the necessary groundwork for a future Government ideologically committed on the Left.

On the democratic front the argument can no longer be restricted to the constitutional issue. The Crowther Committee is expected to report sometime in mid-1971. This should be immensely valuable but it cannot itself solve what must be political decisions. The best it can do, the best it *should do* at any rate, is to blueprint the three or four basic formulae of possible change. All of them are fraught with difficulties. All are virtually already known in essence, though the Crowther Committee should be able to spell out in greater detail for all of us the structure and, I would hope, some of the possible consequences of each. The Federal solution has the basic blocking quarter dilemma. The top tier local Government solution may be made unnecessary by the Wheatley recommendations. Curiously, the "Stormont" solution seems the most feasible of all. What is wrong with Stormont is, of course, Stormont. But it has two great disadvantages for Scotland. One is the absence of a Scottish say by right on the Cabinet through the Secretary of State and secondly that it does not seem to have had the effect, claimed by proponents of a separate Parliament, that it would attract better representatives. There is a third, and that is that a block grant system would tend to leave Scotland with a lesser share of U.K. resources than she at present gets and indeed requires.

And this of course brings us to the crux of the whole thing. We cannot have a constitutional discussion in a vacuum. If Scotland suffers from the uneven development of capitalism in common with other areas then it is right that the entire U.K. resources should be used to restore the imbalance. This should be a matter neither for shame nor pride but a matter of historical justice and of good sound regional economic policy. It is for this reason among others that I must reject the economic separatism of the Nationalists. The key argument is that if we remove all Scottish political control and influence over what all accept is a single economic entity in the United Kingdom, then we are left inevitably to be controlled by that total economy. Consequently we would have less say than we have now over our own fate. Paradoxically, total separation means less real independence.

It is because of this understanding, I believe, that the Labour Party has seen the difficulty in the present situation of implementing the earlier "Keir Hardie" view of a kind of Commonwealth status. It is not just that the implications at that time were in any case never thought through, but because since then there has been increasing intermeshing of the capitalist economy and its interlinking with Government agencies. Hence the weakness of the jibe thrown at the Labour Party, that if they had created an independent Scotland they could have had a Socialist Scotland. The concept is superficially attractive. And in some minor ways it could no doubt have constituted some kind of protective force in Scotland against Tory policies in the U.K. But basically it would have been devoid of real control and power, and, in the ensuing difficulties, the consequent disappointment and bitterness could only have discredited the concept of socialism, if indeed not directly leading to a Right Wing anti-democratic and chauvinist backlash. In other words, the best way of extending Scottish democracy is not through abstract constitutionalism but by Scotland playing a full part in establishing socialism in Britain.

The weakness of the abstract, "vacuum", approach is spotlighted by the Report of the Constitutional Committee of the Conservative Party, *Scotland's Government*. This was produced not so much in panic reaction to the rise of Nationalism as most commentators said, but in order to isolate the Labour Party as the only partly apparently unconcerned about Scottish devolution. It had a huge and irreparable hole blown in it at the moment of publication by the Notes of Dissent from committee members, Professor Mitchell and Sir Charles Wilson. Of all the possible formulae this is precisely the one that could not work inside the present political situation. Indeed, the harsh realities of politics have already cruelly exposed its weakness. As a minority party in Scotland the Tories are already acutely embarrassed in carrying through their policies in the existing Westminster structure, involving them, as it does, in a permanent minority on the Scottish Grand Committee. Their difficulties and embarrassment would be re-doubled if a Labour-dominated Assembly in Edinburgh were established, sharing in, but neither initiating nor controlling, the legislative process. Speaking on the Second Reading of the Tory Government Bill to reintroduce fee-paying into certain local authority schools in Scotland, the former Labour Secretary of State, Willie Ross, said : "By their behaviour in ignoring the decision of the Scottish people, the Government can only achieve a weakening of confidence in British Parliamentary life and cast serious doubt on their sincerity and concern to attune the machinery of Government more closely to Scotland's needs. If the Government do this before the reform, how worthy will the reform be?"[2]

Constitutional reform therefore can only be seen within the context of the political, social and economic totality. It is a part, but only a part, of the real task, which is to extend Scottish democracy.

91

And that means the devolution of effective power not just horizon-
tally in the sense of decentralisation, but downwards, more and
more into the hands of ordinary people. It is not just about Parliament, whether Scotland or U.K., but about planning procedures,
industrial democracy, the extension of popular control over the
major economic decisions. It is because I believe in the possibility
and, more important, the rightness, of this kind of democracy that
I am a socialist. Someone once said that all political questions
boiled down to "Who, whom?" In other words, which group
(class) had power over which other group. I would put it less
crudely as "Who, what?" The what, in a Bevanite phrase, is the
commanding heights of the economy, and the who is the ordinary
people. It is to the political and economic achievement of this that
our minds should be devoted, and for its economic consequences I
cannot see this kind of meaningful democracy being established
without an extension of public ownership in one form or another.
And that is certainly within the radical Scottish democratic tradition! It has been curious to notice how the exponents of the constitutional panacea have been invoking the names of Keir Hardie
and John Maclean in that one context—while ignoring in both of
them their real radical content. Their priorities, too, were socialism
first and devolution second.

A partial model already exists for a move in this direction in the
powers and structure of the Highlands and Islands Development
Board. A major battle will need to be waged to defend its existence
over the next few years for it is clear that while the Tory Government will not dare to kill it, their ideological commitment will certainly not stimulate them officiously to keep it alive. Though it
achieved more in its first five years than I had initially thought possible, we were still too timid in using its very wide powers. And
certainly we failed to use it as an instrument of conscious socialist
planning. (A pungent letter from Ian McInnes in the *New Statesman* (23 October 1970) in reply to an article of mine makes the
point in relation to fishing. He argues that the main effect was to
create a series of "petty capitalists", saddled with loans, instead of
creating home-based co-operatives.) This aspect has to be strengthened, but the main lesson is that the H.I.D.B. should be studied
as a potential model for much wider regional planning elsewhere
in Scotland.

Secondly, the use of public purchasing policy as an instrument of conscious economic change must be developed. In 1965 the total public sector purchasing from the private sector amounted to around £6,000 million in the U.K. Clearly, "The public sector's position as a purchaser is potentially, therefore, a most powerful government weapon; used as an instrument of regional policy its effect could be revolutionary."[3]

Thirdly, we should extend public ownership into the manufacturing sector. As a starting point this could be in the manufacture of tools, equipment and products required because of acts of Government policy, or in the field of import substitution. *Regional Planning Policy* points out, for example, that two-thirds of our electro-medical equipment is imported. And clearly some such impulse is needed in areas such as Scotland in order both to strengthen planning mechanism, compensate for the decline in the traditional industries and to create the growth conditions needed to foster the development of elements of industrial democracy.

Despite the example of the nationalisation of the steel industry, which has something of the characteristics of a service industry to the rest of manufacturing, we have tended to fight shy of other such inroads into the private sector. This has been partly on political grounds, partly because of the "But what should we manufacture?" problem. But the second is becoming increasingly less difficult to answer in a period of accelerating technological change with its consequent demands for new tools and new products. There is no reason why there should not be a publicly owned organisation for the commercial exploitation of the products of Government Research and Development establishments—such as the National Engineering Laboratory in East Kilbride or the National Institute of Agricultural Engineering at Bush in Edinburgh. This would have the added advantage of speeding up the process of getting more rapidly into use the research products, at present having to wait for a private manufacturer to produce under licence.

And the ending of consensus politics from the Right means that the political argument against pushing for such developments is no longer valid. Indeed even an O.E.C.D. publication says : "In general when the primary objective is to accelerate national development, the State should not hesitate to establish productive enterprises wherever private enterprise is unable to exploit fully the national resources. Such government or public enterprise need not be limited to establishing infrastructures; it may include developing certain manufacturing industries."[4]

In such circumstances, given a move towards effective popular democracy, and when there has been a decisive move towards greater control over the commanding heights, then, of course, devolution, in the structural constitutional sense, also begins to make some sense. And this both because of the sense of national identity which can give strength, or élan, to such a development, but also because there is nothing inherently efficient in large scale organisation. The very smallness of the Scottish Office structure leads to the overall efficiency that comes from one Department knowing what the other is about. Jane Morton commented on this point in the *New Society*: "An official in education will know not only how the school building programme is distributed; he will know what else is being built in these areas. . . . Officials know problems at first hand, not only on paper; and a visit to the north east farming area tells the man who makes it not only about output and investment potential, but about the economic balance, the rate of out-migration and the adequacy of transport facilities in the area."[5]

And, if Government is about people, the point is even truer on a Ministerial or political level. I remember meeting a deputation coming to discuss with me a forthcoming closure in Scotland. It was composed of civic, industrial and Trade Union representatives. I knew personally every one of the delegation, and all but one by their first name. This just couldn't happen on a U.K. basis, and it makes for better government. But the real moral is that in the present balance of the mixed economy, and with an inadequate rate of growth, we didn't have the powers to stop the closure. Democracy has an economic content.

II

Esmond Wright

I am writing this essay soon after the General Election of June 1970, and from the singular vantage point of seeing my own party triumph, even if I did not triumph myself. That is, so they tell me, an enriching experience. If I do not as yet find it so myself and am far from sure whither I am myself going, at least part of the question set by this book's title is answered: for five years or so Scotland will go along a Conservative path, as steered by a Government at Westminster which has clear policies and a clear mandate from the people.

At the middle point in the lifetime of the last Parliament there came a Scottish Nationalist wave, which put Mrs Ewing into the House of Commons for a, till then, safe Labour seat, and, in the euphoria of Hamilton in 1967, the S.N.P. talked of winning many seats in 1970. In fact they have won one, the Western Isles, hardly a typical one, and they lost Hamilton. They contested 66 seats, and they had no less than 46 lost deposits. They polled, it is true, 308,000 votes as against 130,000 in 1966, 64,000 in 1964, 22,000 in 1959, 12,000 in 1955 and 7,000 in 1951, but these mathematics mean little in a political system where the dominant fact is election of M.P.s in single-member constituencies, and on a plurality not a majority vote. To form a Scottish Government, a party in Scotland needs to win 36 out of 71 constituencies. From the 1970 result I draw my first conclusion. If, after six years of highly centralised and incompetent government in London, this is the best the S.N.P. can do, then in my lifetime there will never be a politically separate Scotland. It is as clear as that and it is folly to pretend otherwise. I am glad of it, because it would be economically, and, in my view, politically ruinous. The S.N.P. won a by-election in 1967 with mammoth publicity, a lot of youthful enthusiasm and a lot of money. These things were conspicuously missing from the 1970 campaign. In Scotland as a whole they did badly in 1970.

But there is a second conclusion. Hitherto many observers, myself included, have seen the S.N.P. as a party of protest heavily concentrated in the Lowland industrial belt, and in those enclaves of Stirling and Falkirk that evoke the magic of William Wallace, Robert Bruce and the Bannockburn syndrome. I and many others have spoken of Scottish Nationalism as if, in policy and orientation, it was a variant of the I.L.P. with a St Andrew's flag out in front. This view now needs a correction. In the 26 "urban" constituencies in Scotland (15 Glasgow, 7 Edinburgh, 2 Dundee, 2 Aberdeen) the S.N.P. was all but destroyed. They contested 23 of

95

the 26, and lost 20 deposits. Only in Glasgow Central (too small to be of significance and soon to disappear), Shettleston and Springburn, did they save their deposits. If we include the five Ayrshire seats with these 26 the position is even truer: all five were lost S.N.P. deposits.

But in the non-industrial belt they did well. Retaining some strength—perhaps personal to their candidates in West Lothian, Hamilton and the Stirling country—it was in the North West and the Borders that they made their mark. They won the Western Isles, where they had not even stood in 1966, although it was not a party but a popular Provost who won. In Aberdeenshire East and South Angus they came second, and cut the Conservative majority back. They won second place in seven other seats. They were the real alternative party in Argyll and Banff and Moray and Nairn and Hamilton. Outside the big cities they saved as many deposits as they lost. And in some key constituencies they were probably responsible for a change in the verdict.

The appearance of a S.N.P. candidate in Ross and Cromarty probably lost Alasdair Mackenzie his seat, and the same factor probably cost George Mackie Caithness and Sutherland, and probably "sank" Donald Dewar in South Aberdeen. However impressive their vote in safe seats—like Bothwell or Dumfries or Galloway—it makes little difference there. But in marginals—South Aberdeen, Ross and Cromarty, Caithness and Sutherland, Berwick and East Lothian, Roxburgh, and Pollok—the S.N.P. vote can be decisive. Verdict: they did badly, but not as badly in the rural as in the industrial belt, and where they have personable and responsible candidates they are still a force to reckon with. But if they want to do any better, to be something more than a spanner in the political works, they should re-think their policy, abandon the economic nonsense of separation and the radicalism of the Clyde, where they will never outmatch Labour, and develop a distinct brand of policies more suited to the Highlands and the Borders.

And conclusion number three follows logically. What is true of the S.N.P. is far more sharply true of the Liberals. They are now reduced to three seats in Scotland, and almost as soon as the count was over David Steel was calling—as did Jo Grimond unsuccessfully, and somewhat hesitantly, three years ago—for a pact with the S.N.P. The Liberals need it far more urgently than the

Nationalists, but on at least one issue (the Common Market) they differ totally. The Liberals contested 26 seats in Scotland—not one in Glasgow and only one in Ayrshire (Kilmarnock)—and lost 18 deposits. They lost two seats to the Conservatives; Jo Grimond's and David Steel's majorities were sharply dented; they offered no distinctive policies for Scotland; they have ceased to be relevant. It is hard in today's industrial world to see the significance or the dynamism of profit sharing, or to treat seriously a party that proposes the abandonment of the nuclear deterrent.

These conclusions emerge clearly from the figures of the 1970 results. These results however do not give a clear indication "whither" Scotland is going politically, because in the course of the present Parliament the boundaries of the present constituencies will be recast. It ought to have happened before the last election, but was blocked by Jim Callaghan and Labour's fear at the loss of some 20 seats, and not before time : Kelvingrove, Woodside, Central and Gorbals are absurdly small, and will disappear. New constituencies, especially for the new towns of East Kilbride and Cumbernauld, will emerge. And with these will come new dispositions, new forces, and not least new men.

But Scotland changes slowly. That is conclusion four from an examination of the June 1970 result. At a time when England was clearly swinging to the right, Scotland moved only slightly in that direction (2.8 per cent against the South of England's 5 per cent). With 44 Labour seats out of 71, Labour had the giant share of the votes—46 per cent—to the Conservatives 38 per cent, 11 per cent for the Nationalists, and 4.5 per cent for the Liberals. And there remains the imponderable fact, in 1970 as in 1959, that the U.K. (and therefore the Scottish) Government is Conservative because of England's vote; in the House of Commons' Scottish Grand Committee and in all Scottish Standing Committees only the weighting by English members will secure a majority for Government bills. This allows delay and obstruction and those politics of nagging and narking of which Willie Ross is a past master. It will be easier for Ted Heath to get his business through the House than it will be for Gordon Campbell in Committee Room 14.

The Conservatives have spelt out very clearly what their policies are to be for Scotland. S.E.T. will go, with immensely beneficial results for hotels and tourism, for prices and for trade. The fee-paying schools of Glasgow and Edinburgh will be saved—and the threat averted to the 29 grant-aided schools that would almost certainly have followed. The Wheatley proposals of 7 units in local government and some 30 second-tier authorities are likely to be modified—most Conservatives favour the minority report of Miss Betty Harvie Anderson and Mr Russell Johnston, with its suggestion of some 100 second-tier authorities. And, though much will depend on the timetable and the content of the Wheatley and Crowther proposals, it is likely that there will be a serious attempt during this Parliament to implement Sir Alec Douglas Home's report on a Scottish Convention.

These are predictable. But central to the future of Scotland is the problem of Glasgow and the Clyde. Unemployment there is still higher than the national average. There are recurrent labour disputes—at Bathgate and Linwood in the "new" motor car industry, in U.C.S. in the old shipbuilding industry. There has been an over-rapid rundown of older jobs—in coalmining and forestry much more rapid than was ever anticipated. Labour policies for six years, especially S.E.T., hurt. In the last four months of the Labour Government, 216 building firms went bankrupt in Britain, and one in ten of Glasgow's joiners and building workers was unemployed. Millions of bricks were lying unused when 50,000 people were on Glasgow council waiting lists for houses. But there was not only a failure of Labour policy, there was also a Labour legacy. There are 150,000 council houses now in the city, and more people in Glasgow live in subsidised council houses than in owner-occupied or rented property : but the rents from them meet only half the interest on Glasgow's housing debt. Yet many older council houses are insanitary and shoddy and little is spent on repairs and maintenance.

Building for private purchase or for rent is all-but-totally absent, and very expensive. This is the major and thus far intractable problem facing the present Government. That Government is committed to re-negotiating housing subsidies with local authorities on a basis of need, and giving aid to people not to bricks and mortar. In my own campaign in Pollok in June 1970 I spelt out a 10 point programme for housing that seemed to me to have value.

1. End S.E.T. and thus free the building industry from a crippling tax.
2. Exempt the building societies from Corporation Tax.

3. Lower mortgage interest rates to allow more people to buy their own homes, and begin buy-as-you-rent schemes. This will relieve the pressure on council house lists.

4. Re-negotiate housing subsidies so that help goes to tenants who really need it, and assist with rent rebates those groups with special needs such as the elderly and the chronically disabled.

5. Encourage Housing Associations, whether S.S.H.A. or voluntary co-partnership or *Shelter* to improve older houses or build new ones.

6. Set up Housing Advisory Centres to advise families on the cost and benefit of different types of housing.

7. Ensure that tenants in the privately-rented sector get a fair deal and that their houses can be improved, and kept in good repair.

8. The Glasgow Corporation Housing Department needs improvement by :
    (a) More effective housing exchange arrangements.
    (b) More resources for house maintenance and repair.
    (c) More individual information to tenants and owner-occupiers when plans are made for "treatment areas". They should be given the facts by house-to-house visits.
    (d) More attention to environment, landscaping and the provision of essential public services, like doctors' surgeries and chemists' shops in the housing schemes.
    (c) More individual information to tenants and owner-remote housing schemes.

9. Tenants to be allowed to buy their council houses, if they wish.

10. The long term solution depends on a larger scale of region, to allow more "out-of-Glasgow" sites for houses, and on a new system of local government finance less rigid than the rates.

Something like this must I believe be tried.

Government aid will have to take note of the fact that much of the urban renewal programme in Glasgow means not only a loss of amenity and a loss of rating and rent contributions as property disappears, but constitutes also in itself a heavy financial burden, with few matching benefits. The new Kingston Bridge for example cost over £11½ millions to build but involved the demolition of much old property. It will unleash fast heavy traffic through areas north and south of the river that were, until then, areas of high amenity and high property values. It will bring noise and dirt and accidents in its train. The sooner the planning of Glasgow is put in the context of the major plans for the Lowlands as a whole the better; the sooner a Wheatley-style region is set up, the better.

Even when this is done, even when a new approach to the housing problem is begun, there remains a dominant fact about Glasgow, and that is that it remains stubbornly working class in its character and ethos. Its middle class areas like Pollokshields and Hyndland are becoming ghettoes of affluence surrounded by acres of multi-storeys or tenement buildings. In the last 15 years the Glasgow electorate has fallen by just on 10 per cent, but the conservative vote in the same period has fallen by 40 per cent. And the "multis" or the older perimeter housing schemes are short of pubs and clubs, trees and grass. It is this grimness of stone and weather, allied in places to an equally stubborn Calvinism in its licensing laws, that produces not only in Glasgow but in Ayrshire, Dunbartonshire and Lanarkshire an atmosphere very different from England. Economic change has been made but at a slower pace. The motor car industry came into Scotland reluctantly under the last Conservative Government; a few local ancillary industries have grown up to supply it. The electronics and computer, typewriter and tractor firms are "foreigners" too. The West of Scotland has only slowly matched the pacemaker developments that are the mark of the English Midlands. Until this economic pattern changes, Glasgow will stay a Labour city, its folk memory set firmly in the bitter legendry of the 'twenties and 'thirties, fighting not the next election but folk-myth elections still haunted by the names of Keir Hardie and Jimmy Maxton, Manny Shinwell and Willie Gallacher.

England voted Conservative in 1970, and the reasons it did so were well captured by Mr. Eldon Griffiths, M.P. for Bury St Edmunds, who wrote :

There are seven million salaried employees in the United Kingdom—managers, technologists, accountants, civil servants, salesmen, teachers, scientists, and administrators. . . . One out of three of all employees in Britain will fall into the "Salariat" category by the early 1970's. The key people are the under-

forties—those up and coming young salaried people who until
1964 had never known what it was to live as adults, under
Socialist rule. The great majority of these young salaried folk
passed the eleven-plus and went on to the sixth form. They are
beneficiaries of the great Butler Act—products of the post-war
expansion in secondary and college education. By this expansion, in Charles Curran's phrase, "the Tories built an escalator
from Coronation Street". . . . The most striking feature about
these new arrivals is that they are competitive. . . . They are of
incalculable value to the nation because success did not come to
them, any more than it will to Britain, by birthright, tradition or
connections. It came the hard way—by self-help. . . . The new
competitors want no part of cloth caps, cups of char, pigeon rac-
ing, miners' galas, tinned salmon teas and greyhounds. . . . They
feel a total lack of kinship with the post-war world of anonymous housing estates, collective holiday camps, fish and chips
and Bingo.

It is this spirit that is missing in the West of Scotland, the spirit
of adventure and opportunity and challenge. What is missing is
the contemporary classlessness of England, that could produce a
Conservative leader like Ted Heath. Yet Scotland has its examples and its advertisements : in Sir Hugh Fraser, the headquarters
of whose empire is still in Buchanan Street, and Hugh Stenhouse,
whose headquarters is still in St Vincent Street, in Sir William
Lithgow, on the lower reaches of the Clyde, in Pringles in the Borders, in Ferranti and Bartholomews in Edinburgh. But we need
more, and we need them in politics as in industry and commerce.
And it is in dear, dirty, volatile, febrile Glasgow that the Conservatives must do their real hard thinking, and tap this spirit of challenge. Glasgow must be set free from its own prison of memory and
legend. If it is to be dragged from the 1920's and into the 1970's it
will be not only by an economic but by a psychological revolution.
Until it is done the policies of Scotland will be permanently unbal-
anced.

The tackling of "the Glasgow problem" is the major task facing
this Conservative Government in Scotland. In the six years of the
Labour Government there came not a glimmer of an idea about it.
The city's housing debt worsened. Bureaucracy increased. The one
contribution made was to declare the whole of Scotland a

development area, to pour out subsidies and premiums regardless of whether they produced new jobs and regardless of cost, to equip new towns (like East Kilbride) and some old ones (like Motherwell) with ornate civic centres some of which are little more than expensive white elephants. The Welfare State became the Open Subsidy State.

Nor have the 40-odd Labour M.P.s from Scotland made as a group any special contribution either to the solutions of these problems of democratic government or to the dialogue of democratic debate. Its solitary intellectual has been ignored. Scotland has sent its sons across the world. But in the last two decades its own voice has been curiously mute. Not only in Scotland but in Britain whole areas of debate have been ignored. Why has there been an all-but-total indifference to the changed character of secondary and higher education? Why have we shown so little interest in urban problems compared to the U.S.? Why, when the Redcliffe-Maud and the Wheatley Commission were set up, deprive them of the chance to consider how the recast local government is to be financed? In a world in which space has been conquered, what is our role in the Commonwealth and the Underdeveloped World? What are our policies on population control, on food supplies for a world of 7,000 million (by the year 2000)? And what will our welfare policies be by 1990 when one in three of the population will be over the age of 65, and another one-third will be under 21.

In the 1970 election the Labour M.P.s in Scotland, like their U.K. leader, held few meetings, raised no arguments, put forward no proposals. They hoped to lull the electorate by bread and circuses. It was a deliberate strategy, and the opinion polls suggested that it was successful. But the electorate asked searching questions at meetings, and were not deceived. And the Conservative victory was a worthy one, and won on merit. It was a personal triumph for Mr Heath. Mr Wilson and Mr Ross learned that you cannot fool all the people all the time.

Although Scotland has twice as many Labour M.P.s as Conservative, its future depends on the Conservatives for they are suggesting the methods and pointing out the goals. Labour tap a folk memory that is now irrelevant to the Scotland of tomorrow. Their housing programmes are determined by notions that were valid 50 years ago, but not now. Socialism has ceased to offer any solutions relevant to contemporary Scotland. You cannot solve today's problems by using the slogans of 40 years ago. The important thing today is not the redistribution of the national wealth, but its creation; here Socialism is killing the goose that lays the golden eggs. Nationalisation, whether by front door or back, has come to mean Bureaucracy, Expense and Inefficiency. To deny the wage increases that personal effort can genuinely bring, to deny increases in dividends to successful firms, and to do so by decree, is to erect a further series of dogmas which will, by force of nature, be—as they are—untenable. We urgently need, in the short term, tax and Trade Union reform, in Scotland as elsewhere. More than this we need for the next 40 years freedom from dogma and from cliché. We need to restore pride in work, pride in self, pride in country, to swing the emphasis back from rights to responsibilities. We don't need appeals to doctrine or to heredity, but plain intelligence and plain integrity. There is nothing wrong with the adage from each according to his ability, to each according to his need, but Harold Wilson's Socialism in practice became the corruption of what was originally a dream of justice. With Ted Heath in power, we have a reform government that has the spirit of a Peel and of a Pitt the Younger, with a taste for efficiency, for effort, for reward and for high endeavour.

We need these qualities in Scotland even more than in England and Wales. We have needed them for a long time. We need to blow away the cobwebs of feudalism in East and North, of class war and religious and social tensions in the West. We need to lift our sights, to release the spirit of the people who were the first true democrats 400 years ago, and to tap the genius of the land. We cannot afford to wait too long.

III

John Herdman

In spite of the fool whom I heard on television recently suggesting that to be a Scottish nationalist was to be indifferent to "the problems facing the rest of humanity", it is my belief that no Scotsman who is truly concerned with these problems, problems of human values and their survival, can be other than a nationalist. For if the future of Scotland is not to be the future of the Scottish people, if their individual life and culture are to be eclipsed and their creative potential destroyed, then there must undeniably be an absolute human loss. The destruction, moreover, will be at the hands of a nation which has become the very embodiment of anti-civilisation, of an amorphous mass culture which is ignoble, ugly and debased. Indeed it seems to me that the struggle to save Scotland and its culture is a precise moral analogue to the fight against environmental pollution, the central and symbolic struggle of the age. Throughout the world today there must be many thousands of such analogues; but this is ours, here and now.

The future of Scotland considered merely as a geographical expression interests me little; certainly not enough to persuade me to write about it. What does concern me is the creative future of the Scottish people; and I believe that without their freedom they will have none, that they will be utterly absorbed into an anti-culture not only alien but corrupt. I therefore have to call myself a nationalist, when it should be sufficient for me to be a Scotsman. Which brings me to politics.

Before making a bleak judgment on the possibility of the S.N.P's achieving a healthy future for Scotland, I want to make a brief but relevant diversion. It is a common tactic of various pedlars of myths with a desire to play down nationalism to object that the S.N.P. is a "bourgeois" party and as such unconcerned with changing the fundamental nature of society in Scotland. There are two differences between this criticism as voiced by the pedlars of myths and the same criticism as voiced by Hugh MacDiarmid: one is that he has earned the right to make it by having proved in terms of personal hardship and intellectual struggle that he himself is not a bourgeois, and the other is that he quite clearly isn't making an implicit—and illicit—extension from the S.N.P. to nationalism in general. It is, moreover, true that the S.N.P. is for the most part a crassly philistine body whose obsessive worship of economics is only a little less nauseating than that of the unionist parties. At least, though, its *raison d'être* is to address itself actively to a situation central to Scotland's plight and to make at any rate one fundamental change in the present order. The point is that when we hear that trigger word "bourgeois" being emitted from certain quarters as a criticism of the S.N.P., we can be sure that what we are going to be offered is a great stress on radicalism—entirely admirable—the din of which overlays a profound silence on the question of independence. Before proceeding to attack the S.N.P. myself I therefore make this little leap to its defence, even at the risk of securing to myself the dire title of "Bourgeois nationalist". I cannot, after all, feel that opposition to apartheid and dislike of certain Edinburgh councillors are sufficient qualifications for any-one to think of themselves as other than "bourgeois". We all live in a bourgeois society, and personally I like it little enough to have no more wish to be classified by opposition than by adherence to it. The truth of mere opposition is always a limited truth, and if Scot-land is to have any creative future it must lie not only beyond capitalist society but beyond all systems conditioned by the need to oppose it. I mistrust fashionable left-wingery from the point of view of radicalism as much as from that of nationalism.

After Mrs Ewing's victory at Hamilton, it seemed that liberal democracy should be given a chance. Undoubtedly there was some sort of revival of national consciousness going on, and perhaps it might through the S.N.P. express itself sufficiently in political action to effect a change in the constitutional position of Scotland, which in its turn would stimulate a genuine spiritual development in the Scottish people. Although I have been a nationalist for ten years, it was not until Hamilton that I felt there was any real pos-sibility of the S.N.P's achieving anything worthwhile for Scot-land. But like many other nationalists I was overtaken at that time by the psychological affliction since diagnosed as "post-Hamilton euphoria"; so, in spite of all my reservations, I became an S.N.P. activist. Subsequent developments have dispersed the euphoria (which is survived however by a sense of extreme urgency), and though I still believe that the S.N.P. must be supported at the bal-lot-box, the reservations about both the quality of what they are trying to achieve and the likelihood of their achieving even that, are once again uppermost in my mind. These reservations refer particularly to the impenetrable stupidity and despicable fickleness of the electorate, to their apparently total inability to cope with any idea not directly related to their pockets, and the consequent hopelessness of any thinking about the future which turns upon an appeal to the electorate or a pandering to their will. If the people expect their will to be respected for much longer, then they must set about getting themselves a will which merits respect (and before anyone starts calling me a fascist for saying this, I think they should ponder how far they themselves think the will of the people should be respected on problems such as capital punishment, coloured immigration, and "law and order").

On the other hand, I think that the consequences of rejecting liberal democracy are too serious for it to be justifiable to dismiss it without taking a look at what it has to offer Scotland. I do not propose to waste space on discussing the unionist parties (among which number I include the Liberals), since all that they project for this country can lead only to its miserable and protracted death. The S.N.P., however, is founded upon a just cause, and remains activated by its kernel of truth beneath all the tired accretions of policy. Its attitudes therefore merit the courtesy of examination. The General Election of June 1970 necessitated the postponement of the Party's Annual Conference, which would have been asked to approve as its election manifesto a document entitled *The New Scotland*, which embodies all the basic positions on which the election was in the event fought, consists largely of policies already approved, and undoubtedly represents the thinking of the dominant elements in the S.N.P. Most of this pamphlet is devoted to such subjects as Local Government; Money; the Common Market; Industry, Employment and Technology; Transport; Fuel and Power; and Housing. Towards the end, however, two small paragraphs can be found dealing with the following categories: "The Quality of Life" and "The Arts". The first of these admits, with some justice, that political debate in Scotland has tended to focus on "the 'bread-and-butter issues' " and that this preoccupation has "diverted political interest from the more fundamental considerations of man's relation to his cultural and natural environment". This can scarcely be gainsaid, but what effort the S.N.P. has made or is making to reverse such a situation is not clear to me. What they mean by "the quality of life" seems to be indicated by the following sentences: "Independence is a pre-requisite of effective planning. A proper balance between industrial development, town planning, recreational facilities and amenity protection and improvement is immensely difficult to achieve but is central to the whole concept of providing the people of Scotland with a pleasant and stimulating environment." Further insights on the subject of the quality of life envisaged for the free nation by the S.N.P. can be obtained by a random glance through the pamphlet, and I quote a few which I find particularly distressing, not necessarily because I violently disagree with them (though I do with some), but because of the qualities of mind and spirit revealed by them in those most actively concerned in creating the future of a free Scotland :

The marriage of modern technology to Scotland's already famed amenities will produce a thriving Scotland.

Tourism is not only a useful source of foreign currency but an opportunity for the provision of amenities which might not otherwise be justified.

In the hands of happy and healthy youth lies Scotland's future.

The opinions of citizens will be obtained by referendum on issues which are not strictly political and to which a "yes" or "no" answer can be give. Capital punishment, for example, is one of these issues.

No society can exist without respect for the law. There are disturbing signs that this respect has diminished in recent years. . . . Unless appropriate punishments are imposed, the work of maintaining the peace could be seriously undermined.

The Scottish National Party welcomes recent moves to establish a Business School in Scotland.

We firmly believe that a special relationship should be established between the countries of the British Isles. The S.N.P's imaginative proposal for an association of British States would enable that relationship to be developed in a way which would allow each member country to protect her own interests.

I shall refrain from commenting individually upon most of these gems, which speak sufficiently for themselves, but I feel that the last-quoted imaginative proposal (it is only surprising that it isn't "bold and imaginative") deserves a special mention. It is patent that this piece of pious hypocrisy is intended to lull the fears of those who are "afraid of being separate from England", Scotland's natural Celtic allies being dragged in only as a matter of off-hand courtesy (or impertinence). What does not seem to have occurred to its architects is that the word "co-operation", which is used elsewhere in the pamphlet in connection with the imaginative proposal, has a very special and limited force for the English nation, a force which renders it almost synonymous with "absorption". Indeed a very similarly imaginative proposal was put into practice once before. The date was 1707.

It is when they turn to the Arts, however, that the S.N.P's imagination really runs riot. Having congratulated themselves on having "in 1964 proposed the foundation of an Academy to provide a new and dynamic impetus for progress", they present the core of their policy as follows: "We must encourage our own poets, musicians, playwrights, dramatists, and other working artists and further an appreciation of their work, so that life of Scotland [*sic*] can be enriched". No sane person, of course, would envisage or desire anything in the nature of a legislative programme for the creative life of a nation; what is so hopeless about these sentences is the attitude of mind they reveal, that the arts are a sort of pleasant appendage of the national life (together with broadcasting, sport and recreation, the quality of life, etc.), not to be forgotten when policies are being framed, and deserving of being allocated a modest quota of lines which must be filled up, by any assortment of vacuous inanities, to appease any troublesome highbrows in the ranks.

What all these proposals have in common, of course, is their determination to appeal to everything that is basest and most inert and complacent in the public mind. The S.N.P. has chosen to recommend freedom by making it seem as like the present order as possible, an attractive proposition for self-satisfied and stupid materialists. The trouble is that the unionists have got more than a head start on them in the respectability stakes, with the additional advantage that they make even fewer demands on the intelligence and initiative of the public—demands inherently unlikely to be satisfied. The dreary platitudes of the only party to be genuinely concerned even at a superficial level with Scotland's future brings home the continuing relevance of Hugh MacDiarmid's protests in 1932 that "the curse of the National Party today . . . is its desire to foresee and guide the course of events. Nothing that can be so foreseen and guided is worth a curse; Scotland needs a great upwelling of the incalculable."

So the inadequacies of liberal democracy to cope with the problems of modern Scotland perhaps go deeper than the surface manifestations of a politically and morally impotent National Party and an electorate which can be led by the nose by the crudest contrivances of unionist sophistry. It is the whole liberal-democratic attitude of mind which is now open to question. This mode of thought has conditioned the approach of most of us to almost any problem, and is the source of a whole range of modern phenomena from the cult of "planning" in politics and sociology (one might add indeed the cult of sociology itself) to humanism as a popular religion. Its essence is the faith that every problem has a solution if only it can be found, that there is no fundamental change that cannot be effected by taking sufficient thought, that the natural order and all spiritual processes are infinitely open to manipulation and domination by the human will. A concomitant of this faith is the frightening confidence that all this manipulation and domination can be achieved, if only we are efficient enough, without any real struggle, sacrifice, or loss, in accordance with the grand object of securing to ourselves more comfortable, healthy and wealthy lives, greater ease, prosperity, productivity and peace.

The Greeks called this "hubris" and knew that it would have its reward. It is no comfort that the practitioners of this philosophy, such as the planners of the S.N.P., undeniably mean well, for that, as my granny used to observe, is the worst thing you can say about anyone. I recognise that they mean well by Scotland and if I seem to be brutal with them it is because I feel that the nation's plight is becoming desperate and may soon be irreversible. (One of the abiding results of the Hamilton resurgence, probably, will be to activate our English rulers into all sorts of subtle moves further destructive of Scottish nationhood.) People who meant well have been responsible for most of the unspeakable developments now threatening humanity, of which it is the sad measure that war is perhaps now marginally the least menacing.

Tom Nairn, in an essay on Scottish Nationalism in *Memoirs of a Modern Scotland*,[6] limits the possible historical justifications of nationalism to two : the "sweeping away of archaic or predatory social forms", and the "mobilising of populations for socio-economic development". To my mind both of these purposes are secondary and subservient to the mobilising of populations for *spiritual* development; I dislike the word but cannot think of a better one for what I mean. But I agree with Mr Nairn (though perhaps not for his reasons) that Scottish Nationalism has been historically inadequate. Scottish history has in many ways dispersed, weakened and diverted the tendencies which should have produced the mature type of nationalism which Scotland now desperately needs; too few have felt sufficiently deeply to create a tradition. We hear a great deal about Scotland being a "Puritan" country; but if without doubt she has more than her fair share of the Puritan vices, she has surely preserved all too few of the complementary Puritan virtues. What in particular she lacks now is any consciousness of the old truth that you cannot gain or enjoy a good thing without having earned it or paid for it with a sufficiency of struggle and suffering.

It would be extremely pleasant, of course, if we could simply walk into possession of the "New Scotland" by persuasively explaining that independence will mean (I quote from the pamphlet again): "the release of the inventive energies of the people of Scotland in every field of human activity—economic, financial, commercial, cultural and social—from the dead and unimaginative hand of remote control"; if, the dead and unimaginative hand having, as in so many other places, obligingly lifted itself at the first hint that it was no longer welcome, we were instantly to find ourselves, with no scars to show for any unseemly contention, in a cloudless paradise of deep-sea ports, millions of acres of forestry, limitless tourist facilities, of business schools turning out thousands of thrusting, dynamic executives capable of generating imaginative concepts by the minute, of happy and healthy youth growing up protected from the lawless and surrounded by famed amenities in a country restored once more to "her rightful place in the councils of the world".

Such a paradise, fortunately, is only a mirage before the eyes of the planners dying in the desert. Scotland's real choice is between the death that comes with a whimper and something infinitely greater than that mirage, the unplannable but human society which would be the reward of the nation which took upon its conscience the cost of an implacable defence of human values, of which freedom is one. For I do not think that Scotland will achieve the regeneration she seeks unless she is prepared to pass through the fire. The choice between the whimper and the cost of breaking by force the vice which holds the Scottish soul fast in the grip of apathy and despair is one which must painfully exercise our individual consciences and the conscience of the nation; at the moment the whimper appears much the likelier outcome. Yet history has always been notoriously unpredictable.

Notes

1. *The Scottish Debate,* edited McCormick, Oxford University Press, 1969. Tragically, Mr Dewar, who had contributed most usefully to the necessary constitutional discussion himself, was defeated by the intervention of a tiny S.N.P. vote sufficient to unseat him. But I doubt if any measurable proportion of that vote stemmed from a basic desire for structural change.
2. *Hansard,* 11 November 1970. Col. 420.
3. *Regional Planning Policy,* Labour Party Study Group, p. 7.
4. *Methods of Industrial Development,* O.E.C.D., p. 326.
5. Jane Morton, "Scottish Office: Regional Rule" *New Society,* 21 September 1967.
6. Edited Karl Miller. London, Faber & Faber, 1970.

6

RESURRECTION
Anthony Ross

T WENTY-EIGHT THOUSAND FEET above the North
Sea in a clear sky. A low smudge visible ahead. Scotland? At any
rate something which rouses pleasurable anticipations of being
home again, and speculation about what has been happening
there. Abbotsinch—and the airport bus into Glasgow. Growing
feeling of depression. Dirt: so many kinds of squalor. Buildings
in different stages of decay. Rubbish littered streets. General election posters—and at a street junction an eloquent and well-
known Scottish National candidate speaking to six people; all
elderly; grey faces; listless. No one in the pedestrian drift even
hesitates or casts a second glance. What must a Swede or a Dane
think, arriving for the first time in Scotland? Probably, of course,
he would arrive in Edinburgh, that mixture of museum and tin-
selled shop window where the shabby myths that Scotland lives
by are still strenuously refurbished and distributed, drawing some
strength from injections of American, Italian, or even English,
ideas and enterprise.

Mind goes back to discussions with Scandinavians about delinquency, crime statistics, drug addiction, alcoholism. Their mildly
expressed astonishment at the punitive outlook so obvious in our
society, at the way our newspapers sensationalise crime and
encourage offenders to assume a criminal identity with some
pride. The contrast in our crime statistics, quantitatively and
qualitatively. Why have we so much more violence? Why is there
so much delinquency, so much mental illness, so much suicide, in
some of our large housing estates? Scotland after all is a country
with a great tradition—Christian, democratic, educated, or so we
have always been told. "On that day democracy was born"—
Edinburgh, round about 1560. "The Scottish education system is
the finest in the world"—even if the rest of the world no longer

thinks so, even though our schools depend on corporal punishment to an extent surpassed perhaps only in Ireland.

Violence. Stronach—gentle, harmless, the backward big boy in the class—thrown against the blackboard: blackboard easel and boy crashing to the floor. Sixteen stone teacher roaring: declares his knee on Fraser's chest will give him something to remember. Children's first memories: "being skelpt"—"hit by ma Dad"—"ma Mum hammered me". A boy's voice bitterly wishing his parents were dead. "Honour thy father and thy mother that thy days may be long upon the land which the Lord thy God giveth thee." "There wiz always fightin, ken? Ma Dad bashin' ma Ma like, A' got bashed tae, Fridays, ken?"

Other voices remembered against the sound of the airport bus. "I was three, or about that, when two of us went to play in the garden and we took all our clothes off, because we were so hot. I got such a beating. My parents were so angry, almost mad with anger. I don't like to think about it, even now." Chastity and the love of God, duty and respect for parents. "Every sin against purity is a mortal sin"—in Scotland as in the Ireland which Joyce left behind. "I've sinned, Father. I was keeping company." Two boys aged about twelve; flogged before the school; for disgusting, perverted, not-to-be-named acts. "When my parents were told they thought I must be queer. I thought, after that, that if you masturbated you must be a homosexual." Mary MacCrimmon was better treated, who sat at the back of the Seceders' Kirk alone with her son born out of wedlock, for seven years, unspoken to at home during that time by her preacher brother. This Christian land of Scotland. But there's another side—there's always another side, excuse for turning away from the unwholesome fact which spoils the pretty picture of Tannochbrae.

Two boys fighting with sticks on a waste ground. Boys used to fight with sticks, branches or broom handles, when I was a boy: Kirkhill and Louisburgh "battling" in the town of Wick, in quiet streets, while adults watched, not interfering unless tempers became too fierce. Not "violence against the person" demanding police action. Crimes of violence against the person made known to the police in Scotland: 1,193 in 1958; 3,586 in 1968. Murders made known to the police in Scotland: 20 victims in 1958; 40 victims in 1968. And the ages of those convicted of murder, 6 under 18; 3 more under 21. Total number of crimes of all kinds made known to the police: 91,983 in 1958: 152,242 in 1968. Not Scandinavia this, but Scotland—where all can be explained away to the satisfaction of the establishment by reference to alcohol, housing, and the Irish ... three problems which, it would seem, baffle Scottish education, law, and religion.

"But there's nothing wrong with the houses!" said a douce Edinburgh baillie: "It's the people who are the trouble." He was talking about a forty year old housing scheme, one of the first to be built in the still continuing process of removing the common people to the fringes of the city. Gradually they have been shifted, farther and farther out, so that the centre may be fumigated, pastel coloured and sedated for the delight of tourists and an elite population which can afford high-rented flats in the heart of the city. The summer guides still spin yarns to the tourists who gape at the high lands of the Royal Mile, telling them with unconscious irony of how all classes mingled on the common stairs of old Edinburgh. Meanwhile the divisive planning goes on. City government and University combine with property speculators from London and elsewhere to drive "John the Commonweal" into the new ghettos. The last thing the city "fathers" and the academic empire-builders want is that all classes should mingle. "Scatter and rule" might be their motto. London burghs can rebuild on the old sites, but not Edinburgh. It is a portent for the future, not to be mentioned in case Edinburgh should appear too like Glasgow, that raiding gangs from the outer fringes have driven into the centre, beating up students in the Meadows and forcing long-haired apprentices in Gorgie to go to the hairdresser, so as to avoid attention from Skinheads.

"The people are the trouble." The people had an identity in the Grassmarket, the Pleasance, the Cowgate, the West Port, Blackfriars Street, and those other places whose names and buildings made them at least to some degree conscious of belonging to the city and its history. They lived round the castle, Holyrood, St Giles and the Parliament House, as they had always done, and still to some extent mingled with the lawyers, the members of the General Assembly of the Kirk and of the University. They were moved into dreary "schemes" with no amenities except what voluntary bodies might provide; with no appreciation of the economic and psychological problems created by the change, and with scant help towards adjustment. Social workers now have to struggle to ameliorate situations from which little seems to have been learned by local politicians and their departments. The people so caustically dismissed by an Edinburgh councillor are the product of an environment created—if the word does not imply too much a conscious activity—by those forces of religion, law, and education which claim to give Scotland some real identity and which must therefore accept some considerable responsibility for the mess in which she is in today.

Scotland is sick and unwilling to admit it. The Scottish establishment at least will not admit it. The tartan sentimentality, the charades at Holyroodhouse, the legends of Bruce and Wallace, Covenanters, Jacobites, John Knox and Mary Stuart, contribute nothing towards a solution. Small wonder that so many of the ablest people she produces emigrate rather than face the struggle of living here in the fog of romantic nostalgia for a world that never existed, and lies and half-truths about the world that does exist. There is no strong image of Scotland to inspire a struggle with the economic and social problems which oppress people here today. There are still powerful elements to frustrate any radical analysis and programme which might be produced.

If there is to be a hopeful future we must first establish our identity. This has always been in doubt, except in so far as it can be established by geographical reference and negatively in hostility to England. "Scots" live in the north of Britain and are not English. Some would add "and not Irish". Racially and geographically, however, we can distinguish regions which are related closely to Scandinavia, or closely to Ireland, or closely to England. In some areas there are people who have acquired English as their mother tongue in place of Gaelic only during this century. In others there are families who have known no Gaelic in the last nine hundred years. Until the eighteenth century Highlanders were commonly described as Irish in the south of Scotland. It is only in the last two centuries that a Scottish image has been distinctly put forward in the familiar terms of Scottish religion, democracy and education. Even as it was being created it was threatened by the massive influx of impoverished Irishmen whose descendants today make up at least a quarter of the total population of Scotland.

The people living in Scotland have indeed been greatly divided for centuries, and by their divisions have brought trouble upon themselves. Their feudal leaders were generally venal and time-serving, and their industrial leaders would have difficulty in proving themselves much better. If the former had served Scotland instead of immediate self-interest we might have achieved greater peace and prosperity between 1300 and 1600. If the latter had been the paragons of Christianity and democracy described in their obituaries we would have been spared much of the squalor and violence which have coloured life for so many people in Scotland and still do. If there is to be a future with any hope we must recognise the evils of the past, abandon the romantic myths and legends which cover them up and which perpetuate divisions. We must give priority to the creation of a true unity and purpose among the people who now live in this country. How far this can be achieved, and how quickly, seems to depend on a number of powerful existing groups still acting divisively in our society. First of all the churches.

These seem to live too much in the past, a past which never existed as they imagine it. Christianity if taken seriously is revolutionary in its effect on individuals and on societies. For most of our history it has been too often a tool of political interests; in return for support of its own institutional structures and property acquiescing in the misery and injustice which it should have made impossible. The main churches in Scotland illustrate the national habit of selective illustration to support a self-justifying apologetic. That prototype of the Dr Finlay series, Ian Maclaren's novel *Beside the Bonnie Briar Bush*, gives a picture of a Scottish presbyterian community which may have had some resemblance to life in a few unusually favoured rural areas, during a comparatively short period—the last hundred and fifty years— but utterly remote from the lives of most people in Scotland then as now. Equally unreal are the tales of the Catholic Highlands published by the Scottish Catholic Truth Society. That sort of literature feeds the complacency of religious groups with false images of themselves. At the same time it panders to the self-righteousness of the two "chosen peoples", the Lowland Scots and the Scots-Irish. We need to rewrite our ecclesiastical history from the beginning, to set religious life in its real context of economic, social and political events. Religion and politics would both benefit from this exercise. It would help to clear religion from that sentimental attachment to institutions, and dubious tradi-

tions, which obscures the teaching of Christ. How would it promote political health?

A study of political attitudes in Scotland suggests that religion
confuses politics. We may have left the period, not so far back,
when any consideration of Scottish Home Rule was bedevilled by
slogans like "Home Rule means Rome Rule", or "Home Rule
means Presbyterian intolerance". Have we really left it? Discussion of entry to the Common Market in Scotland is accompanied
incredibly by the Very Rev. Lord Macleod of Fuinary, former
Moderator of the Church of Scotland, uttering fearful cries about
the prospect of 80,000,000 Protestants being swamped by
120,000,000 Roman Catholics. How wistfully the Pope must sigh
if he ever comes across that picture which so moved a recent
General Assembly of the Kirk, of 120,000,000 Europeans marching in close rank at his command! Yet George Macleod's naïve
fears were plainly shared by about half the Assembly.

At another level there is the political behaviour of Catholics in
the Glasgow area. The majority will vote for the Labour Party
since it is opposition to the party associated with English
(Protestant) imperial ascendancy. On particular issues, however,
there is no consistency and it is a serious error to imagine that the
Scots-Irish Catholics of the industrial belt are dedicated socialists.
Like so many other members of the Labour Party they are chasing in search of bourgeois dreams but with their own special type
of confusion, and with diminishing loyalty to the Christian ideals
which they profess. Their attitudes are reflected in the drop in
recruitment to the "vocations" of priest and schoolteacher. These
two professions no longer give the assurance of power and status
in the community which may have strengthened recruitment to
them in the past. The emerging Catholic middle class with its
eyes on fur coats and fitted carpets, and packaged holidays on the
Costa Brava, looks, like others in Scotland, for more cash with
less social responsibility and less commitment to other people. At
the apex of its growth there are families now established in professions which used to be preserves of the Scottish Protestant
establishment.

The emergence of a professional and aspiring middle class
from the Scottish Catholic proletariat threatens in two directions.
It is disturbing to the security of members of the Presbyterian
Kirk who want to maintain the idea of a "national" church

unchallenged by any other. It is disturbing to Catholic leaders who see their system of separate schools threatened by the fall in recruits to the teaching profession. Both the Kirk and the Catholic Hierarchy are committed to maintaining privileged positions established by legislation in Parliament, which are anachronistic in modern society, harmful to religion and supported with increasing difficulty and at the cost of steady decline in standards. Inflated statistics and evasion of sociological inquiry help to cover up the fact that while a slight majority of people in Scotland maintain some kind of social allegiance to religious institutions and conventions, there is only a minority of sincerely convinced and committed Christians in this country.

Whether people like it or not we are living in a pluralist and essentially secular society whose future depends on the willingness of its members to cross borders and learn from one another, so that differences may be understood and respected, or resolved freely without any kind of pressure towards involuntary or half hearted uniformity. The churches have had their opportunity to create a truly Christian society and have lost it. They must begin again, without that support from the civil power on which they have so much depended in the past. Much of Europe became nominally Christian from fear of fire and sword wielded by Charlemagne and others like him. It was kept in some sort of Christian appearance by institutions like the Inquisition. Protestant Scotland conformed to the general pattern. Its penal laws were subtle in that they removed the possibility of dramatic martyrdom from dissenters. The latter become non-persons before the law, if they persisted in not attending services and refused to subscribe Protestant formularies. Over a very long period religious conformity was ensured in Scotland by the civil power, which compelled people to enter the Kirk. Good citizenship became eventually inseparable from churchgoing, as in the United States today, and until the Disruption of 1843 established the Free Church, democracy was almost as much a fiction in the Kirk as it had been in the state. Things were settled "at the top" and then manipulated to give an appearance of assent from below, particularly in that alliance of vested interests which brought about the Patronage Act of 1712.

At present both the Church of Scotland and the Roman Catholic Church in Scotland are rather like heavyweight boxers eyeing each other at the weigh-in. Both are given to thinking in terms of structures and statistics, of social religious convention rather than deep personal conviction. They base statistics of membership on occasional identification through sacraments received once or twice a year, or even once in a lifetime. They are afraid of losing members. Generally in Scotland there is this fear of people "going over" to other churches or abandoning altogether church association, however tenuous it may be. That regard for conscience which Christians profess and which has been so often extolled in Scotland, is not so much in evidence when a member moves from one church to another or leaves a church altogether. It might help to bring unity of purpose to Scotland if the two main churches were to agree to revision of the legislation which favours them so much. It would suggest more real confidence in the Gospel of Christ and the action of the Holy Spirit if they showed less reliance on political favour as a condition of healthy existence, or even survival. The Kirk is probably afraid that if it lost its privileged position it would be eclipsed by the Roman Catholics, but in any case it is traditionally wedded to the political establishment which it has served so well, setting an example which the Roman Catholic authorities appear eager to emulate in return for preservation of the Catholic school system.

It has been suggested before, often enough, that at least all secondary schools in Scotland should be integrated into a single system; this would mean a major revision of the Education (Scotland) Act of 1918. It does not mean necessarily, as some have suggested, the disappearance of religious education from Scottish schools. Integrated schools could provide a variety of courses in religion and ethics wide enough to meet the wishes of most parents, Catholic, Protestant, Jewish or Humanist, and conducted by specialists in religious and moral education. Such a system might ensure a kind of discussion at staff and pupil levels which is rarely possible now. It might even lead to a broadening of school libraries which at present so often represent the narrowness of outlook expressed in the spontaneous statement of a Scottish educationalist: "Oh! But I wouldn't dream of reading any of *your* books!" This in turn might help to change the bookselling scene in Scotland, where automatic censorship is so effectively illustrated by the head of the history department in one of our largest bookshops who refused to stock a notable work of scholarship, which he imagined to be purely Roman Catholic in character, with the remark: "This is a Protestant bookshop". He might have said also, with equal emphasis at another time: "This is a Right Wing bookshop". It might even affect the highly placed member of the Scottish Education Department who publicly declared that he preferred old myths to more truthful historical analysis.

Integration of schools might come sooner if the Catholic community could be convinced that this was not a move to weaken Catholicism in Scotland for the benefit of the Kirk, which would continue to claim privileges in educational establishments, hospitals and prisons, on the grounds of state establishment as a national church. If the present situation continues, however, it looks as though there will simply be a steady erosion of the existing positions, with Catholic schools changing inevitably through lack of Catholic teachers, and the Kirk retreating slowly through lack of ministers to fill the posts hitherto regarded as its preserve. Meanwhile it would be a useful exercise if some group were to produce detailed plans, just for the sake of discussion, showing how schools might be integrated in certain selected areas; say Fife, Lanarkshire, Glasgow and Edinburgh. Remembering that to secure an educational system which would help the growth of unity in Scotland it is not enough to integrate Catholic and non-Catholic schools. There is still the problem of the socially and culturally divisive fee-paying schools, so cherished by the city oligarchies which have for centuries made a mockery of Scottish claims to democracy.

Our educational system generally is still geared to meeting the needs of an imperial, capitalist bureaucracy directed from London. Adaptations that have taken place to meet technological needs do not seem to have altered its character fundamentally. The spirit is the same. Children are to be taught what they ought to know, rather than educated to search and think for themselves. Most citizens brought up in pre-war Scotland were victims of the principle enunciated to the Vth Form in Dundee High School: "You are not here to think but to learn. You can think when you go to the university". It brought splendid examination results, and in fact could be continued successfully at the universities which played their part in the production of uneducated literacy, drilled to say the acceptable clichés about anything which was

RESURRECTION

not simply dismissed as beneath notice. There were of course exceptions, as I have reason to remember personally with gratitude to a handful of teachers who stood out against the stream. But I was one of the educational elite in Inverness, and on the border of two cultures, one peasant and Gaelic speaking, the other urban and English speaking.

The process of regimented learning probably reached its worst in Scottish Catholic schools. Two factors ensured this. First, the fideist tendency of Scoto-Irish Catholicism, which has distrusted reason and stubbornly maintained an anti-intellectual attitude in everything. Clericalism is inseparable from this attitude which distrusts the intellectual laymen most of all. It was a well-known Monsignor in Glasgow who opposed a series of extra-mural lectures on the thought of Aquinas with the remark that if working-men read Aquinas they would end up as Marxists—a judgment more profound than he could have possibly recognised in the depth of his own ignorance of Aquinas, whom he was accustomed to misquote at third hand from time to time in defence of a capitalist view of private property. In Catholic schools even more than in other schools religious education was a matter of catechism drill, supplemented in the higher classes by two dehydrated packages known as Sheehan's *Apologetic* and Hart's *Christian Doctrine*.

The other factor inhibiting education in Scottish Catholic schools was social. In the struggle for existence the underprivileged minority must conform or get out, unless it developes a revolutionary role. Pressure to conform has been strong in Scotland and not least among Scottish Catholics. Though there has been a flow of members from Catholicism to the Communist Party in Scotland it has been relatively small, like the party itself. There has been involvement sometimes with the IRA, again on the part of a few. The majority of Scots-Irish Catholics have been ready to conform to the society around them in the interest of temporal success. Their schools have been, therefore, even more strongly exam-orientated than the others, less critical of the authoritarian character of the Scottish educational system. That system is itself under strain in the modern world and the value conflicts which characterise it now. The strain is arguably greater in the Catholic sector where the values presented in home, school, pulpit, and the general social environment, are so often in total conflict with one another. For an increasing section of the school population in Scotland, and already for the majority in junior secondary education, what is presented in school is of little help in facing the problem of living in the modern world in which it is virtually impossible to remain any longer warmly sheltered anywhere. The value conflicts in Scottish society must be faced not only to give some clearer identity to Scotland, but first of all to help those who live in the country to find a satisfactory personal identity and a reason for living at all.

Back to the churches. The institutions which have given most semblance of unity to Scotland have been religious. There was some degree of religious unity before there was any appearance of political unification. The two main churches at the present day contain within themselves all the elements which go to make up Scottish society, and they possess still vast resources capable of being used constructively to shape the future. Will they use them? Or waste them in sterile competition with each other? Or in shoring-up structures which have had their day? They still spend too much money on maintaining old buildings and erecting new ones, for the most part all under-employed. They dissipate energy in barren committees filibustering about corporate reunion and in types of ecumenical meeting which avoid coming to grips with the deeper problems, theological and pastoral. Perhaps if they were more independent of the political establishment they might tackle these, and might recognise also their obligation to give a stronger contribution to political discussion and to the formation of a healthy national conscience. It is all very well to declare a position about apartheid or Viet-Nam, or to dispatch subsidies to development projects in underdeveloped countries. It would help the latter more in the long run if there was more political realism here : recognition of the have-nots in this society : a horror of the social apartheid which is perpetuated by education and town planning and the moral apartheid created by the punitive righteousness associated with the Christian community in Scotland. Committees of administrators and fundraisers directing and financing the devoted efforts of small groups of social workers, whose experience they do not personally share, make claims in annual reports that "the Church is doing something" about this or that. Opium for the conscience. It does not alter the fact that the Scottish community has created, and still creates, conditions which will further strain its psychiatric hospitals and already overcrowded jails, exhaust and frustrate understaffed social services, and stimulate emigration.

Before deciding what it is to be Scottish we need to re-examine our ideas as to what it is to be human, and to be Christian, and make at the start an act of contrition for ourselves and the community in which we live. It might help if we could set aside for a time the image of Scotland presented in the glossy magazines which decorate our station bookstalls : looking instead on the distressed girl of sixteen drifting round the city, turned out of what home she had five months ago, pregnant, it was believed by her own brother; or the young man with a history of baby-home, orphanage, approved school, borstal, young offenders institute, and prison, who repeats dutifully that of course it has all been his own fault; or the defeated woman who longs for the day when another of her fourteen children will leave school and she can tell him to go and look after himself; or the young man who lost his job when it became known that he was homosexual and after three wretched years found peace through an overdose of drugs. The list could stretch until this book was full, a roll-call of those people in Scotland whose tragedy is buried in statistics but who challenge all the conceit with which we brag about our great traditions.

These traditions include an obsessive puritanism to which Protestant and Catholic have both contributed; a vindictiveness which pursues offenders against the law long after they have tholed their assize; a system of local government in which decisions vital to the whole community in a city or county may be taken by committees meeting behind closed doors, and composed mainly of people with money or leisure to enable them to devote time to local politics; an educational system whose employees are cowed by the need to keep on good terms with the bosses if they wish for promotion, and whose programmes sacrifice the many in the interest of the few; a jealous professionalism in many fields, which is one of the reflections of the basic insecurity characteristic of so many of our people and shown in the aggressive pride long associated with the Scots in the eyes of other peoples; sectarian and regional jealousies which too often cripple proposals which are in the general interest; a parochial outlook which refuses to admit the possibility of learning from abroad anything of importance;

an intolerance masked by superficial courtesy but revealed in unguarded moments to supposedly safe ears and also in a general reluctance to read or listen to anything that might call one's own position in doubt, or to co-operate in enterprises which might bring credit to groups other than one's own; and a habit of trying to hold down the young, which means now anyone under thirty.

Some suggestions have been put forward in regard to the churches. The school system will be discussed more fully elsewhere. Nevertheless two points are perhaps worth making here; that our teaching should begin with what is given, the experience of the children themselves; and therefore that it should be firmly related to the study of things Scottish. To begin with what is given is not so easy : it does not fit easily into the examination drill; but it is real and can waken and hold interest, and it seems the best way of making school relevant to the deprived lives of so many children in Scotland. If adopted it makes necessary the training of teachers to enable them to extend discussion and study in breadth and depth. This will mean more attention to the study of the Scottish environment, its geography, history and institutions, literature, music and art. Pop art, folk music it may be; but the talents of the under-privileged in regard to the arts are consistently underestimated. And there must be some major effort to help young people to leave school not simply for dead-end jobs, which make absurd the emphasis in the school curricula on literacy and numeracy divorced from any practical training. Some at least among the Scottish universities might devise a first degree in Scottish studies which would be a preparation for the kind of teaching envisaged.

Such a change in the educational field might help to create support for those on whom the future of Scotland depends perhaps most of all, the writers who can present and interpret her image to herself. They have their share of the national virtues and vices; often bitchy and given to jealous vendettas in which truth of any kind vanishes in bile. The long list of defunct literary periodicals witnesses to their tribal wars and their failure to get through to a sufficiently large section of the people. There sticks in the mind a letter from a middle-aged minor poet to the young editor of a new periodical declaring that nothing but disgust was felt about him and his magazine by every writer of note in the country. He professed to quote two in proof of his assertion. Almost by the same post the editor received a letter from one of the two promising support for the new venture : the other had called on him the previous day to discuss possible contributions. Who among the trio was a villain? Such knife work may gratify those who engage in it but is too costly in a country like ours where creative talent needs all the support it can get and where young writers especially should be given the opportunity to experiment. Those born in the last thirty years belong to a new world and should not be expected to imitate what has gone before as a condition of receiving bread and butter.

We need writers who are born into the modern world of technology and the media of communication which it has produced; writers who see literature not as an exercise in belles lettres, a self-conscious production of art for its own sake, but as a creative act of social responsibility. "Art must be of *use*—a coercive rhyme, to strand a whale on the rock, a scratch on stone to make the corn grow." It is they who can introduce most effectively to one another the various human groups who make up Scotland, contributing to the growth of a keener sensitivity and a more general recognition of the diversity of the Scottish scene. Those born since the war have always been aware of the world beyond Scotland; this does not necessarily make them any less aware of Scotland, rather the opposite, but they underline a greater need than ever for writers who will relate Scotland and the world beyond it in a way meaningful to both. Given the writers the problem is how are they to reach the native public, how to get into the schools and universities, given the deadly state of book-selling and publishing in this country. New means of distribution have to be discovered which will get round the indifference of those who dominate the book trade in Scotland and are interested only in what will sell to tourists or prove an acceptable bromide to the suburban middle class. There is a public which they do not touch, illustrated by the local success of *Caithness Books,* or by the sale of 150 volumes of a Gaelic Text Society volume in one day from a grocer's counter in Lochmaddy. Is the idea of a writers' co-operative to handle the publishing and distribution of Scottish books quite impossible? With perhaps its mobile bookshop?

The key to all our problems must be found in Glasgow probably. The future of Scotland depends on that great conurbation on the Clyde where the Gaelic stream from the Highlands and Ireland mingles with the more British people of the Lowlands, and with others from every part of Scotland. It is in Glasgow that the chief divisive elements confront each other most dramatically, and it is there that the sick legacy of the past century of industrialism is found at its worst. If the people of Glasgow strengthen their roots, and they can still do it, having a large section of the population not yet wholly assimilated to the declining culture of bourgeois affluence, they may revitalise the rest. To do so they must turn outwards more. The insecurity that Scots in general show to the rest of the world Glaswegians sometimes display to the rest of Scotland in the form of a prickly parochialism that resents opposition and withdraws into sulks when it cannot have its own way. The rest of Scotland can learn from Glasgow, but Glasgow can learn from other regions and cities, possibly even from Edinburgh—although I am not sure what, in that last case!

In Glasgow, as elsewhere, it is almost certainly a waste of time trying to convert the older generations to new thinking and new effort. They are not without great figures—Hugh MacDiarmid comes most obviously to mind—who have made a contribution for which the future will be deeply grateful. As a whole, however, they will not change, being for the most part deeply committed to old dead ends. It is the younger generation to which we must look and with which all who can must talk and work, to change our society thoroughly and radically in all its parts. Nothing will happen of great or lasting significance unless those who undertake to shape the future can cut themselves loose from the values which dominate our present society, especially its ruthless and competitive materialism. To win freedom we must agree to live simply and be poor, and learn to be open to people and ideas.

One picture remains from the Edinburgh Festival of 1970. Members of Strathclyde University Dramatic Society living rough, like all student companies in the festival Fringe. Working with an energy incredibly sustained day after day for four weeks and in the face of near disaster at times. Cheerful. No self-pity, no ostentation. Almost in tears one rehearsal, so moved by the play from the Orcadian poet George Mackay Brown, *A Spell for Green Corn*,[1] and its theme of love, religion, art and people. Each night the motionless audience listening to the Fiddler. "In that last silence the word moved, and the bird shrieked it out under the furrows. Now was DEARTH transformed, now was the old hag changed to the likeness of a young girl glutted with love. Now BIRTH was a part of the fable. DEATH BREAD BIRTH BREATH circled the poem of man, in all its permutations, and BIRTH fitted in anywhere, a good and acceptable sound. Yet the word that the fiddle found was more than BIRTH, it was altogether different, it was the merging of all those words in the complete dance, a new and holy mystery. It was RESURRECTION."

NOTE

1. London, Chatto & Windus, 1970.

7

GAELIC SCOTLAND
Derick S. Thomson

I F W E L O O K for the origins of Scotland in historical times, there is no doubt that the Gaelic base is the most convincing, the most influential and lasting in the perspective of the last two thousand years. Archaeologists and historians have a good deal of information, some of it tentative enough, about the Picts and the British, who between them settled large areas of Scotland in the Celtic interest. Yet there is little consciousness of this being a Pictish or a British country, although these peoples, and their languages, remained influential until the ninth, tenth and eleventh centuries A.D. Archaeologists and pre-historians can make many deductions about the Celtic peoples' predecessors, whose genes still influence our characteristics and characters in obscure ways, but it is beyond our imagination to see ourselves in this prehistoric light. The Gaelic invasion was an early one also, though later than all those referred to, but its stamp is still on the country. Though much evidence has been lost, we are clear about the nature of the Gaelic system, and although its power and spread have declined disastrously, its language and literature still live, giving reality and immediacy to history.

Gaelic settlement, most probably from an Irish base, began in the fourth century A.D., or possibly a little earlier, and was strongly reinforced in the fifth century, when Dalriada was settled, and when infiltration via Galloway may also have gathered some momentum. We should recall that Scotland and Ireland are separated by quite narrow channels (at the Rhinns of Galloway and at the Mull of Kintyre), only some fourteen miles at the narrowest point, close enough in modern times to see houses on the Irish coast. By the mid-sixth century Iona, the chief Gaelic foundation in Dalriada, was already a centre of influence with an abbacy worthy of an Irish prince, and Columba was able to work from that base, spreading the influence of Irish/Gaelic Christianity not only throughout Dalriada, but in the more easterly and northerly lands then controlled by the Picts.

It was perhaps in this fashion that the Gaelic language first began to take hold in Central and Eastern and Northern Scotland, as a prestige language, associated with the new religion, which was itself associated in the Irish mind with Latin and with the power of Rome. The spread of religious influence was accompanied, or followed shortly, by that of more secular interests, and although these developments have not been worked out in any detail yet it is clear that they lead in time to that intertwining of political and temporal interests on the one hand, and of language habits on the other, which resulted in the union of the kingdoms of the Picts and the Scots in the mid-ninth century, and the blanket of Gaelic place-names over Central, Eastern and Northern Scotland. The political union practically succeeded in obliterating the Pictish nation, but British and Pictish place-names, or place-name elements, in the stubborn way these have, still survive, in such instances as *Perth*, Kin*cardine*, Strath*peffer*, *Aber*deen, and the scores, indeed hundreds of names containing the Pictish element *pit*, as *Pit*lochry, *Pitt*odrie, *Petty*.

Yet Gaelic names, and by inference the Gaelic language and way of life, spread east and north, and eventually south also, reaching the east and north-east coast, the north coast, the Western Isles, Renfrewshire and Ayrshire, Dumfries and Galloway (mainly here by the direct sea-route from Ireland, in all probability). Gaelic had a merely marginal influence in one area, and one area only, in Scotland: the Lothians, where there are indeed Gaelic names, but where the nomenclature is predominantly Teutonic. Elsewhere in Scotland, signs of earlier Gaelic influence are thick on the ground.

By contrast, when we look at the area of Scotland in which Gaelic speech predominates at the present time, we find it severely restricted: virtually to the extreme western seaboard and the Inner and Outer Hebrides. There are pockets of Gaelic speech elsewhere, and some large if dispersed colonies of Gaelic emigrés still, as in Glasgow, using Gaelic on a daily basis, and in many cases passing on the language to their Lowland-born children, and occasionally grandchildren.

This contrast, between the linguistic map of Scotland in

129

medieval times and in the present century, is not difficult to explain in historical terms. It matches, to some extent, the ebb and flow of power in the country, the rise of centralised power, and its ultimate consolidation in the hands of French- (in the earlier period) and English-speaking nobles. Such an explanation would be on the right lines until late medieval times at any rate, and in some respects, until the early seventeenth century and later, although the central focus begins to move away from Scotland thereafter. But from the eighteenth century onwards, the decline of Gaelic is to be explained in those socio-economic terms that we apply particularly to the era of the Industrial Revolution. Although no short summary is likely to be accurate, we might consider that in the earlier period the status of Gaelic was undermined by infiltration; in the later, by exfiltration, by the enforced clearance, and voluntary (or involuntary, in Marxist terms) emigration of people from the Highlands, which had by the later period become the locale of the Gaelic-speaking population. This clearance and emigration was on a vast scale, and the incidence of emigration is still high, as is that of its correlative unemployment, and these form the major part of the explanation of why Gaelic speech has declined. We are about to observe the wheel coming full circle, and see the drastically weakened base of Gaelic speech infiltrated once more, as a result of government policies, especially those of the Highlands and Islands Development Board.

The Gaelic Census

The decennial census figures plot these movements of population and speech only in modern times, from 1881, and more accurately from 1891. The population of Scotland has grown steadily in this period, with approximately a million and a half being added to it over these last ninety years, and the percentage of that population which is Gaelic-speaking has declined from just under 7 to 1.7. Whereas in 1891 it was estimated that 254,415 persons could speak Gaelic, by 1961 there were just under 81,000, and by 1971 there will presumably be a further decline, since emigration figures (especially from the Gaelic west) have remained high for most of the intervening decade.

The distribution of the Gaelic-speaking population shows some interesting patterns. In 1961, the percentage of Gaelic speakers in Glasgow as a whole was 1.1, but in certain wards, such as Park and

Partick, was between 4 and 5, well above the national average. In fact, over an eighth of the Gaelic population resides in Glasgow. More significantly, slightly over a quarter of that population live in Lewis and Harris. There were still, in 1961, parishes with close on 100 per cent of Gaelic speakers, that of Lochs (Park) in Lewis having 99.2 per cent, Barvas 98.8 per cent, Harris (Middle) 98.2 per cent, Stornoway (Back), Stornoway (Point) and North Uist (North) over 97 per cent, Barra (North) 94.7 per cent, to give the highest percentages only. It is interesting to note that a few parishes, notably Lochs and Barvas, showed a small but steady *rise* in the percentage of Gaelic-speaking population over the period 1901–61. It would appear to be true that until quite recent times, at least in the islands, only unemployment and lack of economic opportunity reduced the number and percentage of Gaelic speakers, while these communities seemed to have made the transition from a monoglot to a bilingual situation without jeopardising the position of Gaelic seriously. The 1981 Census may begin to reflect the influence of English-dominated television on the scene, and a serious worsening of the situation can be expected, unless ambitious plans (much more ambitious plans than have been discussed in B.B.C. or Government circles) for Gaelic T.V. are implemented in the early 1970's.

Myths and Definitions

I doubt if Scotland has ever been so conscious of its possession of Gaelic language and culture as it is at the present time : conscious and yet mystified; perhaps conscience-stricken. Scots have become curious about Gaelic, instead of regarding it as a curiosity. This change has taken place in the last thirty to forty years, and has been accelerated in the last ten. It can scarcely be unconnected with the growth of tourism and nationalism, both concerned with the discovery, or rediscovery, of Scotland.

This growth of interest and concern is based partly on detailed understanding, partly on myth. There is, for example, a phenomenal growth of interest in learning Gaelic, with classes all over Scotland, and learners of Gaelic scattered over many countries in the world. A radio course some twenty years ago attracted an audience of about 50,000, and the interest would certainly be wider now. Nationalists often declare their interest in Gaelic, as might perhaps be expected, for language is one of the clearest criteria that can be used to distinguish a nation. I would not claim that it is an essential criterion, but (to put the matter loosely and briefly) if it is there one need not look further. Gaelic therefore has become in one sense, in one context, a badge of nationality. This growth of interest in Gaelic language is in process of creating what may soon be a powerful myth : a Scottish myth. Like all myths, it is now self-generating : it is not promoted in the style of a Billy Graham campaign; it simply grows.

It is a significant myth. I say this not because I think it will lead to a significant change in the linguistic texture of Scotland, but because it signifies a new interest in things of the mind and of the spirit rather than in material things. It suggests also that we may have turned aside (as indeed we were forced to do) from empire-building, and begun to think of building at home.

With this language myth we can clearly associate other myths, such as those connected with music and tartan. Pipe-music has become identified with Scotland rather than with Celtic Scotland, and in the process Scotland has become Celtic in terms of myth. The processes by which this stage has been reached are delightful to contemplate. William Pitt the Younger encouraged the growth of Highland regiments in order to canalise the martial ardour of the Highlanders, and did not worry unduly (it seems reasonable to believe) if these Highlanders had their ardour extinguished on foreign soil. The pipes were introduced in war to boost courage and enthusiasm; they established a secure place in the army system, and elaborate arrangements for teaching, and indeed fresh composition evolved. The pipes and the kilt became useful recruiting devices, and Lowlanders joined Highland regiments, while Lowland regiments acquired pipe-bands and kilts. Not as many soldiers died as had been anticipated, especially in peace-time; thus, many kilts and pipers infiltrated the civilian population of Scotland. The myth has become so powerful that now a massive demonstration can be staged when a Highland regiment is threatened with disbandment. It is true that in this latter instance the myth is being exploited, largely for political purposes, and funnily enough by unionist forces. But there are, in fact, more kilts and bagpipes about than ever before, and the disease shows no sign of abatement. In such ways does Time bring in its revenges.

The people who partake in such popular developments as these are not usually acutely conscious of historical processes. Yet there

has also been a growth of interest in Scotland's history, and especially in Highland aspects of that history. The most notable example is that of the Clearances, which have now become a myth. I do
not for a moment suggest that the Clearances were a myth, but
these developments of the eighteenth and nineteenth centuries
(and some related phenomena in the twentieth), sometimes brutal,
sometimes hypocritical, usually selfish and perhaps in a handful of
instances well-meaning, have developed, as it were, a life of their
own, and are lodged uncomfortably in the conscience of most
Scots. So too are Culloden and Glencoe, and we can see in the
wings, as these myths are enacted afresh, the modern producer of
the trilogy, John Prebble. But Prebble did not produce the myths
from nothing : he is merely the contemporary medium for them.

There are perhaps other myths in the making, in which we
could see further fusions of the historically separate elements of
Scottish life, but these examples are the most striking. The myths
are to some extent resisted, and rightly so, for myths should not be
allowed to control too many aspects of our lives. Some of the resistance is reasoned, some querulous. We frequently see references to
the "tartan image" of Scotland, in commerce, politics, literature
and the arts generally. Political commentators who are hostile to
nationalism, often bracket "tartan" and "Celtic", hoping to suggest, I suppose, that these terms imply a lower degree of political
sophistication than, for example, "pin-stripe" and "Teutonic". As
I write, I see that someone in the current issue of the *Radio Times*
refers to Mr Alexander Gibson, conductor of the Scottish National
Orchestra, with obvious approval because he is not a
"tartan-trimmed haggis-basher". It is to be hoped that the image,
negative as it is, does not stick, for it has entertaining possibilities.
It reveals, clearly, more about the writer's attitudes than about
Alexander Gibson's. Few would expect him to devote his marked
talents entirely to tartan and haggis (metaphorically of course), but
the alternative need not be a surfeit of pin-stripe and salami. In
literature also, or rather on its journalistic fringes, there are some
cosmopolitans whose eyes are on the ends of the earth, as well as
securely based Scots who are interested in foreign developments,
and the reader must learn to distinguish between serious com-
plaints or warnings and bleak or prejudiced bleatings.

It is clear already that there are various ways of defining Gaelic
Scotland, and that one's reaction to it may depend on the defini-

tion being used. Thus the planner (at any rate the historically innocent, drawing-board type of planner) may define it as a geographical area, or an amalgam of development sites, recreational space and communication networks. The historian may define it in historical terms, according to his area of interest, so that the idea of a Gaelic Scotland we arrive at may be appropriate to the seventh or the fifteenth or the eighteenth century rather than the present day. The Romantic or the Propagandist (for quite different motives) may define it as the physical entity (preferably left vague and unexplored) which corresponds to such symbols as the kilt, the glengarry, the caber and the pipes. The linguist may define it as a patchwork of dialect areas criss-crossed by isoglosses. The demographer counts the human units in the Gaelic area or in Gaelic Scotland, and here we see the term taking on a new significance, for part of Gaelic Scotland is in the Lowlands. The B.B.C. caters for a part of Gaelic Scotland which the demographer misses, for many listen to Gaelic music even if they speak no Gaelic. The Gaelic publisher caters for a market which is restricted in many senses, but has a world-wide extension in some, and the writer addresses himself to all or part of these various Gaelic communities mentioned, depending on his interests, and sometimes on whether he adds an English gloss to his Gaelic work.

The truth lies in some central position, except in the case of fanatical truth, and no one can ever see or express the whole truth, because he gets in his own light. This essay strives to look at the subject of Gaelic Scotland from a large number and variety of angles, but the balance imposed on the view must be imposed subjectively. Emphasis on the past is restricted, although it cannot be ignored, and the main emphasis is distributed between the present and the future of Gaelic Scotland.

Gaelic Institutions and Gaelic in Scottish Institutions

When Scotland was split in two, culturally, split between the Gaelic and the Lowland Scots languages and cultures, or split in three if we bring English into the picture, as we must from the sixteenth century onwards, the Gaelic arts flourished in relative isolation and obscurity. Occasionally curious observers peeped behind the curtain, and saw what James Macpherson saw, or what Sir Walter Scott saw, or later what Fiona MacLeod or Mrs Kennedy Fraser or John Duncan or Sir Compton Mackenzie or Hugh Mac-

Diarmid or Norman MacCaig saw. Some of these curious sympa-
thisers saw more than others, occasionally understanding at least
one aspect of Gaelic life quite thoroughly, but for the most part
even they saw only one corner of the stage, and for most people the
curtain always hung in the way.

There are two ways of promoting understanding between different races or cultures. Both involve investigation and exposition :
one is by means of the native explaining his culture to the
foreigner, and the other is by means of the foreigner acquiring
much of the culture and explaining it to his own ethnic or linguistic group. Usually both ways are used. We are still too short of
this kind of exposition in the Gaelic/Scots (English) context. I
would recommend, for the attention of the first Scottish Government, the setting up of some agency to promote such investiga-
tions and expositions.

Physically, the Highlands are now fully accessible to enquiring
visitors. Indeed, they are now too accessible, and in summer the
loud conversation of tourists drowns out the less strident tones of
the dwindling native population. The Highlands and Islands
Development Board sees nothing wrong or dangerous in this, and
brings expertise and finance to bear mightily, to increase the
dilemma. Thus the ease of physical contact has reduced the possibility of spiritual contact, for the spirit lies quiet when there is a
clatter of dishes and coins.

Gaelic Scotland, however, is not simply, and not only, a geographical area where a close season could be applied in order to allow
the human stock to replenish, or refresh, itself. It is much more
amorphous than that, and must be considered on a national scale.
It is, indeed, truer to say this now than it would have been twenty
or thirty years ago. This will become clearer as we examine the
place of Gaelic in Scottish life.

It is not the case that Gaelic has a strong hold on Scottish institutions, although it has a foothold in several. Sometimes these foot-
holds are constitutional, sometimes personal. There are Gaelic
members of the Inland Revenue and of Customs and Excise, but
their Gaelic is irrelevant to their appointment : it is not, however, a
handicap ! The Scottish Land Court, however, has statutorily one
Gaelic-speaking member, and has often conducted its business in
Gaelic, particularly its perambulation of the marches in the
Western Isles. In the Sheriff Courts also the accused and witnesses

can offer evidence in Gaelic, claiming the services of an interpreter. This falls considerably short of the principle of equal validity for Gaelic and English, and this principle has not been conceded as yet. The Scottish Governors of the B.B.C. include a Gaelic-speaking Governor. The Crofters Commission are strongly Highland and Gaelic in their sympathies. The Highlands and Islands Development Board, possibly because it has been chided for this, does not include a Gaelic-speaking member, although at least three of its full-time members have toyed with Gaelic grammar (if I may refer in this perhaps over-modest way to their linguistic achievements). The libraries of the country provide some Gaelic service, with fine collections in the National Library and in Glasgow's Mitchell Library, in addition to the university collections. The Scottish Central Library is at the present time making arrangements for a Union Catalogue of Gaelic Books. Yet neither the National Library nor the Central Library, nor indeed any Scottish library has a designated Gaelic post. The same is true of Register House. There is clearly some room for improvement here, and no doubt this will come shortly. Gaelic holds an important place in the schools and the universities and the B.B.C., and there are Gaelic publishing societies, such as the Gaelic Society of Inverness and the Scottish Gaelic Texts Society, which are by now Scottish institutions. We shall look at some of these in detail.

Probably the nearest we have to full-scale Gaelic institutions are the Free Church of Scotland and the National Mod. Even these are not free of English influence. The Free Church has been conducting many of its Sunday Schools in English because *The Instructor* uses English, and there is no Gaelic equivalent: it is to be hoped that this gap can be filled. The Mod has for long appealed rather more to non-Gaels and partially denationalised Gaels than to full Gaels.

Yet the Free Church is nearer to being a Gaelic institution, in terms of numbers and of ethos, than any other. Its chief numerical strength lies in strongly Gaelic-speaking areas—the northern Hebrides (Outer and Inner) and the West Coast of Ross-shire—and a large number of the 24,000 members and adherents credited to it in 1966 (I take the figure from James Kellas, *Modern Scotland*, p. 248) must be Gaelic-speaking. I would suspect that the whole future of this church is intrinsically bound up with the fate of the language, and there are times when I reflect uneasily that the fate of the language is similarly bound up with the fate of the church. It is true that the Free Church can survive, and flourish, for a time in a non-Gaelic environment, but that would probably be a transitional phase. The other larger denominations in Gaelic Scotland—the Church of Scotland and the Roman Catholic Church—may be said to have Highland or Gaelic divisions, but the influence of these divisions is a waning one. The character of these churches is not significantly affected by their Gaelic wings : the main feedback of influence is indeed in the other direction. By contrast, the Free Church could enjoy, and largely does enjoy, independence within Gaelic Scotland. It has a warm family life of its own, although it sometimes presents itself, and is invariably presented by the press, in an eccentric and somewhat priggish light, as though it were the chief (or the only) bastion of religious truth in a corrupt, permissive and stupid society. Yet the Free Church is a very real part of Scotland's conscience, and it should not be stilled.

The Church of Scotland provides an interesting spectrum of social attitudes, and of Gaelic and English attitudes, if we consider it in its Gaelic setting. There are recognised gradations in charges : some may be held by "men of the people" only, or alternatively by ministers whose theology is close to that of the Free Church; others may tolerate some freedom of movement (social as well as ecclesiastical); others again may be largely dominated by middle-class (and mainly non-Gaelic) values and attitudes. City and town and country, mainland and island, help to define these nuances, but the definition is influenced by other elements also. It may help to understand the range if the extremes are defined, and they are here defined with a hint of caricature, as (1) the suave city minister, who mixes easily in middle-class society (Gaelic or English), adjudicates at Mods, goes to concerts, and is on one of the Church's ecumenical committees, and (2) the sombrely dressed, black-hatted minister, at home mainly in his village society, who cannot afford (spiritually and socially) to appear at any form of public entertainment, and probably has no desire to do so, who sees the scarlet woman of Rome in the background of any inter-church dialogue.

The Gael is a good actor, and his mental processes are subtle and devious; he is on the look-out for contradictions and inconsistencies, can savour hypocrisy, and loves gossip with the love of a rural society. There are the makings here, in the ecclesiastical sphere, of a delightful Chinese puzzle, and it is savoured until the time comes to crack it. By then there is another in the making.

Gaelic in Schools, Colleges and Universities

The possibilities of educational as of other theory are not end-less, and it can be observed periodically that there are cycles of change which lead one back almost to the original starting-point. It is interesting to think of the recent history of Gaelic education in this light. It is not suggested that in many senses it is back to its pre-1872 state, but the movements of the last century in this field are instructive. Before 1872 there were Gaelic schools, and I have known personally many old people who attended them in their youth, or whose parents did. It is a measure not only of the inade-quacy of these schools but of the oddity of our own thinking that we tend to regard these Gaelic schools as eccentric establishments. One of them is graphically described by Donald MacKinnon (later Professor of Celtic at Edinburgh) in a Gaelic essay "Seann Sgoil". He describes a Gaelic school in Colonsay in the 1840's. The building was a humble one : long and low, thatched, doorways closed against the prevailing weather by a bundle of heather, earthen floor, two fires burning on the floor in the middle of the house, and the seats consisting of deal planks resting on slabs of stone. The pupil's equipment comprised a slate, cheap writing paper, ink made from oak sap, a quill pen, *Gray*, the Shorter Catechism, a Gaelic Bible covered in sheepskin and a good shinty stick. The old schoolmaster had been in the Army in his youth. He would take a share in the game of shinty before calling his scholars into school, when the day's work began with a Gaelic prayer, followed by a Bible reading, and catechism; then writing and counting, counting and writing, until afternoon, when there was a Bible reading, a prayer, and more shinty.

MacKinnon, writing shortly after the introduction of the new system following the 1872 Act, is critical of the lack of range in that old school he remembered, but is appalled by the basic tenet of the new system : that the education of Gaelic children should be conducted in English. He was something of a lone voice in this, and not a sufficiently influential one, and the new system, with its neglect of the children's native language, and often a crude per-secution of it, took a firm hold on Gaelic Scotland. This leading tenet of the new system was in close accord with its basic utilitarian purpose, which was to give the abler pupils educational passports and export them to the cities or abroad. As the Gaelic area went through this period of degradation, sustained by this cynical educational philosophy, it did indeed send out a host of young people armed with passports, lost much of its vital population, and bred a depressed economy and a history of mental depression as well.

There is a sense in which the revival of Gaelic interest and opportunity can be regarded as an indicator of spiritual and social and economic health in the community. The story of this revival is now becoming a long one, and I can only refer to some salient points in its course. In 1918, a Gaelic Clause was added to the Educational Act of that year, giving parents in the Gaelic area the right to demand facilities for the study of Gaelic in the schools. Gaelic had already asserted a place in the schools examination system (in the old Queen's Scholarship, and later in the Higher Leaving Certificate examinations), and as a result of these developments, backed up by Gaelic Teachers' Conferences and the publication of new text-books, mainly by An Comunn Gaidhealach, Gaelic gradually won a position of respect and prestige in at least the senior secondary schools. Its progress in the primary and junior schools was much more erratic and arbitrary. Meantime, provision in the universities and training colleges (in some of these at least) had improved greatly, and a more or less adequate supply of Gaelic teachers became available.

The next advance came from about 1950 onwards, and is still in progress. It has many separate aspects, but all combine to give Gaelic in education greatly enhanced opportunity and prestige. The last twenty years or so have seen much re-shaping and freeing of the Gaelic curriculum, many advances in teaching method, and a restructuring of the examination system, the latter carried out mainly by the Gaelic Panel of the Examination Board, and including separate provision for ordinary and higher courses for both native speakers and learners, as well as an examination in sixth year studies. This period has seen also an almost complete replacement of text-books, with many new types of books appearing and about to appear, and a basically different attitude to the role of Gaelic in schools, and the role of education in the Gaelic area. In this period Gaelic as a subject has begun to make its way into both primary and secondary schools in Lowland areas, notably Glasgow, spasmodically in Edinburgh and Greenock, Inverness, Aberdeen, Perthshire and Stirlingshire. Gaelic is now taught in some three or four senior secondary schools in Glasgow, for example, in some ten or more primary schools, and in one further education college there. More recently still, Gaelic broadcasts for schools, on the V.H.F. service, have been inaugurated. There have been useful school developments also in such activities as inter-school debates and quizzes, participation in Mods and drama festivals, and in the development of the Gaelic sections of school magazines.

In the mid-1950's Inverness-shire, at the instigation of Dr John A. Maclean, the Director of Education of the time, began to place a new emphasis on the place of Gaelic in the schools, appointing a Supervisor of Gaelic, setting up panels and working parties of Gaelic teachers, and in general stimulating interest in the subject and in new ways of teaching it and using it as a medium of instruction. The results of this policy have been very encouraging, and excellent work was done by the first Supervisor, Mr Murdo MacLeod, who has only recently moved to the School Inspectorate. There was, I think, only one aspect in which the Inverness-shire scheme fell short: it shirked the boldest step of all, that of setting up, even on an experimental basis, schools in which Gaelic would be the sole medium of instruction for the early years of the course, or for the whole of the primary course. The scheme did go so far as to teach Gaelic reading before English reading, at any rate in selected schools, and apparently with highly encouraging results, but there seems to have been a partial failure of nerve, and incomplete backing from older teachers. Yet it is clear that this has been the most comprehensive and the most successful venture in Gaelic school education this century, and it is still in progress.

Largely arising out of the success of this scheme, the Scottish Education Department encouraged the Highlands counties to set up a Joint Committee on Gaelic Text-books, to consider the provision of new and varied books which would be guaranteed a sale, thus meeting the schools' needs for new material and the publishers' need of a stable market. This scheme has now become a very successful co-operative venture between the Gaelic counties (including Glasgow for this purpose), Jordanhill College of Education, which has run workshop courses for teachers, a number of active panels of Gaelic teachers, especially in Inverness-shire, and the main publishers, Gairm Publications, who have also been producing school text-books independently. The Gaelic text-book position has been revolutionised, and the stage is being set for further advances in the schools.

Jordanhill College of Education has played an important part in training primary teachers to man the schools in which these new policies are being carried out, and these teachers owe much to the infectious enthusiasm of Mr John A. MacDonald, the lecturer in Gaelic at Jordanhill. Meantime the universities, particularly Aberdeen and Glasgow, have been producing a steady stream of honours candidates in Celtic, so that the serious shortage of students with this qualification is now mitigated. These universities have freed the Celtic curriculum to such an extent that their courses can cater for both the dedicated academic and the more vocationally minded student, and the benefits of this unshackling are being felt in the schools, as ordinary and honours graduates take up their posts. There are still areas of opposition in the schools, where the strong English bias of the past hundred years still has a hold, particularly among older headmasters, but the position is steadily improving. A school such as the Nicolson Institute in Stornoway, which has an open-minded rector, can do much to change the climate of opinion, and there seems little doubt that this will happen, and in due course the change will spread.

In the universities, in addition to important changes in Celtic and Gaelic curricula, and the growth of honours schools, there has been a growth of staff in the Celtic Departments and a good deal of diversification of research interests and specific research projects. Lecturing staff in the Celtic Departments has increased from the meagre figure of 3 in the immediate post-war years to 10 or 11 now, and with such research projects as are pursued by the School of Scottish Studies, the Linguistic Survey of Scotland, and the Historical Dictionary of Scottish Gaelic, another half-dozen specialist posts are in existence. The range of Celtic, and more specifically Gaelic studies in the Scottish universites has thus increased greatly in the last twenty years, and this is reflected in a welcome increase in postgraduate work : it is to be hoped that this trend will continue.

Only three of the Scottish universities—Glasgow, Aberdeen and Edinburgh—offer courses in Gaelic and Celtic. Courses in

Celtic are offered in many universities throughout the world. Many of these concentrate on Old and Middle Irish : specifically Scottish Gaelic courses are offered in at least the following universities abroad : Oslo, Freiburg, Harvard, St Francis Xavier, Oxford, Trinity College Dublin, University College Dublin, and Galway.

This century, especially the post-1918 period, and more especially the post-1945 period, has seen a steady strengthening of the position of Gaelic in schools, colleges and universities—in contrast to its decline as a spoken language. This has been done with conspicuous success on the level of organisation, in the provision, for example, of opportunities to study Gaelic, with the appropriate examination incentives, practically at all levels. Yet the place of Gaelic in the schools still remains unsatisfactory, for lack of the final step. This final step perhaps requires an act of faith, and preferably of communal faith. This is why we hesitate, collectively. The faith is hardly to be won in isolation, as faith simply in a language. This is not a satisfactory basis for faith. It must be linked to something else, a whole culture or way of life perhaps, more probably a nationality. National idealism is a strong buttress for language, and language for national idealism, and further advance, if it comes, will come from that direction.

Gaelic in the Communications Media

A language which has only peripheral exposure in the press, and on radio and T.V., must fight an unequal fight for survival, let alone growth. Even with the rise of T.V. the extent to which people are conditioned to read is formidable : we read compulsively, whenever print or lettering comes within our range of vision. Quite young children acquire this compulsive habit : it is not confined to the highly literate. It should therefore be an important part of any language movement to increase that language's exposure rate, even at the risk of charges of indecency. In the Gaelic context, Gaelic should be mercilessly and continuously exposed to the public gaze, in print, on television, on signs, posters and hoardings, in advertising literature, on the packaging of goods, and so on. It is an understanding of this situation that has prompted recent militant campaigns on behalf of the Welsh language, and the recent demand to have the 1971 census forms printed in Welsh. But the Gaelic movement in Scotland has not as yet seen the full urgency of this approach, and can still take up a great deal of slack in exploiting it.

Constant use and exposure of the language is also of great importance in expanding its resources, in fitting it for use in changing circumstances. It is often said, by those who have no means of knowing about it, that Gaelic has no vocabulary for a wide range of contemporary purposes. This is far from true, but it is true to say that it needs to expand and adapt its vocabulary constantly. In earlier times, before widespread literacy and instant communication, language changed and grew relatively slowly. Now it can grow or change very rapidly, at least in certain aspects of vocabulary. Successful coinages can become current almost overnight— but only when there are writers working through the night on the morning's copy, papers to print it, and newsmen to broadcast it.

Gaelic is not well placed to take advantage of this situation, which requires a sizeable number of writers and media if it is to be exploited. The position of Gaelic in the media is a highly inadequate one, as can be seen from the following table (as of May 1970):

Media	Titles, etc.	Extent, nature of use
Daily press	—	No use of Gaelic.
Weekly press	*Stornoway Gazette*	Minimum of two columns, frequently exceeded; occasionally a full page. Occasional snippets or features in other Highland weeklies.
Fortnightly press	*Sruth*	Between 2 and 4 pages of Gaelic, i.e. from one-sixth to one-third of the total. (Now ½ page in *Stornoway Gazette*).
Monthly periodicals	Church magazine Supplement *An t-Eileanach*	Entirely in Gaelic, ranging from an 8-page printed Supplement, *Na Duilleagan Gàidhlig*, to occasional features.
Quarterly periodical	*Gairm*	100-page magazine. All text in Gaelic. Approximately half advertising in Gaelic.
Annual	School magazines	Separate Gaelic sections or interspersed Gaelic items in approximately 8 annuals.

Media	Titles, etc.	Extent, nature of use
Radio		Average of 3½ hours per week, made up normally of an average of 40 minutes of religious services, 25 minutes news, 60 minutes talk, 85 minutes songs (Now reduced).
Television		15 minutes a week for part of the year only. Songs.

Clearly the main deficiency occurs in the high-frequency publications, especially the daily and weekly press, radio and television. It would certainly have been helpful if *Sruth* had increased the proportion of Gaelic material it used, and increased the quality and range of this material at the same time, but its incorporation into the *Stornoway Gazette* was, of course, a move in the other direction. It would be even more helpful if the weekly and daily press could increase, or introduce, Gaelic, and if the daily and weekly Gaelic coverage on radio and television could be increased, so that we approached nearer to an effective degree and frequency of exposure. The weekly 3½ hours of Gaelic radio, (now seriously reduced to approximately 2½ hours) out of the 378 hours of broadcasting by the B.B.C., is an offensively meagre total. For all that, a good deal of coinage, adaptation and general innovation takes place, and the current vocabulary of Gaelic has changed significantly to adapt to contemporary trends in manufacture, technology and science, as well as to innovations in entertainment, public interests and current affairs generally. All this innovation has still to be made definitive by the issue of a new dictionary or dictionaries. The truly creative coinage and adaptation is that carried out under practical writing conditions, and happily it is mainly innovation of this kind that we have. There has been some more abstract coinage, as for instance a list of literary and other technical terms compiled by the Gaelic Panel of the Examination Board, for use in examination papers (and by implication in Gaelic teaching!); or the late John Paterson's publication *The Gaels have a word for it!*, something of a misnomer, since many of the words listed might have been described as John Paterson's private property.

Apart from the more technical matter of coinage and adaptation, it is important to realise the range of Gaelic material appearing in these media, and the gaps in that range. News forms an important part of the range, and is represented mainly in radio news bulletins and items in *Sruth*. We have still to attain daily news coverage, and perhaps as important, fresh-news coverage, for much of the news content of both radio programmes and *Sruth* is already familiar from an English hearing or reading. Until January 1971 *Sruth* ran an effective column of Church News in Gaelic, and this was to a large extent fresh news; its ecumenicity, however, is no doubt a cause of offence in certain quarters. Other regular features can be classified as causerie and/or belles lettres, political comment, and book reviews, and there are occasional articles on foreign affairs. At the level of the quarterly, there is a good deal of exposition of a wide range of topics : nuclear developments, space travel, medical topics, cell biology, painting, to name only a few. The exposition here tends to be in greater depth. In addition there is regular comment on fashions and cosmetics, and some limited musical criticism. On the more exclusively literary side there is of course regular publication of fiction and poetry.

There is still a considerable lack of "roughage", of the bulk ephemerese which a semi-literate society (and indeed the fully literate sector also) feeds on and excretes daily. It would be as foolish as it would be smug to say that we can simply do without it.

Despite the narrowness of the base, it can be said that the position of Gaelic has improved significantly in this sector in the last twenty years, and the time is fully ripe for further advance. This advance should be along several avenues some of which may be suggested here :

1. Increased radio and T.V. coverage, with emphasis on "daily" coverage of news and comment in Gaelic.
2. Increased Gaelic coverage in weeklies, especially the *Stornoway Gazette*, if necessary with some public subsidy.
3. Children's paper(s), including comic strip(s).
4. A school/V.H.F. publication, to go with the Gaelic radio lessons, each medium to be complementary to the other.
5. A monthly Gaelic or Gaelic/English publication sponsored by the Highlands and Islands Development Board and the Crofters' Commission.
6. A monthly publication, independent of any public organiza-

tion, to promote comment and assessment on current affairs, including politics, government, industrial and other development, and also on matters of literary and artistic interest. This suggestion may be as yet impracticable, but it is to be hoped that it will come eventually.

7. A monthly "pulp" magazine, catering for relatively unsophisticated readers, and providing popular fiction and features.

Gaelic in Entertainment

Just as in Gaelic literature there has been a strong emphasis on poetry, so in Gaelic entertainment there was and is a strong emphasis on song. It can scarcely be denied that here what was once a rich tradition is sadly impoverished and has virtually lost all sign of creative vigour. The processes by which this change developed are clearly understood historical processes, and the remedy is not too difficult to see, though perhaps very difficult to apply.

When the Gaelic society of Scotland was more whole, in the sense of enjoying its own range of institutions, and its own functional divisions—classes if you like—the arts in general flourished more than in modern times, when the society is broken and fragmented, and when competing loyalties make for incomplete development. This incomplete development is caused both by a failure to define artistic goals, and by fragmentation of the effort needed to reach them. When there were Gaelic leaders (then called chiefs) who were, by the law and custom of their society, patrons also, certain forms of art and entertainment flourished : as juggling and fooling, sculpture and silverwork, harp and pipe music, and certain kinds of literature.

Society is no longer organised on these lines, and although aspects of the old tradition have been kept alive by performers, performing in a different milieu and so differently, the creative aspects of the tradition have largely withered. It was rather a conservative tradition at the best of times, and its rate of adaptation was not high : had it been, the tradition would have changed and evolved steadily instead of fossilising. Had this happened, there would have been a continuing emphasis on creation rather than simply on performance, and a consequent toning-up of the whole system.

As the mass of the Gaelic people became more and more divorced from their own literary and musical tradition, aspects of

that tradition receded into limbo, or were at best recalled and re-
vered in an esoteric way. The consequence was that the central
popular tradition became an unambitious one, without sufficient
strength either to create or to resist easy imitation. Sometime in the
nineteenth century, with the greatly increased contacts between the
Gaels and other peoples, especially in urban centres such as Glasgow, this new popular tradition was consolidated, and its symbol
became the *céilidh*, and the *céilidh* came gradually to consist of a
succession of good-going songs, with choruses for the most part,
and solo performances on instruments such as the fiddle and the
pipes and the accordion. There were gradations of *céilidh*, some
more sophisticated than others, some appreciating a different range
or indeed complexity of songs than others, for territorial or historical or personal reasons. But basically the *céilidh* came to be
thought of as the symbol of Gaelic entertainment, and finally almost as the whole of Gaelic entertainment. I am including under
the term *céilidh* the vast majority of more formal concerts staged
in the cities in particular, and elsewhere; although these may often
have had their platform parties in evening dress, their long-winded
chairmen and voters-of-thanks, and been followed by balls or
dances, with Masters of Ceremony as well as chuckers-out, in an
artistic sense there was seldom much to choose between one function and another. I am not discussing the social enjoyment of
these occasions, which was high, and which provided their *raison
d'être*, but the artistic, or specifically musical content, and in
particular their contribution to a developing or stagnating tradition of Gaelic music.

The *céilidh*/concert tradition was influenced to some extent by
the tradition of "variety" in the music-hall sense, and Gaelic has
impinged more directly on that tradition in one or two ways, for
example in the persons of Allan Macritchie, Calum Kennedy and
Alasdair Gillies, who have trod the boards, and in the case of the
latter two, starred in television shows; or by direct imitation of the
form of the variety show, in older and more recent performances,
especially in Glasgow. The island of Lewis, perhaps because of its
strong links with Glasgow, seemed to specialise in a line of native
comedians who were and are very much of the soil in their
humour : there are some signs of successful adaptation rather than
plain imitation in this instance.

Pulling in a different direction, and at times achieving some eccentricity too, were the devotees of the folksong cult, with their slogans, explicit or implicit, of "Back to the Seventeenth Century" or "Back to Barra" or "Back to Gapped Scales" or "Back to Catholicism": usually if not always, back somewhere. There was a clear need for an assertion of the value and beauty (and perhaps even the purity) of the folksong tradition, but art and bigotry are not good bedfellows, and both the *céilidh*-mongers and the folksong-bashers tend to be myopic and bigoted. Music cannot flourish long, in either milieu, without fresh creation, without experiment, and there is virtually none, scarcely even a recognition of the need for it. This desperate musical poverty is depressing. To dispel the attitudes that underlie it we need more education.

The role of the B.B.C. in this matter, in recent years, has been largely to follow popular leads. This has been dictated partly by lack of knowledge and appreciation, partly by prejudice. There are one or two Gaelic musical programmes which are good of their kind: the MacDonald Sisters' T.V. programme and the folksong programme entitled "Craobh nan Ubhal". In between there is much dullness of presentation, repetition of items, and a general lack of artistic imagination and integrity.

The National Mod also merits the charge of dullness and lack of imagination, and is too blatantly competitive to carry much artistic weight. The Mod has done a great deal to foster the development of choral singing in Gaelic, and at its best this has been perhaps its greatest glory. There have been adventurous settings, and although fresh musical experience has been achieved largely or entirely by the grafting on of an alien style, it can be said that here—and almost here alone—Gaelic music has grown in the last thirty years. If the National Mod could somehow develop its function as an Exhibition of Gaelic music, and cut itself adrift from its pot-hunters and its late-night rabble, it could still do exciting and valuable things. It would be untrue as well as ungracious not to add that it has stirred interest and enthusiasm in Gaelic music in many parts of Scotland, helped to keep alive the tradition of the *òran-mór* or art-song, and brought many fine artists to the public over its seventy to eighty years of existence.

There are various recording companies which issue Gaelic recordings, of song and pipe-music. These live in the same climate, basically, as has been described, and cater to much the same audience.

The piping public, as was indicated earlier, is not co-extensive with the Gaelic public. Here again, the art has become almost exclusively a performing art, with little fresh creation, at any rate in the classical music of the pipes, although a recent B.B.C. competition did attract a good number of entries : this was a quite exceptional flurry of creative interest in piping. It is suspected that a piping mystique is rather deliberately fostered, and there seems little doubt that there are great gains to be made, both for the musical public at large and for the serious pipers, from deeper study, more cross-fertilisation, and more communication. Mr Seumas Mac-Neill has taken a prominent part in spreading knowledge : the bridge he and others are building need not project from only one side of the river.

There is no permanent or repertory stage in Gaelic, only an amateur stage, and the history of Gaelic drama is brief, being virtually confined to the twentieth century. Gaelic plays are often presented in the competitive festivals of the S.C.D.A., and sometimes reach an advanced stage of the competition. More significantly perhaps, there is the body called the Glasgow Gaelic Drama Association, which stages an annual festival of short plays in Glasgow, attracting entries from various parts of Scotland. Clubs had to rely heavily on translated plays in the early years of this festival, but it has always attracted a proportion of original work, both in plays and in production. These plays and productions often win prizes, and the public is being gradually acclimatised to work other than farce and kitchen comedy. One hopes that this movement will grow; there are clearly grave difficulties in the way of development in this field so long as the opportunities for theatre are so restricted.

It seems to me that there has been one serious omission in the Scottish Arts Council's activities and forward planning : the setting up of a serious enquiry into the potential of the Gaelic arts, and a more vigorous policy of fostering and supporting them at the present time. It is hard to avoid the impression that although there is goodwill, it is so vague and fusionless as to amount to very little in practical terms. Perhaps it is not too late to look a good deal more purposefully at the possibilities of this kind of patronage, which is of course the successor of the patronage of wealth and caste, and might be held to apply to Scotland as a whole, Gaelic Scotland included.

Gaelic in Publishing and Literature

Talent and achievement are not the prerogative of the big powers, nor is their incidence relative to the size of the societies in which they are found. There are exceptions, of course : space exploration is undertaken with most success by the big powers. But the Nobel prizes for Literature or for Peace do not always, or usually, go there.

The smallness of the Gaelic society is not quite so severe a handicap as might be expected, in the literary sense. In practical terms it is a handicap, but once practical difficulties are overcome (as they can often be by practical measures) literature and writing, and publishing, can flourish. Two of the prime examples of this are Iceland and the Faroes; Iceland with approximately double the Gaelic population of Scotland, the Faroes with approximately half. Both maintain a steady and well diversified flow of books in their own languages. Gaelic Scotland, as we shall see, has begun to solve its publishing problem.

It would be fair to say that modern Gaelic society has been, in general, more aware of literature, or at least some forms of litera-ture, than English society has. This situation comes about from historical causes : the largely classless nature of modern Gaelic society, the earlier merging from the seventeenth and eighteenth centuries of professional literary artists in the surrounding society, the innate conservatism which fosters literary traditions as part of the precious past. These were the factors which helped to preserve the stories of Dark Age and Medieval times on the lips of story-tellers in Uist and Barra and Tiree, and elsewhere, into the middle of the twentieth century. They kept alive the Ossianic ballads, with their echoes of the Norse Invasions. But above all they fostered an interest in poetry and song of all kinds, in the art of verse-making, so that an impressive volume of verse was carried orally from one generation to another, and from one century to another. This includes the chants and prayers of medieval and late medieval times, represented in Carmichael's *Carmina Gadelica*, the very fine range of folksongs dating from the sixteenth century onwards, the poetry of elegy and eulogy, especially that of the seventeenth and eighteenth centuries, and the verse which cele-brates local incidents, preoccupations and characters, still current and still being composed. It is only in the present century, and indeed since the 1920's, that this tide of verse of many kinds has begun to run less strongly. In some areas, where spoken Gaelic has lost its hold, or its strength, both the oral tradition and the widespread facility in verse-making have weakened or disappeared, but in much of the Outer Isles, and in pockets elsewhere, this has not happened yet.

On this background, in the present century in particular, there was superimposed another linguistic and literary system, that of English, making a two-colour print, and sometimes other colours were added from further afield. In the areas of high vitality in Gaelic Scotland this seems to have produced a fresh and novel type of literature, ready to use themes and techniques tried out in other literatures, but with strong, recognisable echoes from the Gaelic literary past. It is a literature that, in tune with modern developments, can speak across borders, yet is recognisably Gaelic. Very occasionally—Iain Crichton Smith is the chief example of this—the writer uses English as well as Gaelic as a main medium; usually it is a bilingual experience and sensibility which underlies the work, and its clearest appeal may be to a bilingual public. I daresay the same is true of modern Irish literature. The writers who fall into this category are clearly the most creative and innovatory of contemporary writers in Gaelic : they are the sensitive antennae of the Gaelic system, and sometimes they have a blind arc behind them, but more usually they receive messages from the past as well as from the future.

These are not the only, or by a long way the most popular, Gaelic writers. They have often been ridiculed, or sniped at, by those who receive messages only from the past, and whose blind arc is in front of them, and sometimes to their flanks also. These crab-like bats, if I may be pardoned so crudely exuberant a metaphor, seldom say quite what is in their minds, but try to deliver glancing blows. They sometimes set themselves up as experts in language, especially grammar, and may have great though superficial knowledge of metrics, but the central genius of language is a closed book to them. Some of these blind bats pass for literary critics.

I place in an entirely different category the practising writers, mainly poets, who still follow an older tradition in their work. There have been some fine representatives of this class in recent years. Donald Macintyre, whose poetry was published under the title *Sporan Dhòmhnaill,* was one, and Donald MacDonald (*Dòmhnall Ruadh Chorùna*) was another; there are many still living and writing. The best of these poets write with a fine instinct for traditional metrical craftsmanship, using rich lexical resources with ease, producing echoes and adding nuances, mostly within a well-defined tradition. It is a tradition that can assimilate fresh experience superficially, without quite assimilating it in poetic terms : the sniper at the Battle of the Somme is the North Uist fowler wearing a different hat, and the poet seems to see them both in much the same perspective. In this way the verse continues to serve its purpose, in a social sense, holding public interest. The main way, however, in which verse of this kind holds its public is by topicality and humour : the poet is the village or district or island laureate, who responds to the contemporary stimuli, formulates a view, or simply entertains. Verse of this kind still has a waiting public, and a large quantity of it still awaits collection and publication. The late Norman MacLeod of Lionel in Lewis (his nom-de-plume was Am Bàrd Bochd) collected much Lewis verse of this kind, some of which was recently published with the title *Bàrdachd á Leódhas.* Similar collections are in preparation for Skye, South Uist and Tiree, and any of the Outer Hebrides, and some mainland districts, could produce comparable work. It would be savoured in all these places for its craftsmanship, topicality, humour, and a greater or lesser degree of lexical virtuosity. There are some interesting resemblances between work of this kind and the ballad verse which is composed in the Lowlands, notably in Glasgow : some very fine examples by writers such as Jim Mac-Lean and Maurice Blythman may be referred to.

There is no prose equivalent of this truly popular verse which exists basically in an oral context, and it hardly seems likely that there can be any longer. For the verse derives a good deal of its popularity from the fact that it can be used orally : it is an extension, even in book form, of the oral tradition. This tradition once encompassed prose with almost equal ease—the prose of the sagas and tales of all kinds—and the tradition still lingers, especially in pockets in Barra, South Uist, Benbecula and Tiree, but it seems to need more cultivation, a more strenuous application on the part of the tradition-bearer, and our society is on the point of abandoning it. If a full transition is to be made from a society "literate" in oral literature to one literate in the conventional sense (but in Gaelic) some body of work must take the place of the oral prose. It is not likely that this will take the form of written transcriptions of traditional tales, however much the antiquarians and traditionalists might wish it.

Development of written literary, as opposed to oral literary, work has in the last thirty years or so been concentrated in a rather different area, and the developments in this area have been noteworthy. We have already glanced at the diversification that has taken place in prose of exposition, and in periodical writing generally, and it might be added that in the process there has been a considerable freeing of Gaelic prose, a distinct move towards the informality and the rhythms of speech. When this is well done it does, of course, involve much art. This movement is, I suppose, a positive response to the increased informality of society, as well as a reaction against the ornate and somewhat pompous prose of an earlier period. There is a tendency, still resisted by many, to make one phrase do where three would have been used before.

These tendencies are equally marked in the short story, and also in the non-traditional verse of this century, particularly that of the last thirty years, and there can be little doubt that it was the poets who gave the lead in this matter. The innovation which was the product, or the occasion, of this leadership was connected with styles and developments in other literatures, for the innovating writers in Gaelic have all, without exception, had ready access to one or more non-Gaelic literatures. Either directly or through some sort of mediation they have been aware of the work of symbolists and imagists, of developments in French poetry, or Czech and Russian fiction, of Joyce and Pound. As a result of all these influences, and the changing climate of Gaelic Scotland, major changes of direction occurred in both poetry and the short story, which both became rather cosmopolitan in form and style, although still clearly belonging in many ways to the Gaelic tradition. This set up tensions in Gaelic literary circles, and in the fifties and early sixties there was much debate over the old and the new, the *seann nòs* and the *nòs ùr*. Some of this debate was shadow-boxing, since the underlying processes and motivations were not well understood or defined. For example, one form which the debate took was to oppose the merits of traditional Gaelic grammar, or metrics, to the demerits of slackened standards of grammar and metre; whereas the new-style writers were usually not careless craftsmen but writers responding to a new situation and a new set of stimuli of which their critics were unaware. Current Gaelic speech has changed from that of the nineteenth century, or the earlier twentieth, the case-inflections of nouns are steadily disappearing, grammatical gender is becoming less rigid, backchat is more appreciated than debate, our minds are more open to nuances and so there is less need to labour ideas. The debate should have been about these underlying movements, rather than about grammar and so on. The debate has died down to some extent now, and in many ways the revolution has been accepted, and a new one should therefore be in the making. For the involved, committed Gaelic writer, the last thirty years have been an interesting, at times an exciting period—perhaps one of the most exciting in the whole history of Scottish Gaelic literature.

Gaelic Publishing

It is appropriate at this point to discuss developments in Gaelic publishing in the period we have been looking at, and to speculate about the future. The post-1945 period has seen large scale reorganisation of publishing in Scotland. Here as in a long and dreary list of Scottish industries, firms and organisations, there has been one take-over bid after another, with the monotony relieved only by closures and liquidations. There is not much sign, in the publishing field, of take-over leading to expansion in Scottish terms. Here, as in many other fields, it must be hoped that political independence will lead to rejuvenation : at any rate the miserable devastation produced by centralism becomes clearer every year.

Gaelic publishing was not in a strong position in 1945. Some firms which had shown an interest, or developed a specialism, in Gaelic publishing were already closed, or were pulling in their horns : Alexander Gardner of Paisley, Aeneas MacKay of Stirling, even Alexander MacLaren of Glasgow, the leading Gaelic publisher of the inter-war period. Since then MacLarens have gone out of business, and Oliver and Boyd would appear to have no further interest in Gaelic publishing. An Comunn Gaidhealach, which rivalled MacLarens for part of this century, have lost much of their publishing impetus. The place of leading Gaelic publishers in recent years has been taken by Gairm Publications, who have produced a list of Gaelic school texts, and works of poetry and fiction. Some of the school texts are in part sponsored by the Joint Committee on Gaelic Text-books, and published by Gairm Publications. (In July 1970 Gairm Publications took over Alexander MacLaren.)

A significant new factor has begun to influence the course of Gaelic publishing. In 1968, following on two or three years of consultation and planning, a grant in aid of Gaelic publishing was given to the University of Glasgow by the Scottish Education Department. This grant is at the level of £5,000 a year for an experimental period of four years. A Gaelic Books Council has been set up, being provided with office accomodation in the Celtic Department of the University, with a full-time Editorial Officer, and with clerical assistance. The larger part of the grant is to be devoted to the support of Gaelic publishing : the remit is confined to new and original work in Gaelic. The intention is that the economic strait-jacket imposed by a small reading public should be eased by these arrangements, which allow for a modest subvention to publishers, and through them, via royalties, to authors. In addition, the Editorial Officer provides liaison between authors and publishers, and to some extent between publishers and the reading public, helping to provide information and certain technical services where these are required to bring a book to the point of production. The Gaelic Books Council is concerned, then, to some extent with stimulating fresh activity in Gaelic writing, and with easing the problems which beset authors, publishers and readers in a restricted, under-organised market. Predictably the scheme had a slow start, since books do not appear overnight, but it is now quite clear that it is having the stimulatory effect that was anticipated. Grants are now being awarded at what promises to be the average rate of fifteen a year, and already there has been a healthy diversification in the range of books published, some improvement in the design of books, and some improvement in the flow of books to the Gaelic public. The grants are hardly on a scale which would seem attractive to commercial publishers, and it is very difficult to attract newcomers to this field, but there are modest signs of development here too. The Highland Book Club has issued its first Gaelic publications, and one or two other publishing enterprises are about to appear. The grants do allow the small or private publishers to use the services of designers and illustrators, and to publicise their books more effectively. If development continues at the present rate we could anticipate the grant-aided publication of some twenty to twenty-five books per year in three or four years' time. This would be a significant achievement, and would almost certainly lead to an enrichment of the life of Gaelic Scotland.

The present Gaelic Books Council scheme does not cater for translation, either from Gaelic into other languages or from other languages into Gaelic. The Council might reasonably take translation into Gaelic under its wing at some time in the future (as the Welsh Books Council does already); it is to be hoped that translation from Gaelic might be encouraged by other means.

In Conclusion

It may well be that the role of public subsidy in relation to Gaelic Scotland will have to be radically re-thought. Under the present system there is considerable support by subsidy for the Highlands as a whole (more support than there is even for London transport). It may be that a part of this subsidy is not well directed. It may be that its basic aims are not the right ones for the area and its future development, as opposed to its quiesence or run-down or preservation as an area for overspill or amenity. It will be clear to all but the most bigoted that development of the Highlands for the benefit of the rest of the country is one possible answer to the Highland problem, but not the answer that men of good will have been expecting all this century. It will be at least as clear that the Highlands should be developed with regard for their own conditions and traditions, and not least for their language, and if this raises in the planner's mind the vast complication of English being dominant in certain parts of the area, then a separate policy can be devised for the Gaelic area. But it will, furthermore, be clear also that Gaelic Scotland is not simply a geographical expression, and that its development problem is one that has to be faced more resolutely than at the present time, although laissez-faire policies are already yielding to policies of limited intervention and support. The greatly increased awareness of Scottish nationality and the Gaelic element in that, will ensure that greater attention is paid to such matters in the near future, and that the adverse balance from which Gaelic in Scotland has suffered for a lengthy period will be convincingly redressed.

BIBLIOGRAPHY

HISTORICAL

Dillon, M. and Chadwick, N. *The Celtic Realms*. London, 1967.

Gregory, D. *History of the Western Highlands and Isles of Scotland*. Edinburgh, 1836.

Kellas, James G. *Modern Scotland*. London, 1968.

Kermack, W. R. *The Scottish Highlands, A Short History*. Edinburgh, 1957.

Prebble, John. *The Highland Clearances*. London, 1963.

LINGUISTIC

A Linguistic Survey of the Gaelic Dialects of Scotland, in Vols. supplementary to *Norsk Tidsskrift for Sprogvidenskap* (by C. H. Borgstrøm and M. Oftedal). Oslo, 1937, 1940, 1941, 1956.

Calder, George. *A Gaelic Grammar*. Glasgow, 1923.

Dwelly, Edward. *The Illustrated Gaelic-English Dictionary*. Glasgow, 1971.

Holmer, N. M. *Studies on Argyllshire Gaelic*. Uppsala, 1938.

——. *The Gaelic of Arran*. Dublin, 1957.

——. *The Gaelic of Kintyre*. Dublin, 1962.

Jackson, Kenneth H. *Common Gaelic: The Evolution of the Goedelic Languages*. London, 1961.

Learners' Gaelic Courses are published by *Gairm* (*The Learners Pack*), *Sruth*, and Gaelfonn (59 St Vincent Crescent, Glasgow, C.2), the latter with long-playing records.

Linguistic Atlas and Survey of Irish Dialects, Vol. IV (including specimens of Scottish Gaelic Dialects). Dublin, 1969.

Maclennan, Gordon. *Gàidhlig Uidhist a Deas*. Dublin, 1966.

Paterson, J. M. *The Gaels have a Word for it!* Glasgow, 1964.

Wainwright, F. T. *The Problem of the Picts*. Edinburgh, 1955.

Watson, W. J. *The History of the Celtic Place Names of Scotland*. Edinburgh, 1926.

SOCIAL AND ECONOMIC

Campbell, John Lorne. *Gaelic in Scottish Education and Life*, Edinburgh, 1950.

Census 1961. Scotland. Vol. 7. Gaelic. Edinburgh, 1966.

——. Gaelic. Supplementary Leaflet (No. 27). Edinburgh, 1966.

Gaelic-speaking Children in Highland Schools. Vol. XLVII. Scottish Council for Research in Education. London, 1961.

Grant, I. F. *Highland Folk Ways. London,* 1961.

Maclean, Calum. *The Highlands.* London, 1959.

O'Dell, A. C. and Walton, K. *The Highlands and Islands of Scotland.* London and Edinburgh, 1962.

LITERATURE AND MUSIC

Campbell, John Lorne. *Gaelic Folksongs from the Isle of Barra.* Linguaphone : London, 1950.

——. (and Francis Collinson). *Hebridean Folksongs.* Oxford, 1969.

Coisir a' Mhòid. Gaelic part-songs. Glasgow, 1953.

Collinson, Francis. *The Traditional and National Music of Scotland.* Routledge : London, 1966.

Craig, K. C. *Orain Luaidh Màiri Nighean Alasdair.* Glasgow, 1949.

Eilean Fraoich: Lewis Gaelic Songs and Melodies. Comunn Gaidhealach Leódhais. Stornoway, 1938.

Gairm. Gaelic Quarterly. Gairm Publications, 29 Waterloo Street, Glasgow, C.2, 1952—.

Hay, George Campbell. *Fuaran Sléibh.* Maclellan : Glasgow, 1947.

——. *O na Ceithir Airdean.* Oliver and Boyd : Edinburgh, 1952.

Kennedy-Fraser, Marjory. *Songs of the Hebrides.* London, 1909, 1917, 1921, etc.

Literary Criticism : the main media have been *An Gaidheal* (no longer published), *Gairm, Scottish Gaelic Studies* and the *Transactions of the Gaelic Society of Inverness.*

MacAskill, Alex. *Rosg 'nan Eilean.* University of Glasgow : Glasgow, 1966.

MacAulay, Donald. *Seòbhrach ás a' Chlaich.* Gairm Publications : Glasgow, 1967.

MacDonald, Donald. *Dòmhnall Ruadh Chorùna.* Gairm Publications : Glasgow, 1969.

Mackenzie, Colin. *Oirthir Tìm.* Gairm Publications : Glasgow, 1969.

Maclean, Sorley. *17 Poems for Sixpence*, 2nd ed. Edinburgh, 1940.

——. *Dàin do Eimhir agus Dàin Eile*. William Maclellan: Glasgow, 1943.

MacLeod, Norman (Am Bàrd Bochd). *Bàrdachd á Leódhas*. Gairm Publications: Glasgow, 1969.

Scottish Gaelic Studies. Aberdeen University: Aberdeen, 1926—.

Scottish Gaelic Texts Society. Publishers of texts of Gaelic classics and some modern works such as *The Prose Writings of Donald Lamont* (Edinburgh, 1960) and Donald Macintyre, *Sporan Dhòmbnaill* (Edinburgh, 1968). The editions of poetry have English translations. (Secretary, Mr. J. A. Smith, 108 Queen Victoria Drive, Glasgow W.3.)

Shaw, Margaret Fay, *Folksongs and Folklore of South Uist*. Routledge: London, 1955.

Smith, Iain Crichton. *A' Chùirt* and *An Coileach*. Plays, both published by An Comunn Gaidhealach: Glasgow, 1966.

——. *An Dubh is an Gorm*. University of Glasgow: Glasgow, 1968.

——. *Bùrn is Aran*. Gairm Publications: Glasgow, 1960.

——. *Bìobuill is Sanasan-reice*. Gairm Publications: Glasgow, 1965.

——. *Iain am measg nan Reultan*. Gairm Publications: Glasgow, 1970.

Sruth. Fortnightly bilingual newspaper, published by An Comunn Gaidhealach: Inverness, 1967—and now incorporated within the pages of *Stornoway Gazette*.

Thomson, Derick S. *An Dealbh Briste*. Serif Books: Edinburgh, 1951.

——. *An Rathad Cian*. Gairm Publications: Glasgow, 1970.

——. *Eadar Samhradh is Foghar*. Gairm Publications: Glasgow, 1967.

——. (and Ian Grimble). *The Future of the Highlands*. Routledge: London, 1968.

Thomson, James. *Fasgnadh*. Stirling, 1953.

Transactions of the Gaelic Society of Inverness. Inverness, 1872—.

Wittig, Kurt. *The Scottish Tradition in Literature*. Oliver and Boyd: Edinburgh, 1958.

8

ORKNEY : THE GIRL

George Mackay Brown

IN THE HIGH narrow rocky sea-inlet on the north coast of the island the men were making ready for the fishing. Ploughing and sowing were finished. The cattle, let out of the dark byres, drifted among the new sweet grass like tranced creatures. Down here, hidden from the women and the animals, the crofters turned their faces to the dazzle of the sea. It was a beautiful morning in April.

"Well," said an old silky-bearded man, "that was some day, I'm telling you. That was a day that will not be forgotten in this parish for a long time. I spat salt for a year after."

Carefully he applied a brushful of tar in long fluent strokes to the flank of an upturned boat. When the tar thinned out he thrust his brush once more into the metal tar drum.

A thin dark twist of a man lifted his head from the rock and the pool where he was gathering limpets.

"Tell us, James of Dale," he said. He turned and winked at the other men as much as to say, *Wait till you hear this lie.*

A girl appeared at the high seabank above the beach. She was shawled and she wore a long gray worsted skirt. She looked at the group of crofter-fishermen working below. She lingered uncertainly, as if she heard from far off the voices of women calling to her from the wells and peat stacks. Then she crouched down on the grass, half turned away from the men, her hand on her bare instep.

"I was fishing that day," said James of Dale, "with my father and my grandfather under Scabra Head in Rousay. We were fishing for haddocks. That was all of fifty years ago. I wasn't long finished with the school. The razor had maybe touched my cheek once. Well, it was a fine day and we fished and we fished and we caught nothing. 'Now', said my grandfather—he's been in the kirkyard thirty-two years come Michaelmas—'that's a funny thing', said he. 'I could tell from the look of the sea beyond

Scabra there were haddocks here, any God's amount of them.'
We drew in our lines and still there was not a fish on the hooks.
After a time my father said, 'There's a queer motion on the sea
today.' Then a shadow fell on us and I looked round and there
beside the boat rose an island as big as the Brough of Birsay. And
this whale, he hosed the sky through his blowhole. And he sent
sheet after sheet of spray flying over us. I'm telling you. And his
wash nearly turned us right over. I sat at the tiller and I never
saw men rowing like my father and my grandfather. One
moment they would be closed up on the thwart like jack-knives
and the next they would be straight as boards, leaning far back.
The blades sang like fiddlestrings. And the boat—*Dayspring*, that
was her name—she skimmed the sea like a skarfie till we got back
to this beach where we are now."

The limpet-gatherer sat down on the flat dry rock and his shoulders jerked with merriment. The laughter came out of him in a
thin wheeze that ended in a bout of coughing. Then he wiped his
distracted eyes on the back of his hand.

"Thu may laugh, Sander Groat," said James of Dale gravely,
"but what I'm telling thee is the God's honest truth." He sank his
brush deep into the jet-black lake, and began to stroke the *Mary
Jane* tenderly and sensuously.

The girl on the sea bank laid off her shawl. She plucked a long
stalk of grass and put it in her mouth. From far inland came the
fragile bleat of a sheep; nearer at hand a croft woman cried
sharply to a child to keep out of the cornfield. The girl's hair was
drawn back in a tight coil of bronze.

The youngest fisherman left his line and hooks on the rock
where he was sitting and looked out to sea. It was still ebbing fast;
he could hear the slow suck and drench of the sea as it was withdrawn from tangle and sand and rock crannies. He put his elbows
on his knees and his face in his hands and looked out over the
slowly shrinking ocean.

"Thu won't fill thee belly that way, Tom", said Sander Groat.
"Thu has a hundred hooks to bait yet if thu has one".

Tom rose to his feet and walked down to the ebb. Sometimes his
bare feet slipped in the seaweed and then he described a wild pir-
ouette and his hand would seize a spur of rock to keep himself from
falling. Gracefully he swayed across the glittering red swathes,

161

down to the shrinking edge of the water. Sometimes he would linger beside a rockpool and angle his face in that mirror, pushing out his lips, touching his curled blond hair with his fingers. On he swayed and slithered and hesitated to the sea fringe.

"Far too good for the likes of us, that one," said Sander Groat. "They're poor folk up at Estquoy, but this one, you'd think from the way he carries on his mother had given some duke or prince a night's lodging. He's going to Canada, fancy that! He's written to the emigration agent in Liverpool. His fingers are far too long and white to rip the guts out of a herring. He wants to sit at some office desk in Toronto. Then some summer he'll come home to Estquoy for a holiday and he'll be wearing tweed knickerbockers, and by God, he'll look at us like the far end of a fiddle."

Sander Groat turned and spat among the shells. Then he raised his blunt stone and began rhythmically to knock limpets off the rock.

Up above on the sea bank, the girl had strewn her lap with a scatter of daisies, and she began to link them together, slow and silent and totally absorbed, a long thin pink-and-white halter.

Occasionally the silence of the boat noust was split by the rasp of a saw. Two men were working beside an upturned boat with a rectangular gap in it. A long white board lay on the stones. One man, stout and breathless with the exertion of sawing, hovered between the board and the gap in the boat, making anxious measurements and calculations. He marked the board with a crumble of red sandstone. Then he and the other man lifted the board and leaned it against a flat rock. He began to saw furiously. The song of the saw rose to a thin high shriek. A white stub fell off and the stout man once more fitted the board against the hole in the *Sea Harvest*. "She'll need a thumb-length off yet," he said.

"Have a rest now, Howie," said his mate. "Smoke thee pipe."

"And by God I need a rest, Peter", said the fat man. "I'm all silver under my sark with sweat."

"There is never any need to take the name of the Lord in vain," said Peter.

Howie filled a clay pipe with tobacco from his pouch. "It was done deliberately," he said. "Who would have done a thing like that now? If I get hold of him I'll twist his bloody neck."

"Swearing never did any good at all," said Peter. "Nor uncharitable thinking either. The strake was rotten. Look at the pieces. You can crumble them in your hand like a bit of old bannock."

Howie held the still flame of the lucifer over his pipe and sucked it down into the bowl. He blew out three clouds of smoke. "I'll murder the bastard," he said. "Somebody smashed it in with a stone in the winter time."

Up above, the girl brushed the daisies out of her lap, petulantly. She leaned forward from her haunches, looking out to sea, her face tilted high, lips apart, looking far out over the heads of the fishermen as if she saw a splendid ship on the horizon. Her eyes moved slowly over the delicate thin line of the horizon. Her brow fell, a shutter, and made shadows of her eyes. She was utterly absorbed in the furthest reaches of the ocean.

"For God's sake," said Sander Groat, his stone hammer poised over a cluster of limpets, "a seal."

A sleek head flashed in the water, sank, rose again, shook a scatter of salt from its tight burnished pelt. A hand rose and arched and clutched at the water and disappeared. Then another hand. Arms beat the water like slow millwheels. The feet made a long rhythmic agitation. A shoulder flashed and sank, flashed and sank. Tom of Estquoy swam leisurely between the two skerries.

"I suppose he wants to wash the glut and the dung off him," said Sander Groat. "He can't go to Canada smelling like us poor folk. O no, that would never do."

Old James of Dale dipped his brush, very finicky, around and between the faded blue letters MARY JANE at the bow of his boat. "I mind the time," he said, "I swam from this same noust here to the island of Rousay for a bet. It was a winter day. Benjie Berstane wagered me a half-crown I couldn't do it. I had to swim against sea and snow."

Nobody encouraged him this time. It was getting towards noon and the sun fell hot into the deep cove. They were beginning to feel hungry.

The old man mumbled away over the shining black curves of his boat.

There was one shed on the beach where two young men were working. They were so very like each other that they must be brothers; they might well be twins, for they seemed to be equal in possessiveness and authority. They kept themselves somewhat apart from the other fishermen. They spoke to each other privately, in harsh whispers; occasionally one or the other would look round to see if they were being overheard.

One brother was carrying out of the shed, three by three, a stack of lobster creels, and piling them against the outside wall. The other examined every creel carefully. Every now and again he would take a defective creel and lay it aside; it would have to be repaired with twine, perhaps, or the eye was twisted so that a lobster couldn't get in, or the frame was smashed. And all the time they kept up their low harsh secret dialogue. Sometimes they would break off and face each other. Then it was like a man possessed glaring deep into a mirror.

"The shed is mine," shouted one of them at last. "He always said that. The shed and the creels and the tackle are mine."

"Is that so?" said the other. "I never heard him saying that. All right, then. You can have them, so long as the boat comes to me."

They both realised at once that they had spoken too loud. They looked round guiltily at the other fishermen. They moved closer to each other, whispering, gesturing wildly with their hands, pointing inside the shed, pointing over the rim of the noust to their croft hidden in a fold of the hills. But even though they kept their voices down, the other men could hear an occasional word, "ox" and "plough" and "spinning-wheel". At last one of them gripped the other by the shoulder and their faces were close together, transfixed and yawing like cats.

Peter Simison rose to his feet and went over to the shed. "Come now, Abel and Harald," he said. "What kind of way is this to behave? Your father's still not cold in his grave. Think shame of yourselves."

"The two cows are mine," shouted Abel to Peter. He still had a creel in his hand. "Daddo took me into the byre one day just after New Year and he said, *Be good to them, Abel, after I'm gone*". . .

"Right", cried Harald. "I get the barn then. That's only fair."

Peter stood between them. "It's a great pity," he said, "that thee father died without making a proper will. What was he thinking of? He might have known it would come to this."

"The fiddle on the wall is mine," shouted Abel.

"The sensible thing to do," said Peter, "is for one of you to take the croft of Lombist and for the other to take the fishing boat *Trust* and all her gear."

164

"A croft is ten times more valuable than a fishing boat," said Howie the carpenter, his face like two immense apples behind a drift of tobacco smoke. "That's the trouble."

"And they're twins," said Sander Groat from the rockpool. "That makes it worse than ever."

"Twins, maybe," said Howie. "But they didn't burst on the world at exactly the same time. One must have been dropped before the other. Who was the midwife? She would know."

"My wife Mary Jane was the midwife," said James of Dale. "She's been in the kirkyard twelve years come the fourth of March. So we won't get much enlightenment from her."

"Settle the business peaceably between yourselves," said Peter to Abel and Harald of Lombist, "or I'll tell you what way it'll end—you'll be two old tramps on the road eating a crust here and a fishhead there. Take charitable counsel one with the other." He admonished them gravely, shaking his finger between them like a referee at a fight.

Chidden, the twins returned silently to their work. Harald brought out, four by four, the creels from the shed. Abel examined every creel carefully; every now and then he would lay one aside to be repaired. They did not look at each other. But the air seethed between them in the hot noon.

The girl stretched herself out in the new grass. She lay down and writhed about slowly like a cat. Then she was still, her eyes closed against the sun. Her eyelids pulsed slowly. She stretched her legs apart. Her closed fists lay on each side of her head like a child asleep. There was a faint puzzled smile on her face. All that could be noted of her existence now from the noust was a trembling in the tallest grasses.

"We won't get the new plank in her today," said Howie the carpenter. "I doubt it." He scraped the dottle out of his clay pipe carefully and put it in the pouch with his roll of tobacco.

"It's just past noon," said Peter Simison. "There's a whole day before us."

"I know," said Howie. "But I have to take this board home, and I have to plane the ends of it. Two miles there and two miles back. Then the riveting and the putty and the tar."

"Well," said Peter. "There's no hurry."

"And even then," said Howie, "she won't be tight till she's been in the water a day or two."

Tom of Estquoy came up from the sea, shuddering with cold and fastening the band of his trousers. His worsted shirt was flung about his shoulders.

"Were thu trying to slip away quiet-like to Canada?" said Sander Groat. "Losh, man, that'll never do at all. There must be a lot of cermonial for an important chap like thee. I'm telling thee, the pier'll be black with folk the day thu leaves Orkney. The road to Hamnavoe will be one long lamentation of women." Sander Groat gave a little snirt of mockery.

Tom of Estquoy let on never to hear. He spread his gray shirt on the rock and lay back on it. His long arms gleamed like marble in the sun. The new red-blond hairs across his chest flickered like fire. His ribs were pearled with water. He closed his eyes against the light. He still shivered occasionally from the whetting of the ocean.

"Canada or no Canada," said Sander Groat, "thee father's a poor man like the rest of us. He'll have to go on fishing from this coast to keep thee mother and sister out of the poorhouse. He'll be wanting his lines baited for tomorrow morning."

Presently, taking his time, as if the other fishermen in the noust didn't exist, Tom sat up and looked about him. He reached for his shirt and pulled it on. He yawned. He lifted a hook from the coiled line. He drew the tin of bait towards him. He stuck a piece of mussel on the barb. His nose wrinkled.

The last of the creels was out of the shed now. Abel and Harald sat against the black wall with one ball of twine between them. They worked expertly at the holes in the creels, knitting and knotting, passing the knife from one to the other. Whenever one had finished a repair job he held up the creel for the other's approval. Then they would nod, one after the other; and the mended creel would be added to the stack of sound ones.

They whispered together like two grudging ghosts.

"I don't want her at all," whispered Harald. "You can have her."

"Are you sure?" whispered Abel.

"Him that's dead would have wanted it," whispered Harald. "His heart was set on that. I heard him speaking about it at the last Dounby Show to Tor her father, in the whisky tent."

"But I thought you liked her," whispered Abel. "You danced with her all night in the barn at Estquoy last harvest home."

"No, I don't like her that much," whispered Harald. "You can have her."

"Well then," whispered Abel, "in that case the croft's yours. That's fair enough."

"No", whispered Harald, "what way would you both live? You're not tinkers, you couldn't live in a ditch. I'll take the boat and the shed and the creels."

"You heard what Howie said just now," whispered Abel. "Lombist is ten times more valuable than the *Trust*."

"I don't care," whispered Harald. "Fishermen should be bachelors. The sea's no place for a new-married man. Look what happened last November to the *Jewel*. One wave made a new widow and three new orphans up at Clodberry."

"Well, then," whispered Abel, "you can bide with us up at Lombist. You'll eat and sleep there."

"I will not," whispered Harald. "We can't abide the sight of one another. You know that fine. And with *her* at my mother's hearth it would be worse than ever."

"Where will you bide then?" whispered Abel.

Harald nodded at the shed. "In there," he whispered. "I'll get a stove put in it."

"It's falling to pieces," whispered Abel.

"A few nails," whispered Harald. "A board or two. That's all it needs. I'd like fine to live here, next the sea."

"You wouldn't last a winter," whispered Abel. "The cold and the damp."

"Mind your own bloody business," whispered Harald. "Don't try to dictate to me."

They worked together in silence for a while.

"Pass the knife," said Abel.

James of Dale laid his tar brush carefully across the tar bucket. The *Mary Jane* was all tarred now except for the stern, and the name had to be painted in in blue. James sat down in the shade of the boat. He took a length of twist from his tobacco pouch and began to cut thin dark slivers with a knife into his half-closed palm.

"Did I ever tell you men," he said, "about the time I put down the travelling wrestler at the Hamnavoe Market? I put him down three times."

"An old man like you will soon have his Maker to meet," said

Peter Simison gravely. "You should be thinking thoughts of peace and of truth."

Peter set the board along a flat rock with a bit of the end protruding.

"Ten bob this fair-man offered," said James of Dale, "to any man in the crowd who could beat his champion. You never saw such a girth on a man, like a hogshead he was, twice as big as Howie over there. Nobody stirred in the crowd for a while. Then, thinks I, the whole of Orkney will be disgraced—"

Howie put his knee to the board. He squinted along the pencil mark and applied the saw. The wood shrieked its torture between the high walls of the noust. For two minutes nothing else could be heard. Old James of Dale's mouth opened and shut silently, telling the story of how he beat the fair-ground wrestler.

At last the board was shorter by another thumb-length.

"—and so," said James of Dale, "there he lay in the centre of the ring, that great ox, panting and groaning, and me on top of him pressing his shoulders flat down on the canvas. You should have heard the cheers of the crowd. This man with the check suit and the cigar steps up and puts a half-sovereign in my hand. Next day the wrestling tent was away from the fair-ground. It was never seen in Orkney again."

A sweet tremulous cry possessed the air. A cluster of kittiwakes dipped and circled above them. They had risen from the loch a mile inland; and now they hovered and dropped, a flashing disordered throng, and furled themselves on the still sea beyond the weeded rocks. The girl's startled face watched their flight through a screen of grasses.

"The tide's turned," said Sander Groat. He wiped his slimy hands on his trousers and walked over to the crag. He took from a sandstone fissure a large stone jar. He prised the cork out of the neck and sniffed the contents. "This is strong stuff," he said. "It's been in the jar since before Christmas." He set the jar down on the flat rock in the centre of the noust.

The fishermen gathered round it, unwrapping their pieces. James of Dale sank his gums into a wedge of new cheese; the pale juice ran down into his beard. Abel Bews of Lombist had two cold smoked cuithes. Harald Bews cracked the delicate gray-blue shell of a duck egg on a stone. Peter Simison took from under his jacket a large round bannock, thickly buttered. Howie the carpenter had two boiled crabs. Peter and Howie shared their food. Tom of Estquoy sat slightly apart from the other men. He had a slice of bread from the baker's in Hamnavoe, doubled over, with honey in the middle. "I never eat when I'm drinking," said Sander Groat, and winked, and raised the ale-jar.

Peter laid his bonnet on his knee. He bowed his head and murmured a grace. When he looked up again Sander Groat's throat was convulsing with the ale. Old James of Dale took the ale-jar from him. He tilted it till it eclipsed the sun. He sighed. He was very content. His tongue licked one amber drop from his moustache. He offered the jar to Abel Bews of Lombist. Abel drank, scowling, as if it was bitter herbs. He would not pass on the jar to his brother. Instead he reached it back to the provider, Sander Groat. Sander Groat lurched to his feet and stooped with his precious burden over Harald Bews. Harald wiped the mouth of the jar on his shirt sleeve as if his brother had contaminated it; he tilted first his head and then the jar at their different angles, and his adam's-apple jerked thrice in his well-sculpted throat. He sighed bitterly and gave the ale-jar to Peter Simison. Peter passed it on at once to Howie the carpenter; he did not drink himself. Howie drank for both of them. He held the fat jar with great tenderness to his mouth, as if he was dandling his first-born, his heart's-desire, the marvellous fruit of his loins, with a prolonged passionate kiss. "I think thu're drunk enough," said Sander Groat anxiously. Howie yielded up the jar reluctantly. Sander Groat stood in front of Tom of Estquoy whose mouth shone with honey and white crumbs. "Nothing for you," he said. "No work, no drink." He stood in the centre of the rock and drank the last of the ale himself, tilting the stone jar till it was completely upside down and empty. He sighed and scattered the last few drops on the rock.

"I'll tell you what I could do with now," he said. "A woman."

"Sander Groat," said Peter Simison sternly, "thu has a wife and fourteen bairns up at Otterquoy. I'm surprised to hear a man like thee saying such things."

Sander Groat began to laugh. His thin dark face twisted, his shoulders jerked, and the laughter came out of him in thin jets and wheezes. Then they were all laughing in the noust. Even the twins laughed, narrowing their eyes and showing their fine teeth and gums in exactly the same way; the sound of their laughter passed between them wonderingly, like an echo. Tom of Estquoy ate the last of his bread-and-honey and smiled superiorly. Only Peter Simison did not laugh. He waited till Sander Groat's mirth expired in a few coughs and gasps. Then he said, "We'll get back to work now, I think, if it's the will of the Lord."

Howie picked up his saw.

There was a new sound on the sea, as if a wondering hand had strayed over a harp. The lowest rocks were awash with the flowing tide. What had been pools a half-hour before no longer existed. Slowly the flood encroached. Forlorn brown swathes of weed were gathered once more into the great translucent Atlantic garden. The kittiwakes rejoiced in the new cold fecund waters.

There was a new sound on the land too. It began as a faint flutter. The rapid rhythm grew louder. Sometimes it was lost in a fold of the hills, then it came stuttering on, louder than ever. The girl's face flashed with excitement. The new sound came closer. It hammered the afternoon apart.

The girl rose up from her grass couch. She stood for a moment and looked down contemptuously at the fishermen who were turning their refreshed hands to the monotonies of the coming summer. She turned towards the hill and ran up the broken road to the crofts above; and a collie ran across the field to meet her, barking blithely; and a drift of ducks waddled in panic from her bare feet, filling the ditches with their gabble.

A motor cyclist came careering down the broken road towards her.

9

THE FUTURE OF SCOTS

David Murison

In discussing the future of the Scots language, it might be useful at the outset to get our terms right in view of the amount of nonsense that is talked about Scots, ranging from the notion that it is essentially and originally a Gaelic language which has got somewhat mixed up in the course of centuries with English to the view that it is standard English, corrupted by un-educable Scots, clod-hopping peasants and Clydeside hooligans in particular, and I have even heard it described, by a Scottish working-man, as "a kind o' slang".

Gaelic speakers refer to it simply as "English", occasionally ad-ding some epithet like "broken", to imply a degree of aberrancy from the norm of the Sassenach laird or the Free Kirk minister or the local M.P. or other worthy whom they hold in awe, at least in public.

This confusion is due to various causes, partly to deliberate poli-tical obfuscation, partly to social prejudices, partly to deplorable teaching of Scottish history in Scottish schools. So it is necessary first to straighten out the muddle with some historical facts.

Scots began as a dialect of Anglo-Saxon, the language brought over by German tribes to Britain in the sixth century A.D., which many scholars prefer to call Old English, using "English" in a somewhat ambivalent manner which slurs over the fact that modern English is really a kind of Anglo-French, as indeed Scots is also. The northern dialect of Anglo-Saxon established itself in Lothian in the seventh century, where the majority of the place-names are still of Anglic origin, as compared with the reverse situa-tion in the rest of the country with its predominantly Gaelic and British (early Welsh) toponomy. By the tenth century the Gaelic-speaking kingdom of Alba had gained sovereignty over what is Scotland today, the land of the Scots who came from Ireland in the sixth century. But this position was upset a hundred years later when the Norman Conquest of England brought immigrants, from Northern England especially, into Scotland in the wake of the English princess Margaret who married the Celtic King, Malcolm Canmore. The centralising Feudal system and the church which accompanied it radiated out from the Forth area with Edinburgh (a hybrid Celtic-English name) as its chief town, and consolidated its power over the Lowlands of Scotland with French-speaking barons and, more important from our point of view, their stewards, bailiffs and other officials, and the minor clergy who in the main spoke Northern English. The rise of the burghs, an Anglo-Saxon word, as centres of trade, was another major linguistic factor. The native population, not militarily conquered, but peacefully overrun by this well-organised system, were obliged in their own interests to learn the language of authority and business—and so this speech gradually assumed a dominant position in the Northern Kingdom, just as the language of London by stages developed into the southern King's English. It is essentially those old dialect differences between the two that still distinguish Scots from English in form; it was the political independence of Scotland from England that kept the distinctions going and indeed increasing until by the late fourteenth century, after the War of Independence, it had grown into a national language, the official speech of the Kingdom of Scotland. For another century it was still called "Inglis", the northern form of "English", in witness to its origin and it was not materially different from the speech of the parts of England north of the Humber. But it became the vehicle of a considerable and distinguished literature, including the names of Barbour, Henryson and Dunbar, and much anonymous popular verse.

In the early sixteenth century the poet Douglas made the first vernacular translation in Europe of Virgil's *Aeneid* and in extending the vocabulary of Scots by borrowing from other languages, helped to make it adequate for all the purposes of literature, while the same thing was being done simultaneously for English by writers like Lydgate, Sidney and Elyot. Incidentally, Douglas was one of the first to give the national name "Scots" to the speech he was using, and gradually the term "Inglis" was dropped, in recognition of the fact that the two were now distinct languages.

Their distinctness was now indeed such that a group of Lollards in Ayrshire about 1520, anxious to read the New Testament in their vernacular, got one of their number to Scottify the language of Wycliffe's version for surreptitious circulation in defiance of the church, so surreptitious in fact that the manuscript remained out of sight for nearly four centuries; and when the Reformation came to Scotland in 1560, the new church in haste to get the Bible into the hands of the faithful had only the English Genevan Bible available for the purpose. This created a serious problem for Scots, which now had a rival in its own territory, and one that had behind it the authority of the word of God. The Scots became familiar with English, both in their own reading and in hearing it read and in sermons preached in its phraseology. Gradually English was bound to be associated in the minds of the Scots with what was solemn, formal and dignified, while the native tongue would continue to be used for and associated with the everyday, familiar, emotional, comic aspects of life; that is, it was used at a lower intellectual pitch. To what we may call the spiritual prestige which accrued to English after 1560, was added the social prestige which followed the Union of the Crowns in 1603 and the removal of the Scottish court to London. The King, who was himself a poet of some talent and a patron of other poets, adopted English speech and manners and his own work shows continuous anglicising from manuscript to print. The administration of government now directed from London affected the usage of authority at home in Scotland and we can trace the same anglicising process in the public and private documents of the seventeenth century, chancery, town council and law court records, Acts of Parliament, letters and other family papers of the gentry, church records, and so on.

Finally, as a last blow to the survival of Scots as a full curial and national language, the Union of Parliaments in 1707 gave English political prestige as well. It became the language of legislation of the whole island; and the first Scottish M.P.s were rudely reminded of the fact by the laughter of their English colleagues at the barbarous unintelligibility of their parliamentary utterances. Their mortification led to gradual adoption of southern speech partly by simple imitation and partly by organising elocution lessons to purge the Scottish vowels from their phonemic systems, and the Scotticisms from their vocabulary, as Hume, the philosopher, tried to do.

While English had been taught in Scottish schools since the

beginning of the eighteenth century at least, it was of course taught by people who had probably never heard an English voice in their lives; but by the end of the century there was a spate of books on English pronunciation, some by Scotsmen, which ultimately succeeded in bringing the vowel sounds in particular of the two languages into nearer approximation, though not absolute similarity—a state of affairs which has not even yet been achieved, despite the fact that, since the advent of radio and television, the sound of English speech, as well as its written appearance, has penetrated every Scottish home. Nevertheless the whole tendency in the last two hundred years has been towards assimilation, a trend much speeded up by universal state education since 1872 and a code which for two generations took a particular delight in hunting the Scotticism to its death, with a reasonable amount of success. Had this process gone on without hindrance or counterpoise, Scots would have practically ceased to exist, as Cornish, or Manx. The Scots would be speaking more English English and this essay would never have been written.

On the other hand throughout the seventeenth century popular culture, which has always been strong in Scotland, much of it based on oral rather than written, tradition, because it was preserved by people who could not write, kept faithful to the old tongue. The ballad, folksong and comic verse flourished and began to be published at the beginning of the next century, significantly perhaps at the very period of the Union. Later on Allan Ramsay, to whom Scottish culture owes more than it generally acknowledges, reprinted much of this popular verse, as well as a selection of the best of Scottish medieval poetry, and followed it up with poems of his own, songs, poetical epistles, and a pastoral drama, the *Gentle Shepherd*,—all in Scots. Following his example in Scots verse are the poets Fergusson and Burns.

The genius of Burns and his all-pervasive influence on his fellow-countrymen really gave the Scots tongue a new lease of life for another 150 years and restored it to an honoured place among the poetic languages of the world. Hundreds of poets echoed his phrases, used and reused his vocabulary and repeated his themes, and though it is now fashionable to deride their work for its poetical qualities, not indeed without some justification, the fact remains that *linguistically* they kept the old speech going reasonably well till the time of the first World War, when, as Lewis

Grassic Gibbon finely says, "it was the old Scotland that perished then, and we may believe that never again will the old speech and the old songs, the old curses and the old benedictions, rise but with alien efforts to our lips." Burns's success, furthermore, inspired our other literary genius, Scott, to emulate his predecessor in prose." "Burns by his poetry" he said to James Ballantyne "has already attracted attention to everything Scottish, and I confess I can't see why I should not be able to keep the flame alive, merely because I write Scotch in prose, and he wrote it in rhyme."

The trouble was that Scott confined his Scots—and no one has surpassed him in his skill in writing colloquial Scots—to the dialogue of his humbler, though psychologically far greater characters, Edie Ochiltree, the Headriggs, Dandie Dinmont, Jeanie Deans and so on, eschewing any attempt to use Scots for his own narrative.

The achievements of Burns and Scott, great as they were, were nevertheless only partial. There are fundamental differences between the literary speech of Scotland of the sixteenth and that of the eighteenth centuries, namely, that now there was no prose of a serious, philosophical or technical nature; poetry and its language are on a more popular and less intellectual level, with no second David Lindsay, no epic, no metaphysical verse, nothing like Dryden or Pope in England; the vocabulary is much more restricted and personal, more realistic and hence more regional and so encouraging the rise into prominence of local dialects, which naturally thrive in the absence of a standard form of speech and of a national literary centre. The efforts to extend the range and usage of Scots vocabulary, such as Douglas had made, had long been abandoned, in direct contrast to the polishing and refining of contemporary English by Addison, Steele and Johnson. Burns himself provides the classic example of the difference in scope and status of Scots and English in "The Cotter's Saturday Night," where the formal dedication, the family worship, and the moralising are in English, while the descriptive intimate domestic scene and action, the supper, the chat, are in Scots; and one notices in particular the gradual subtle sliding into English when the Bible is brought out, implicitly embodying the historical association of the Bible in Scotland with the English language.

This lengthy preamble has been necessary to explain the

condition of the Scots tongue today. Not merely has the present state of affairs grown logically out of the past but many of the attitudes still prevailing can be parelleled in the eighteenth and nineteenth centuries from which they have come down practically unchanged. The loss of political status, in the first place, has meant that Scots is no longer used in any formal or official capacity and so no attempt is made to think abstractly in Scots *i.e.* to expound new ideas, or reformulate old ones. It is limited now to the expression of the ephemeral emotion, the incidental anecdote, the proverbial platitude, the simple statement, and if someone were really determined to keep his Scots at all costs and in all circumstances he would find his thinking very circumscribed or the utterance of it woefully inadequate. Scots is not used in schools, either as a medium of instruction, or as an object of study in its own right, and the acquisition of it by the Scot is left to chance or the accident of nature. As no attempt was made to keep up any standard, the quality of Scots sadly deteriorated, the grammar got mixed up with English, so that for instance the plural of *cow* became *coos* which is neither English *cows* nor Scots *kye*, and the vocabulary began to melt away. A rough census taken among school-children in Aberdeenshire about 1930 showed that about a sixth of the words had been lost in a generation, and some recent tests tend to confirm the loss of another sixth since then. A simple calculation would indicate that there will be less than half left by the end of the century.

The policy of plain suppression and rigid uniformity, based on a naive unscientific view of language, failed in its objective, as any common sense observer could have foretold; but common sense is not a usual attribute of educational administrators. It was based on the fallacy that a man could have only one language, which he had to discard if he wanted to acquire another—and, besides, in regard to Scots, on the assumption that Scots was some kind of bad English that needed to be restored to its original purity. The theory, if theory it was and not simply ill-informed prejudice, took no account of bilingualism, even less of the polyglot, which the most superficial acquaintance with European conditions would have made obvious. Unfortunately Union in Scotland has merely resulted in provincialism and insularity.

The outcome of this policy has been to get the worst of both worlds, the destruction of Scots but *not* by any means its replacement by good English, for it has been noticed that where bad Scots is spoken, the English is poor also. The modern theory of registers, the variant types of speech that almost every speaker possesses and adapts with great and subconscious subtlety to the occasion, *e.g.* as between close friends and strangers, children and adults, when making a speech or speaking informally, etc., has shown that people have a surprising versatility in speech and that, if their speech inhibitions are removed, can acquire a remarkable fluency. The trouble has been, that in Scotland, in particular, official policy has increased rather than diminished these inhibitions—and it is far more probable that the common complaint against Scottish children of inarticulateness is due not to the fact that they naturally spoke Scots but that they were strongly discouraged from doing so.

Now admittedly much of this criticism of the official educational attitude is outdated. Professional linguists are far more understanding in their outlook on speech, and this, and the historical events of the last generation, above all the spread of American rather than English speech over so much of the world, have led to a more tolerant view of non-standard speech. Now in fact a teacher is almost afraid to call any locution wrong or impermissible, and indeed a list has been made with the blessing of the Department, of Scots words which may be allowed in a child's exercise. But a realistic appraisal of the state of Scots today makes one feel that repentance may have come too late.

Fewer and fewer *speak* Scots regularly and as a matter of course; the language of formality is English, good, bad or indifferent, but English, not Scots, and as the need for formality arises more frequently in industrial areas, the majority of the Scots use this language most of the time. It is only the rural and depopulated minority that keep their Scots with any degree of vitality. This can be seen from the findings of the Scottish Dialect Survey and the *Scottish National Dictionary* where the conurbations of Glasgow and Edinburgh return blanks to so many questions about Scots word-usage in these areas. This has unfortunate repercussions on such bodies as radio and television and the theatre, where the purely mechanical principle of counting of heads seems to prevail and a watered down version of Trongate Glesca, chiefly with emphasis on the characteristic tone pattern, and a few glottal shops thrown in, passes for modern Scots. Middle Scots fares even worse, for it is often too painfully obvious that the actors have never heard real Scots spoken, anglicise the consonants and reduce the vowels to a complete confusion which is neither Scots nor English. So much for spoken Scots.

When it comes to written Scots, the position is equally unpromising. The Lallans practitioners apart, who will be discussed later, the output of Scots writing is shrinking. An odd novel appears from time to time with a sprinkling of dialogue of the debased industrial variety which, as we have seen, can hardly be described as Scots—we must guard against the all too frequent assumption that any form of speech used in Scotland, that is not standard English is *ipso facto* Scots—and incidentally there is often in these works a *nostalgie de la boue* which reminds one of the Scottish novel of the 1890's with the dunny substituted for the kailyard. But the old weekly column in Scots of the local newspaper has pratically disappeared. The mildly Scots-spoken flavour of the type of story published by the Dundee school of literature has evaporated in the last twenty years and Scots entries in competitions for poems, short stories and the like, have dropped on an average to two or three per cent.

On top of all this and arising out of the political situation in which English is the language of the establishment, are powerful social and economic pressures militating against Scots. The "best" people have not spoken Scots since the eighteenth century. It is the language of rustics, servants, lay-abouts, stick-in-the-muds, backward-looking sentimentalists *et hoc genus omne* who have made no headway in the rat race, and anyone who uses it except to make a joke must take the consequences of his social backwardness, in betraying his vulgar origins or his inability to benefit from comprehensive education, and obviously a young man who speaks Scots as of nature should not raise his sights higher than the career of a navvy. The haunting fear of every Scots mamma is that her dear offspring at an interview for some consequential position, in the south of course, should perpetrate a Scotticism or utter a rather broad "a" and so slam the door to advancement in his own face. This explains why in so many Scottish homes Mamma is constantly on guard on the speech front against infiltration into the redoubt of what she thinks is pure English.

The language indeed has become so déclassé, that those who

ER O F   S C O T S

are politically most vocal about class consciousness avoid it like
the plague and deliver themselves of their sentiments invariably
in the most polysyllabic English they can muster. Not many years
ago a distinguished or, to be strictly accurate, prominent politician was telling the pupils at a school prizegiving that their first
essential objective to strive for was "good English," that along
this route alone hung "the plums at the top of the tree," adding
in a voice breaking with emotion—"maybe even a job in
London."

The average Scot is probably not quite so provincially minded
or so besotted with worldly wisdom as this and retains some
shreds of national self-respect to cover his spiritual nakedness. He
will learn to speak English because it is to his advantage to do so
but not being a politician he sees no reason to discard or
deliberately forget his Scots, not having a seat in London to lose
he does not smell a diabolical Scottish Nationalist plot every time
he hears a Scots word, and being a bit of a sentimentalist, he even
likes to be reminded from time to time of how Grannie used to
speak, and he usually *dis*likes the intrusive *r* and the *w* for *wh* of
standard English. He may even in his relaxed moments, when he
is not acting as the local representative of his London firm or
trade union or being the civil servant or the teacher or the
uncertificated intellectual and when no one of any consequence is
listening, drop into the Scots of his youth. It has indeed been
noted by linguists that when people grow old and cease to bother
about their social status they tend to revert to the older forms of
speech they learned as children.

What is also abundantly clear is that the Scot *understands* a
good deal more Scots than he actually speaks, as an observation
of the audience at any Scots play will substantiate. Nonetheless
the stark fact remains that the Scots language is in a bad state of
decay and will assuredly pass into such a vestigial condition as to
be virtually dead. There will of course be a distinctive form of
English spoken in Scotland for a very long time yet and already
there are people who speak of this as Scots. As one who can
remember the speech of people who were born about the time
that Queen Victoria ascended the throne and who never left their
native district in North-East Scotland, I consider this use of
"Scots" to be a serious misnomer which only serves to confuse the
issue.

As for the future I have already forecast one solution, to let things take their course, the easy way out, the line of least resistance, the one that is being followed in most things Scottish. One need do nothing but wait until all that separates us from acceptability and headships of departments in the south will be a trilled *r* (already on its way out in Edinburgh). When we all speak like one another, it will not be possible to distinguish a Scotsman from an Englishman, a navvy from a nobleman, we shall all appear to be educated (and the notion that to be educated one must abandon Scots is one of the most cherished, especially by the Scottish working-class) and in consequence we shall all live happily ever after.

Of course it will mean that most of our best literature before say 1880 will become less and less intelligible. The poems of Barbour, Henryson, Dunbar and Lindsay will be as remote as the thoughts of Kung Fu Tse (not to be confused with Mao Tse Tung) in the original Chinese. Burns and Scott can soon expect the same fate and our Scottish songs will ultimately be unsingable in the original. Indeed much of this has already been achieved by our Scottish educational system and the B.B.C. between them. After all, is there any real alternative, so long as a hundred of us are left alive who might want to keep the Scots tongue going as part of a national identity and a link with the country's past, and even to make it a vehicle of Scottish literature of the future?

For the rest of this essay I shall assume that there are such people. To discuss the rightness or otherwise of their view is beyond its scope, for the answer to it lies outside the field of philology. But the Lallans movement which was in full swing in the 1950's is sufficient witness to the existence of such a feeling and the rationale of it has been amply expounded by Dr C. M. Grieve ("Hugh MacDiarmid") and Professor Douglas Young. The problems of the revival of a decayed language and its restoration to international status were in fact discussed in reference to Scots by that distinguished Scottish philologist Sir William Craigie in a paper to the Vernacular Circle of London in 1921, and much of what follows is a recapitulation of Craigie's arguments which are still sound today, though progressive atrophy in the language has occurred in the intervening half-century.

There is of course nothing new or unusual in the recreation of a language, and internationally-informed Scots are aware that all over the world minority or socially depressed languages have fought or are still fighting their way back to literary status like Croat and Czech in the old Austrian empire, Nynorsk in Norway, now on an equal footing with Danish, which was the Rigsmaal or official speech of the kingdom, Faroese and Icelandic which also won their place against Danish, Flemish likewise in Belgium and Frisian in the Netherlands, the Basque and Catalan of Anarchist Spain which at the moment gets short shrift from the Castilian of Franco's regime. Dutch is now in the ascendant in South Africa, thanks to English imperialism in the Boer War, and Hindi and Urdu in India for like reasons. Hebrew is being recreated as the national language of Israel and the emergent African nations are all busy with similar tasks : Greece and Turkey with national languages of their own started on the more dubious business of ridding their vocabularies of foreign elements with considerable success.

Of course these cases are not entirely parallel with Scots, which has to face up to competition, not with a minor tongue like Dutch or Danish, but with the most powerful international language of the world, with a huge and magnificent literature and the political prestige of America as well as Britain to support it. Any idea which may lurk in the mind of an ultra-Nationalist of a Scotland which may someday speak nothing but Scots, is a mere chimera. For good and all, every Scot is now bilingual in some kind of Scots and English or Gaelic and English, a few more fortunate are trilingual, understanding (and speaking) all three, an increasing number linguistically impoverished have English only. It can hardly be stressed too much that bilingualism is a common feature of everyday life in Belgium, Holland. Alsace-Lorraine, South Africa, India, Norway, Canada and U.S.A., and above all Switzerland, where the case is most nearly parallel to Scotland, and where trilingualism, as between High German, Swiss German and French, or Romansch, is frequent enough. In German Switzerland the *spoken* tongue is the Swiss dialect of German. This is not normally written (though there *are* dialect authors), and business correspondence and journalism is carried on in High German. Public lectures and speeches are made in High German, though *some* members of Parliament use Swiss in the Rathaus, and all use it in the lobbies. University professors lecture in German but interview their students privately in Swiss; a civil servant will read out a regulation to an inquirer in German and proceed to explain it informally in Swiss. Any attempt to speak German out of turn would be looked upon as eccentric, if not offensive. We have come a very long way from this state of affairs in Scotland.

Assuming that this a moderate and practical goal, what can be done to get there? To begin with the problem of spoken non-literary Scots, obviously it will have to be restored to some kind of social status, to be made respectable in the eyes of our class-conscious society, and after generations of snobbish prejudice this will be no easy job. Since however the prestige of English in Scotland is very largely linked with education, conceivably if Scots were placed firmly in the curriculum and counted for something in the Leaving Certificate, one might find a new respect for it in the eyes of ambitious Scottish parents. I say "firmly" because when the Advisory Council on Scottish Education in 1946 recommended that one period a week should be devoted to Scottish subjects, this specific and, by European standards, natural and reasonable suggestion was sidetracked by educational politicians into the expression of a nebulous hope that *all* Scottish education might be infused with Scottish sentiment.

Nothing less than the introduction of Scottish literature as an integral part of teaching and of the examination structure will do. In Scotland things are so arranged that Scottish subjects, even if on the curriculum, can always be avoided in examinations. The present haphazard "do it if you like but only if you think you can spare the time from the essentials" attitude in schools will *not* do. The conscientious teacher cannot give Scots adequate treatment, the lazy will use the loopholes left open for him. What is more, the unpalatable fact has to be faced that there are very many teachers who in their own day never had the chance or the inclination to study Scottish subjects at school and are quite incapable of teaching them.

This means that the universities and colleges of education must also give similar attention to their curricula. While considerable progress has already been made recently in this direction, there is still at the moment no way of inescapably confronting the intending teacher with the obligation of passing on his country's culture and traditions to the next generation. One can take a horse to the water but not make him drink, as the Irish have discovered in their linguistic revivalism, and this of itself will not save the Scots language. But at least it will keep some knowledge of it going and some understanding of what has been said and written in it and incidentally some idea of what it really sounds like, and not the B.B.C. version of it. Nevertheless whether this policy of re-educating the Scots is to succeed depends ultimately on breaking down the psychological inhibitions of the parents against permitting it and the teachers against teaching it and against stupidity even the gods may strive in vain.

Finally there is the question of written Scots as a vehicle for a new national literature, the avowed purpose of the Lallans movement. It might be said at the outset that there is not much hope for or point in a written Scots that has no spoken form to back it up, and a Scots that is merely dictionary-dredging, and not always accurate at that, will be simply a dilettante exercise. Yet the state of Scots is such that the dictionary is indispensable and it is noticeable that the Lallans poets invariably add a glossary for their readers. There is also a kind of a paradox in MacDiarmid's demand for a more intellectual type of poetry to be expressed in a language of lowered intellectual pitch—a blunted tool which needs to be given a new edge and temper. That he succeeded so well in his earlier work and in *A Drunk Man Looks at the Thistle* (1926) is not only a tribute to his own genius but to the inherent possibility of the attempt.

At the moment the Lallans poets, now mostly in their fifties and over, seem to have fallen silent and the younger generation of bards with few exceptions, vociferously repudiate Scots, no doubt partly as a gesture of revolt against their predecessors, though it is sometimes difficult to see what advantage is gained by replacing "unintelligible" Scots with an equally unintelligible English. Nor is there much in the argument that a poet must use only the language that comes natural to him. If this were really so, no poetry would ever be written, for poetry requires art in words as well as feeling and Wordsworth himself lived to refute the theory of the *Lyrical Ballads*.

All the same the Lallans writers cannot be said to have raised Scots very far out of the rut it had run in since the seventeenth century. Few of them have the linguistic skill of Burns, who incidentally borrows more than is generally supposed from his predecessors and, more seriously, they have restricted themselves almost entirely to poetry, thus perpetuating the lop-sided development of Scots as a literary language noted above. There is no hope for Scots until it can be used for prose and drama as well, including the short story, the radio sketch and documentary.

This is a much more difficult business. In contrast to poetry, continuity in Scots prose was broken in the sixteenth century. There are no real models later than that date; and the old historical prose of a feudalised rural society cannot be simply adapted to the needs of modern industrial life, having missed the evolutionary development which English underwent in the interval. To short-circuit or condense this is a highly complex matter which would have to be left in large measure to the professional philologist, the grammarian, the lexicographer, to do for Scots in this century what was done for English in the eighteenth. It is by no means impossible, given the will and the encouragement. Craigie is quite emphatic on this and points to the irrefutable success of a similar policy in Norway, the Faroes and Friesland; and the work on two large-scale Scottish dictionaries is already a monumental step in this direction for anyone who knows how to use them.

But it needs the practitioner as well as the technician and we cannot just whistle up literature when we like although we can create a climate for it, as the Irish did at the beginning of this century. The short story is a particularly suitable field for linguistic experiment and it is worth noting that one of the world's great short stories, Scott's *Wandering Willie's Tale*, is precisely an experiment of this nature in Scots, which Stevenson followed in *Thrawn Janet* and *The Tale of Tod Lapraik*. Then the drama, which could be a halfway house between verse and narrative prose, presents another opportunity for the writing of Scots as Robert Maclellan, Sydney Goodsir Smith and the late Robert Kemp have shown in their plays.

Hitherto the mistake made by so many Lallans experimenters has been in an unskilful, indiscriminate and, too frequently, unidiomatic splashing about of Scots words taken at random from a dictionary, or concocted, not always correctly, out of their own heads or incongruously assorted from a variety of dialects. Two things should be borne in mind about literary Scots: firstly, that it has the same origin as English, that its differences from English are regular and not haphazard, and numerous as these are, the similarities are still more so, and that English and Scots have roughly the same relationship and should have the same degree of mutual intelligibility as Dutch and German, Spanish and Portuguese, and Polish and Czech or Russian; secondly, that a metropolitan Scots still exists, decayed though it is, and should be restored as a standard.

As it so happens, this problem of resuscitating Scots prose is not a new one. Most recently Lewis Grassic Gibbon in the greatest Scots novel of the twentieth century, *A Scots Quair*, makes an attempt to reproduce the rhythms and cadences of Scots along with some of its vocabulary; earlier there were Stevenson, Mrs. Oliphant and Moir. But the most serious attempt at a kind of Scottish English was made by the novelist John Galt, who obviously gave much thought and care to the matter, experimented with it in *The Annals of the Parish* and *The Provost*, and when criticised for it went on to make a spirited reply in a postscript to his Scots historical novel *Ringan Gilhaize*, in which significantly enough he quotes the Arbroath Declaration; and his later work continues to explore the possibilities of this half-Scots, half-English style.

While this hybrid is not the *final* answer to the problem of a revived Scots, it does point in the general direction of the solution and it shows what can be done; and so Galt's works are essential reading for those who would follow suit. It should be remembered also that one of the last remaining repositories of the old Scotland is our legal system, though of course there are people busy pulling it about our ears too, and in much of the phraseology of Scots law we can heart faint echoes of the old curial speech of the kingdom. Here too is an idiom to be closely looked at. Yet another model worth study is Basic English, which has now somewhat gone out of fashion. But in a sense Basic English was an attempt to recreate a new kind of English prose as an antidote to the amalgam of cliché and jargon which is now so stultifying a noble language, as well as bamboozling the minds of those who read it. A similar discipline in a new Lallans would do the Scots no harm, and possibly some good.

When the technological revolution reaches its zenith, presumably we shall all have time and money galore and have to think hard about what to do with our affluence and leisure, and it is conceivable that a few Scottish souls might even want to learn Scots. No doubt the usual chorus will arise about "wanting to turn the clock back" from those for whom time stopped for ever in 1707, and there will be vociferations about Babel from those who forget that Babel was the result, not the cause, of the presumptuous stupidity of mono-minded men who thought to reach heaven in one great multi-storey high-density tower block.

10

LITERATURE
Alexander Scott

Even Scotland, where the poets have always out-numbered the novelists—and most of *them* have been poets too—has never experienced such a pullulation of poetry as in the last decade, and while the cascade of slim volumes continues to pour from the presses there seems no reason to believe that anything short of a major slump, and a consequent catastrophic cut in Arts Council subsidies, can stem the flood in the foreseeable future. An anthology of Scottish verse 1959-1969 compiled in the spring of the latter year contains no less than 240 poems by no fewer than 51 writers, and any editor attempting a similar compilation only a year later would have found himself compelled to add yet other authors to the list. Successive numbers of the *Scottish Poetry* annual volumes published by Edinburgh University Press since 1966 have never failed to give tongue with new voices; our most venerable verse magazine, *Lines Review,* which for all too many of the years since its foundation in 1952 appeared rather less frequently than once a twelvemonth, has recently been compelled to become a quarterly in order to cope with the Niagara of contributions; and our other poetry periodical, *Akros,* which is published three times a year, has had to quadruple its size since Duncan Glen first issued it in 1965.

While quantity need not indicate quality, there is no doubt about the prestige of contemporary Scottish verse, which is exceptionally high. This is due, first and foremost and above all, to the presence of a great poet, Hugh MacDiarmid, whose seventieth birthday in 1962 was celebrated by the much-too-belated publication (in New York) of his *Collected Poems*—an event which caused even the ranks of Suddronry to raise the semblance of a cheer—and whose subsequent collections of mainly early work, *A Lap of Honour* (1967), *A Clyack-Sheaf* (1969), and *More Collected*

Poems (1970) have consolidated a reputation so formidable that most criticism has quailed before its superlative brilliance and versatility.

After half a century of creative endeavour, during by far the greater part of which his work was neglected or denigrated by all the critical establishment except the particularly discerning—while at the same time he was never without disciples, some of whom have themselves attained distinction in poetry—MacDiarmid has now become an institution, in ironic fulfilment of his own early prophecy that he would "aye be whaur/Extremes meet". Books and pamphlets on his work and influence multiply; articles and essays and "special MacDiarmid issues" of magazines abound; his occasional prose is selected twice over, introduced and reintroduced; his early masterpiece, *A Drunk Man Looks at the Thistle* (1926), is reissued (1971) in a would-be-standard Scots spelling supervised by an American scholar; and recording companies vie with one another to put his verse on disc in his own voice. But, again ironically, all this fame has been thrust upon him during the very decade when many—although by no means all—of the younger generation of Scottish poets, those born in the later thirties and the early forties, have dismissed his achievement as being no longer relevant to their contemporary aims, which are concentrated on the creation of a poetry in English rather than in Scots.

That Scots—the variant of Northern English developed in the Scottish Lowlands over the past fourteen centuries—has not only survived but revived as a language for poetry in the twentieth century, despite all the pressures towards Anglicisation and/or Americanisation resulting from exploitation of the mass media, is principally due to MacDiarmid's genius. When he began his literary career in the years immediately following the First World War—which, fought in the cause of "gallant little Serbia" (or read "Belgium"), had shocked him into concern with his own small country—the Scots poetical tradition was in ruins after more than a century of slavish imitation of Burns by versifiers content to sketch only the surface mannerisms of the Scottish scene, and much of its more intellectual vocabulary had fallen into desuetude. MacDiarmid had to achieve nothing less than the restoration of Lowland Scots as a literary language at the same time as he sought to employ it to express the highest reaches of spiritual and intellectual awareness and the deepest levels of emotional and physical experience, matters which had all too seldom found utterance in Scots since the work of the medieval poets. His success—attained not without struggle, the signs of which are occasionally all to evident—brought him numerous disciples, none of them lacking talent, but few of those who emerged during the thirties and forties have survived as poets in Scots until the present day. Some have fallen silent (Douglas Young), some have concentrated on Gaelic (George Campbell Hay), and some have reverted to English (Maurice Lindsay). Of those who remain, Robert Garioch and Sydney Goodsir Smith are the most outstanding modern poets in Scots apart from MacDiarmid and William Soutar (1898-1943).

Garioch crowned his career with *Selected Poems* (1966), by far the funniest collection of the decade, with more belly-laughs per stanza than there are nips in a gill. Although he is not only a native of Edinburgh but a graduate of its university—he used to be a schoolmaster—Garioch identifies neither with the professional class nor with the bourgeoisie but presents himself as a drop-out, speaking dialect, writing in the language of the pub, and preferring the company of drouthy drinkers to the acquaintance of the respectable. The underdog who bites the ankles of the powerful and the pretentious is, in various sizes, shapes and forms, the truly dominant character in most of the hilarious contributions to his series of "Sixteen Edinburgh Sonnets". In "Glisk of the Great" a famous singer, fat and flushed with wine, cracks doubtful jokes with a trio of "notorious baillies" as they sally forth from an expensive hotel and sail away in a municipal Rolls-Royce, followed by an unprivileged spectator's sardonic comment that such behaviour "gies our toun some tone". In "Queer Ongauns", the official mace is dismissively described as "a muckle siller cosh" and the activities of the office-bearers are presented as being both scandalous and incomprehensible. In "Heard in the Cougate", a reception for the King of Norway is reduced to absurdity by being discussed in gutter-Scots liberally interspersed with gobs of spit. Even in "Elegy", where Garioch appears in person as "a new-cleckit dominie," he represents himself as biting the hands that fed him inadequate fodder, the headmasters who criticised his aptitude and his appearance and his inability to live on his salary—"Weill, gin they arena deid, it's time they were"—while in "Did Ye See

Me?", where he gives a public performance clad in complete academic regalia, he blows up the bubble of professional pomposity by means of a ludicrously-persistent employment of archaistic rhymes, then pricks it with the pin of illiterate ribaldry. Garioch's comic contempt for his own profession, the poorest-paid and the least privileged in the land—expressed at its most ferocious in his "Repone til George Buchanan"—has led him to identify himself with the underpaid and the underprivileged in general, and in "Sisyphus" he transforms that mythical sufferer of eternal torment into a Scottish labourer-cum-layabout.

Despite the contemporaneity of his subject-matter, however, Garioch's treatment of it is by no means novel. On the contrary, it is at least as old as the eighteenth century, since it exemplifies what a perceptive critic of Ramsay, Fergusson and Burns has called "the reductive idiom"[1]—in other words, "Kaa the feet frae the High-Heid-Yins." Like his earlier exemplars, Garioch empties the ash-can over "the unco guid" and hurls sticks and stones at Holy Willie—even although, in modern terms, the unco guid have developed into "the cognoscenti, a hie-brou clan," and Holy Willie has dwindled into "some pacing provost" inaugurating the start of yet another Edinburgh Festival by entering the High Kirk of St Giles "fu sanctimonious . . . to music frae *Die Meistersinger*" while the lesser breeds outwith the law mistake him for Shostakovich. Garioch even attempts the poem of communal celebration, in the style of Fergusson's "Hallow Fair" and Burns's "The Holy Fair," but while "Embro to the Ploy," with its theme of Festival fun, undoubtedly contains some stanzas which are both clever and ironical, its development is extremely disjointed—particularly in the most recent reprints, where new stanzas have been inserted with apparent disregard for their context. For the poet, the occasion is "filled wi synthetic joy"— like the drunks in the Festival Club—and the poem is rather synthetic too, an exercise in the "Christ's Kirk on the Green" stanza which inevitably suggests pastiche.

His mastery of Scots is an essential source of the strength of Garioch's work, but while his Edinburgh poems possess verve, vigour, colloquial command, ironical idiom, comic invention and slashing satirical strength, his style—with all those admirable qualities—seems incapable of achieving the sublime. (His nearest approaches consist of the pathos of "At Robert Fergusson's Grave" and the wry tenderness of "Brither Worm," in the first of which Burns is a character, while the second inevitably reminds the reader of his "To a Mouse.") Despite his formal indebtedness to the Night-town scene from Joyce's *Ulysses* in his dramatic extravaganza, *The Masque of Edinburgh,* Garioch's language shows none of the Irishman's virtuosity in weaving together the vernacular and the literary, but always stays close to the spoken tongue. This, of course, is one of the principal springs of his work's authenticity; but it is also one of the reasons for his comparative narrowness of range.

While Sydney Goodsir Smith admires Garioch's achievement and shares some of his attitudes—particularly the detestation of High Mucky-Mucks—and while he often displays a similar command of the reductive idiom, his work has a wider and deeper range of sensibility, which he is able to express through a linguistic medium of much greater flexibility and variability of style. Another admirer of Joyce, his prose romance *Carotid Cornucopius: The First Echt Fitts* (1964) an attempt to create an Edinburgh equivalent of *Finnegan's Wake*, Goodsir Smith has mastered the art of combining contemporary vernacular Scots with his own equivalent of the aureate (gilded) style of the medieval makars, and that combination enables him to move between the gallus and the glorious with superb speed and manoeuvrability. His Lallans (Lowland Scots) language is very much an individual creation, for one of the impulses behind his verse is the zeal of the convert. Although he is a Scot on his mother's side, Goodsir Smith was born in New Zealand and educated in England and on the Continent, and it was only after he settled in Edinburgh in the later thirties that he became enamoured of Scottish life and letters, espousing the nationalist cause and becoming a disciple of MacDiarmid and the "Scottish Renaissance"—more properly, "resistance"—school of poetry in Scots.

His most effective rcent publication is *Kynd Kittock's Land* (1965), an extended poem on Edinburgh commissioned for B.B.C. television, which plunges from the heights to the depths and then soars off again into the "saumon-reid" of the dawn sky—which the poet sees (as through a glass darkly) only because he has been up all night carousing with his chosen companions, "the bards and lauchin lassies," among whom he can forget that the city is "sair come doun frae its auld heichts . . . smug, complacent, Lost til aa pride of race or spirit." Like most of Goodsir Smith's Edinburgh poems, this one is mainly nocturnal, and his favourite characters are the rejects of a commercial society, Kynd Kittock herself, "a great boozer who died of thirst one night when the taverns were shut," the poverty-stricken pensioners in the slums, and the "penurious scribes" in the pubs. His swift and subtle rhythms and his cunningly-contrived verse paragraphs, with their abrupt transitions between the gay and the grave, the profound and the profane, and with their darting-and-pausing movement that exactly mirrors the ever-changing sense, convey the impression of exceptional emotional energy—and emotional honesty too.

In contrast, his *Fifteen Poems and a Play* (1969), which draws on work written over the past two decades, is his most unequal volume since he ceased to be an apprentice, with a verse play whose predictability of plot is made all the more apparent by the inflation of the dialogue, an extended poem on the Forth Road Bridge which fails to span its length in significant style, a song on whisky which is little more than a catalogue of distilleries, and a song on sex which is neither clean nor clever. But alongside these disasters, the achieved creations are all the more noteworthy. In "Three", (on Lenin's dictum, "Three men make a revolution") Goodsir Smith has written an anti-political poem which puts a whole revolutionary tradition to the question by means of a sequence of queries at once loaded, deadly and direct; in "The Kenless Strand" he sketches a vision of doomed love in lines which are as bare as they are pictorially precise, and where sense and sound are indissolubly fused together; and in "The Reid, Reid Rose" the dragging rhythms echo the despair of the central image of "the weary, burnin rose." Other poems which demonstrate that his hand has not lost its cunning have appeared in the magazine *Akros*—"I Saw the Mune," a moving meditation on the conflict between love and power, and "Spring in the Botanic Gardens," a melancholy declaration of dependence "on anither's strength" which confesses the writer's weakness with all the courage of a mature talent.

Although Tom Scott is only three years younger than Goodsir Smith, he did not begin to publish work in Scots until the fifties, and his single full-length collection to date, *The Ship and Ither Poems*, appeared as late as 1963. Even then, it shows a belated apprenticehood, its Scots sometimes plodding, sometimes lame, and sometimes almost immovably clogged, its images frequently inappropriate, its anger and its irony often uncontrolled, its attempts at sublimity sometimes drowned by an unconscious inclination towards the art of sinking. The main contributions which avoid those technical faults are two love-poems, "Orpheus"—at once simple and sensuous in its vivid evocation of the power of creativity—and "The Bride," a vision-poem whose powerful rhythms drive the conviction of sincerity through its medieval mannerisms. Unfortunately, Scott's next publication, the pamphlet-poem *At the Shrine o the Unkent Sodger* (1968), repeats the worst rather than the best qualities of *The Ship*, since it is a raging anti-war rant in twenty-two pages of high-pitched anger, jolting in movement and near-hysterical in tone, "the imagery . . . burst open by pressure of emotion."[2] Yet this bellicose bard, when not roused to fury, has shown himself capable of expressing a synthesis of satire and sympathy at once subtle and strong, as in his much-anthologised "Brand the Builder," which pulses with organised energy and pictorial power. This is the first of a series of poems on the St Andrews of Scott's youth, and although none of the other contributions to the sequence yet published has quite as much width, depth and balance as "Brand," their varied quality is more than good enough to leave the reader impatient to see the whole complete in print.

Another poet who began to publish in Scots during the fifties, Alastair Mackie, has yet to issue a collection which reveals the full range of his work—there are only two Scots poems in his *Soundings* (1966)—but enough of his verse has appeared in the magazines over the past decade to establish his individual talent. An Aberdonian, from an area where Scots probably remains more secure in the mouths of the people than anywhere else in the country, Mackie has an idiomatic command of his medium which gives him a fine range of themes, from the local to the universal, expressing acrid wit and shuddering desolation as well as dazzling imagistic fire or colloquial comedy.

Colloquial control is an equally notable feature of the work of J. K. Annand, a literary veteran whose first collection of bairn-rhymes, *Sing It Aince for Pleisure* (1965), showed that he was not only a clever contriver of verse for children but a poet who, on occasion, could combine complete simplicity of style with considerable power of passion. In his recent sequence, *Two Voices* (1968), some of the sea poems weld together brutality, tenderness and savage wit in lines of stabbing directness. While the danger of a style so unadorned as Annand's is that the poetry seems forever on the point of crumbling into prose, and collapses into it whenever the emotional pressure is low, at his best he can use a style stripped to the bone in order to express an elemental situation with a ruthless realism that still contrives to sing. Some of his comic verse, too, has force as well as fun.

The writer who has issued many poems, in Scots and in English, under the pseudonym of "Ronald Eadie Munro," has revealed himself in 1969—with the publication of his Scots volume *Kythings*—to be Duncan Glen, editor of *Akros* poetry magazine, publisher of Akros Publications, and author of the biographical-critical-bibliographical study *Hugh MacDiarmid and the Scottish Renaissance* (1964). In Glen's case the use of a pen-name can be justified, or at least excused, on the argument that two poets rather than one are represented in *Kythings*. First there is Glen, who writes autobiographical poems about the actualities of his own experience, as in "My Faither," an elegy of such profound simplicity that it is almost an impertinence to comment on the skill with which the substitution of a single English term for its Scots equivalent transforms the feeling of the whole work; or as in "Ceremonial," where the sight of a dead mouse leads to an appreciation of the intermingledom of "the bricht colours o life and daith" expressed with a delicate restraint which still contains both pity and affirmation. Then there is Munro—a name chosen for its association with Scottish summits?—who writes visionary poems on his relationship with the Muse, where sky-imagery combines and contrasts with images of "glaur" (mud) and brute vitality in his striving to express the paradoxical association of idealism with the foulest fact. None of these latter poems is entirely successful, for their sense is sometimes as clouded as the skies which arch over their maker, but they bear witness to an endeavour to interweave the actual with the imaginative which is all the more admirable for the infrequency with which post-medieval Scots poetry has made the attempt. It is a good augury for Glen's future that his Scots reads like a living language rather than a literary lingo.[3]

A propagandist for Scots as well as a practitioner in it, Glen has recently claimed that there is at present "a revival of writing in Scots" embodying what another critic has called the "stubbornly popular genius of the Scots tradition."[4] This is a point on which the present writer finds it difficult to comment, for if such a revival has in fact occurred during the past few years—after a decade of doldrums since the middle fifties—his own work has had some small share in it, and he has been a frequent contributor, in both Scots and English, to *Akros* and *Catalyst*, the two magazines which Glen adduces in support of his view.[5] It is beyond dispute, however, that since *Akros* was founded in 1965 far more verse in Scots has appeared there than in *Lines Review* (edited since 1967 by Robin Fulton, a younger poet who writes in English) or in the *Scottish Poetry* annuals edited since 1966 by George Bruce, Maurice Lindsay and Edwin Morgan, three poets in the Anglo-Scottish tradition.

But most of the best Scots poems in *Akros*, and in *Catalyst* (since 1967), have been written by established poets in their middle years—who have also appeared, although less frequently, in *Lines* and *Scottish Poetry*—and many of the younger makars have been extremely erratic. Eric Gold (published in pamphlet during 1969) is capable at his best of a fine fusion of wit and feeling, but at other times is unable to avoid clumsiness and pedestrianism; George Hardie (another *Akros* pamphleteer), lacking formal control, is over-dependent on emotional force, and when this fails his poems tend to fall apart into chopped-up prose; and David Morrison (*The White Hind,* 1969 and *The Clay Yird,* 1970) proves all too often that enthusiasm, and even dedication, are no substitute for technical competence. Yet the Scots are, notoriously, "late developers" in poetry—Annand, Tom Scott, and even MacDiarmid, are cases in point—and after every adverse criticism has been levelled against the younger vernacular bards it still remains true that the presence of public platforms, in the shape of *Akros*, *Catalyst*, and (since 1970) Morrison's pamphlet periodical *Scotia*, has brought them on stage in considerably greater numbers than was the case ten years ago. Within the past eighteen months alone, the magazines mentioned above have introduced the present writer to impressive Scots poems by authors previously unknown to him, David Angus, Donald Campbell, Rory Watson and William Neill (who also writes in

English and Gaelic), and whether or not they and the other younger makars prove to possess staying-power, they form a part of the present scene which only prejudice could pretend to be absent. Some effective verses in Glasgow dialect, by Stephen Murine and Tom Leonard, should also be noted.

At the same time, however, it is equally indisputable that English has become the majority language for verse by Scottish writers, a growing number of whom have never spoken anything else, and all of whom are introduced to English at a very early age, both in and out of school. The most distinguished, as well as the most prolific representative of what Glen has called, somewhat pejoratively, "the polite English school," is Norman MacCaig, with five full-scale collections during the last decade. The first of these, *A Round of Applause* (1962), with "all the enchanting wit, the melodic ease, the rhythmical subtlety"[6] and the apparently effortless creation of illuminating metaphors which characterise his work of the fifties, also expresses profound dissatisfaction with his own attempt to establish personal identity through the investigation and domination of natural objects. In the next, *Measures* (1965), MacCaig gives the impression of marking time—there is a lack of rhythmical variety and energy.

But between writing the *Measures* poems and those in his next book, *Surroundings* (1966), MacCaig was able to leave his usual haunts in Edinburgh and Sutherland for Italy, and "The Streets of Florence" expresses his sense of astonished wonder at the revelation he experienced there, when he realised that history—in the form of the faces immortalised in the canvases in the Uffizi Gallery—was also alive in the identical faces of the Florentines he saw about him in the streets. This discovery of the historical sense seems also to have stimulated a novel feeling for other people, as in "Assisi," a moving expression of pity for a complete stranger, where the image of the deformed dwarf who sits outside "the three tiers of churches built/In honour of St Francis" presents an unanswerable dilemma to all charity, human or divine. The apparent simplicity of the writing here is understatement at its most devastating.

Expressing new themes, MacCaig has abandoned the regular metrical forms of his earlier poems and adopted free verse. In a volume so experimental, he can hardly be expected to achieve

invariable success, and failure is particularly apparent in free
verse, which falls flat if a joke doesn't come off, or if ideas don't
ignite when rubbed together, or if the emotional fire is too low to
generate sufficient steam. Yet even the failures are usually illumin-
ated by the fine phrases with which MacCaig captures a fleeting
notion or catches an image on the wing, while the free verse form
permits him to attempt—and often to succeed in—such hitherto-
untouched subjects as literary criticism and such formerly-ignored
themes as the futility of politics. For almost the first time, too, he
has been able to write some really funny poems (as distinct from
his many witty ones).

While expanding his range, MacCaig has also recovered—or
perhaps even increased—the intensity with which he had earlier
expressed his involvement with the Highland landscape and with
love. In "Go-Between," where these themes are compellingly combined, the brief free-verse lines possess a rhythmical force and a
sensuous immediacy which both express and enhance the passion
from which the poem has sprung, and in "Sounds of the Day" the
appeal to the auditory imagination in the opening lines reinforces
the sense of shock when the lover finds himself deserted ("you left
me/Beside the quietest fire in the world"). This poem, again, has
one of MacCaig's most surprising, effective, brutal and exact conclusions, an image of superb tactile expressiveness. "Escapist," on
the other hand, is perhaps the finest of all his poems expressing personal concern, creating its own landscape, a scene which is at once
mythical and all-too-real, and expressing the hallucinatory horror
of a man trapped by his realisation of the inescapability of violence
and death. If this poem is individual in its conception, it is universal in its implications, and shattering in its impact.

The territory gained by MacCaig in *Surroundings* has been
both consolidated and extended in his succeeding volumes. In
Rings on a Tree (1968), with "The Red Well, Harris" he finds an
evocative symbol ("one drained well/on top of another") for the
emigration which has gone far (too far?) towards the ruin of the
Highlands; with "Crossing the Border" he conjures up, through
images of useless violence, the brutal facts behind "ballad" history;
and with a scintillating sequence of nine poems on New York he
counterpoints a strikingly sensuous simplicity of style against the
proliferating confusion of the environment. In *A Man in My Posi-*

tion (1969) he has essayed the extended poem. History is an essential background to his study of Sutherland, "A Man in Assynt," where the passion behind his view of Highland people in their native landscape and seascape gives his free-verse lines their compelling rhythmical force and sensuous energy. Another poem of some length, "No End, No Beginning," is perhaps his most remarkable work to date, combining his subtle perception of natural beauty and his delighted appreciation of the enlivening qualities of love with a profound visionary insight into the fundamental unity of all modes of being. In view of those achievements, it may seem petty to complain that in some of his "metaphysical" love poems—a genre where he has often triumphed in the past— MacCaig nowadays seems to be less concerned with love than with playing conjuring-tricks with ideas about it.

Another poet of MacCaig's generation, Sydney Tremayne, shows a not dissimilar development of new forms in his fifth collection, *The Turning Sky* (1969). His range of feeling is wide, from desolation ("Through all our absences the long tide surges") to half-humorous resolve ("This wilderness supports a hare;/It also may support a man"), from pity and love ("Hares . . . hold their ground by knowing where to run") to the satirical celebration of necessary ignorance ("If I'd known where I was I'd have broken my neck"). A master of the conversational style as well as the more mannered, Tremayne possesses a wit which is sometimes not without an element of brutality, and which sometimes can seem not uncontrived, but which is elsewhere extremely pretty in its point—as in the five-line sketch of his father "Riding, erect and slow, his twenty-six-year-old bicycle." Other parental poems, however are moving elegies for the loss of love, expressed (as in "Stone Walls") with telling simplicity. Throughout his career, Tremayne's control of form has always been notable, and he now shows himself capable of the extended meditation ("Details from a Death Certificate") as well as the brief lyric. It remains to be seen whether the subjects which he has been exploring for a quarter of a century can continue to provide him with novel discoveries.

In *Landscapes and Figures* (1967) by George Bruce, a considerably less prolific contemporary of MacCaig and Tremayne, most of the poems date from the forties and fifties and show his characteristic qualities—which are also those of his native Aberdeenshire

coast, bareness and resistance—in ignoring conventional pretti-
ness in order to concentrate on the shape and line and plane of
Buchan places and people. The more recent poems, however,
show an even finer sharpening of style as well as a widening of
range. "Visitations from a War-Time Childhood" has a glittering
satirical edge to its starkness, and "Laotian Peasant Shot," in its
unsentimental understatement, strangely but successfully combines the heart-cry and the shrug. More recent work still—included in his *Collected Poems* (1970)—is at once surrealist and
rooted in everyday reality, displaying a technical command employed in the exploration of both personal and general experience,
and with much greater emotional scope (rage, despair, passionate love, compassion, and even randiness) than the gravity of his
earlier work allowed.

Bruce's editorial colleague, Maurice Lindsay, is more content
with traditional forms, and more unequal, with a regrettable tendency towards rather trite philosophising and a corresponding
slackness of style, a loss of rhythmical urgency and dexterity, and
a too-apparent juggling with parts of speech. But he is sensuously
aware, and when he refrains from trying to tease the sights and
sounds of the natural world into patterns of metaphysical explanation he is able to allow his gift for seizing upon essential details
to create a design which is itself sufficient interpretation of the
experience which the poem enshrines ("Stones in Sky and
Water"). His best work is as penetratingly perceptive about
humanity as about the world of nature, and the most successful
poems in one of his recent collections, *This Business of Living*
(1969), show a widening and deepening of his range in this kind.
The synthesis of beauty and cruelty, ruthlessness and pity, action
and thought and feeling in "At the Mouth of the Ardyne" is both
admirably economical and evocative, while he expresses the ambiguities of love and art in "A Ballad of Orpheus" and the brutal
defeat of love by hatred in "Glasgow Nocturne," poems which
reveal that his talent is still developing, still discovering new
themes and new ways of expressing them.[7]

There is little that is new in the most recent volume by W. S.
Graham, *Malcolm Mooney's Land* (1970), with which he broke
a silence of fifteen years. In some ways, indeed, the book represents a retreat from the position won with such praiseworthy panache in its predecessor, *The Nightfishing* (1955), for while most

of the contents of that collection were concerned with Graham's principal theme, the difficulty—amounting to virtual impossibility, in his view—of communication between man and man and between poet and public, the title-poem was a triumphant negation of that argument, since its superbly evocative lines expressed with compelling sensuous conviction the cohesive force of a shared experience. But in the title poem of the new book the poet is utterly alone in an Arctic landscape, while elsewhere he is in solitary confinement (after Kafka—not to mention a hundred or a thousand others), trying to "get through" on the plumbing system. He also laments, not for the first time, the impossibility of recapturing his lost childhood, and the otherness of persons apart from himself. While Graham has lost none of his unerring skill in the weaving of verbal music and the creation of images which, while novel, he makes appear inevitable, that music tends to repeat tunes already heard, and those images are all of a kind with earlier metaphors. In some poems, too, he proves his theory of the impossibility of communication not wisely but only too well by presenting word-patterns whose obscurity is total. This volume is the work of a highly professional craftsman, but—with the possible exceptions of a little love-poem and an elegy for a friend—it says nothing which the writer has not said before.

If Graham has ignored Pound's advice to "make it new," an unsympathetic critic has accused Edwin Morgan of being "owre eident in ettlin to be aye in the new guise."[8] But if this is a fault it is one which, in the context of Scottish artistic conservatism, the present writer does not find difficult to forgive. Central to Morgan's only full-length original volume, *The Second Life* (1968), in position as in effect, are his poems on Glasgow. The cry of human agony in "Glasgow Green" pierces beyond the city scene to achieve universality, and "King Billy," on the burial of a "gang-leader in the bad times/of idleness and boredom, lost in better days," is scarcely less intense in the passion of its pity. But such is Morgan's versatility that his humorous poems on Glasgow are equally successful. "The Starlings in George Square" is hilarious in its surrealist description of those shrill beaks, and it combines comedy with a sensitive appreciation of the beauty and mystery of the birds and gratitude for the unknown forces which have led them to associate themselves with the town. Again,

"Good Friday," a burlesque monologue by a drunken proletarian, is also a beautifully understated expression of the pathos of ignorance. Some of the love-poems, too, have a Glasgow setting, and take strength from the association of parochial details with poetical passion. The best of them, however, might be set in any lover's room anywhere—"One Cigarette," with its vivid opening line, "No smoke without you, my fire," has that moving simplicity, that seeming artlessness, which only consummate art can command. But Morgan is also a writer of fantastic imagination, who delights to explore outer (and inner) space as expressed in terms of science-fiction. Time-travel in "From the Domain of Arnheim," and teleportation in "In Sobieski's Shield," are employed not merely fancifully, or to provide opportunities for technological displays, but in order to throw light on fundamental human emotions of pity and terror from new angles.

Beside his thematic variety, Morgan's formal unadventurousness is somewhat surprising. Almost all his work is couched in Whitmanesque free verse, and he does not always avoid the diffuseness encouraged by its apparent ease. Sometimes, too, Whitman's example betrays him into too frequent use of invocation, with the result that a poem may proceed in sudden spurts, jerked along from one ejaculation to the next. On the whole, the less consciously emphatic, the more movingly functional his verse becomes—as in "King Billy," where the scrupulous avoidance of the slightest suspicion of "fine writing" is perfectly suited to the sombre lamentation of the theme. Yet the reader who finds himself yearning for even one "jewel five words long" has some reason for his lack of complete satisfaction with a large volume written in a style so close to prose.

About the so-called "concrete" experiments which occupy more than a third of the book, others must write who find that these verbal cartoons and/or linguistic puzzles constitute a viable poetical form. Neither will the concretions of Ian Hamilton Finlay and Alan Riddell be discussed here. Finlay's orthodox verse, *The Dancers Inherit the Party* (1960 and 1969) and *Glasgow Beasts, an a Burd* (1961), is mostly minor, and mainly whimsical, although not without individual charm; but while Riddell's *The Stopped Landscape* (1968) expresses "a still, small voice" which sometimes lacks energy, for all its gentleness his verse often expresses a haunting sense of loss, all the more poignant for the quietness with which he accepts it. Sometimes his profound dissatisfaction is expressed fancifully, with the semi-surrealist technique which has attracted some attention when employed by such writers as George Mac-Beth and his disciple D. M. Black but which has scarcely been noted in Riddell's work, where it is used with restrained subtlety rather than blatant surface bravura. In MacBeth's earlier volumes, his bizarre imagination, considerable technical skill, emotional power and intellectual ruthlessness have combined to create some splendid poems on his own childhood, on his relationship with his dead father, and on mythological themes; but in *The Night of Stones* (1968) imagination has dwindled into fancy, emotion has atrophied, the intellect has turned inwards, and the bizarre has become the byzantine, with "sound-poems" and "found sound-poems" which are not creations but constructions. On the other hand, the attempts at objectivity in *A War Quarter* (1969) rarely rise above the journalistic.

If MacBeth suggests the rootless cosmopolitan intellectual, George Mackay Brown—born and bred in the Orkney islands, where he still lives, and a convert (in 1961) to Roman Catholicism—has always expressed, both in his verse and in his prose, his insight into the social customs and the individual characters of his local community, as well as his appreciation of the significance and power of religious myth and symbol. In his earliest collection, *The Storm* (1954), these themes are treated separately—in "Orcadians," a sequence of character-sketches written in a free verse which sometimes fails to avoid the pedestrian in its attempt to achieve vernacular simplicity, and in "Saint Magnus on Egilsay," where the measured blank verse and the images of arrested action show the influence of an elder Orcadian, Edwin Muir. But in many of the best poems in his later volumes, *Loaves and Fishes* (1959) and *The Year of the Whale* (1965), he contrives to combine the two themes and thereby to enhance both. At the same time, his voice has become unmistakably his own, without the echoes of Yeatsian lyricism or Muirist mythologising or Dylan Thomas organ-intoning which mar the earlier work, although he often achieves a singing directness not unworthy of Yeats, a legendary richness not inferior to Muir, and a verbal resonance no less remarkable than Thomas. Although most of his poems are intensely local, he neither sees nor presents his characters as provincial oddities, as queer fish in an island backwater, but always as individual souls enshrined in the flesh of Orkney fishermen and farmers, and the implications of their dreams and their deeds, their pursuits and their passions, have width as well as depth of relevance. Again, his fascination with Orkney's patron saint, Magnus, martyred in the twelfth century, has led to a concern with the whole of island history and a consequent enrichment of his work through the interplay of past and present.

His themes, no doubt inevitably with a religious poet living in a small community in close contact with the fields and the fishing-grounds, are the fundamental ones of work and worship, growth and decay, death by land and water, the interweaving of love and lust between the sexes, and under and above and through them all, the divine mercy. His emotional range is wide, not only from poem to poem but also within a single creation, moving from religious devotion to wry realisation of human weakness in "Our Lady of the Waves" and from melancholy acceptance of the inevitability of death to grateful appreciation of the inexhaustible richness of life in "The Year of the Whale." Many of his poems are dramatic, and such is his sensitivity to the feelings of others that he can speak through the mouth of Harald, the agnostic ale-drinking shepherd, with as much sympathetic understanding as when he wears the mask of a medieval abbot, while "Ikey on the People of Hellya" is as ironically revealing on the character of the speaker, a thieving tramp, as on those of the people whom he plunders. The style of these poems is superbly simple, combining conciseness with clarity in phrases which are at once functional and fine.

Orkney Tapestry, Mackay Brown's 1969 volume, is a successful experiment in the interweaving of prose and poetry, expressing a singular vividness of vision. After a series of bird's eye glimpses of landscape and folk, he focuses on how the communal life of shared centuries has shaped place and people in one particular valley, Rackwick, of which he writes a history, in verse and prose, which has all the qualities of legend—an enchantment to read, even although the action is often tragic and the end is emptiness. For the dark irony involved in the kind of "progress" which has resulted in depopulation, he finds the desolate image of the deserted hearth ("The poor and the good fires are all quenched"). But our civilisation has always had some horror at its heart, as Mackay Brown shows himself to be penetratingly aware in his chapter on the Orkney Vikings, where his own poems, "tough, rich, passionate, witty,"[9] enhance the prose narrative as much as his taut translations from the Norse. Against all expectation, however, that Viking horror gave birth to holiness, with the martyrdom of Magnus. Mackay Brown relates this marvellous story partly in narrative, partly in verse, and partly in dramatic form, making it at once historical and contemporary with ourselves. His mastery of the vernacular style, blending simplicity with splendour, is dominant throughout.

Another poet whom an unsympathetic critic might describe as parochial is Iain Crichton Smith, for many of his best poems issue from his personal experience of particular places and people in the Highlands, himself included—he was born in Lewis. This self is much more than a detached observer. He suffers, he rejoices, he celebrates his moments of illumination, and he extends his sympathy to the men and women he meets, even when they humiliate him, and even when they humiliate themselves by their own lack of sympathy. The style of some of the poems in *The Law and the Grace* (1965) is almost prosaic, and can afford to be, for the tension between pity and hatred which vibrates in them needs no embellishment. Other poems, again, consist of a series of statements which are also a series of highly evocative and impassioned images. The finest, perhaps, is "Old Woman"—"Your thorned back/ heavily under the creel/you steadily stamped the rising daffodil." Those three lines embody a vision of a whole life devoted to labour and moral disapproval; and while the old woman's attitude may differ from the poet's he has a profound understanding of it, since he shares with her the same ancestry, the same history (represented by his acrid studies of "The Clearances" and "Highlanders"), and the same daily background. No poet could be more closely involved with his themes than Crichton Smith, and none could express them with more concentrated concern, a bare precision, a subtlety which reveals insight as well as verbal skill, and—at times—a blazing visionary passion of agony and glory.

His most recent collection, *From Bourgeois Land* (1969), a frontal assault on what he regards as the twin curses of Calvinism and capitalism, offers a pound of philosophising for each sixteen ounces of fact. But his speculative intellectualisations are by no means always in harmony with his intuitive intelligence, and some of the links between Calvinism and capitalism are not so much wrought as wrenched together, while there are occasions when the usual taut sensuousness of his style sags beneath a dead-weight of drab generalisations. Yet, among the mish-mash of metaphysics and the limping lines, there are many poems—their connection with the book's ostensible theme usually tenuous—which are both dramatic and disturbing, derived from experience rather than imposed upon it by the imperfectly-analytical intellect, and expressed through images which at once embody and enhance their subjects.

The second poem, contrasting religion's gloom with passion's glory, finds the exact reflection of that contrast by counterpointing the dreariness of a Free Kirk manse against the deliciousness of its garden; in the sixth, "Hamlet," the world is a chaos of distorting mirrors where "Images bounce madly against reason/ as, in a spoon, wide images, fat and jolly;" in the eighteenth, the indissoluble association of horror and beauty is expressed through the savage killing of a zebra, torn to pieces by wild dogs while the rest of the herd retires to safety "Where the great suns of God intensely burn;" in the twenty-first, "At the Sale," the panic fear of time passing pounces from the paraphernalia of an auction in an old house; in the twenty-fifth, a watch presented at retirement reveals "the howling faces of eternity"; and in the thirty-fourth, the other eternity—of great art—is at once a feather and a flame, as "the hammered poetry of Dante turns/light as a wristwatch, bright as a thousand suns." To a poet capable of such revealing insights, far more unequal writing can be forgiven than is contained in *From Bourgeois Land*.

Equally outstanding as a translator, Crichton Smith produced an English version of the greatest of eighteenth-century Gaelic poems on the natural scene, Duncan Ban Macintyre's *Ben Dorain* (1969), which demonstrates a command of verse forms and musical harmonies scarcely inferior to the original *tour de force*. Only a poet possessing superb technical virtuosity could translate Macintyre's variations on a landscape and its denizens with any accuracy, for the work represents—as the the penetrating and provocative preface remarks—"the Gaelic language at its peak." Fortunately, Crichton Smith is not only a technical virtuoso but a man of deep and sensitive feeling, and the result of his translation is a great English poem in its own right—"so clear and so active/so pure and creative/with innocent motive."

While Crichton Smith has been publishing collections since 1955, Tom Buchan, only three years younger, did not produce his first volume, *Dolphins at Cochin*, until 1969. A reason for this delay may be that his starting-point as a writer is from a position of disenchantment so extreme as to be almost total—it is not without significance that one of his most effective poems, a fine fusion of intellectual questioning and sensuous affirm-ation, is called "Doubting Thomas". Too often, perhaps, he remains stuck on the start-line of a rather facile cynicism, but when passion impels him forward his progress is all the more impressive for having to be fought for against the restraints of disillusion. He is capable of both wry external comedy and ironic self-criticism, and his style, for all its bare precision, sel-dom loses touch with sensuous experience. At least equally sen-suous, Stewart Conn is also a talented myth-maker, and in the first half of *Stoats in the Sunlight* (1968) he gives a legendary quality, a universal relevance, to his memories of the Ayr-shire farm where he spent much of his childhood and to the contrasts wrought by time in the place and in the people who lived there. When he writes about contemporary Scotland, how-ever, his work tends to be fanciful or pictorial merely, and when his myths are not so much personal as literary the verse tends to sag beneath "picturesque" imagery. But in at least two of his fables, "Flight" and "Ambush," he achieves a naked strength of style admirably suited to the ruthlessness of his themes. Equally ruthless, and yet tender too, is his love-poem "The Fox in its Lair," with its stark awareness of the common muck out of which all beauty springs.

A similar spare conciseness enables Robin Fulton, in *Instances* (1967) and *Inventories* (1969), to express his insights in the minimum of space and yet with no sacrifice (at his best) of either clarity or passion. A keen-sighted appreciation of the significant details of the Scottish landscape issues in highly indi-vidual poems where appearances become symbols of emotional and intellectual experiences, and a like acute awareness enables him to transform his knowledge of his own weaknesses into a source of strength. But the deliberate understatement of his style does not always provide his verse with sufficient impetus to lift it above a somewhat dry intellectualism. When D. M. Black attempts this kind of understatement, however, as in the second and third sections of *The Educators* (1969), he becomes much more drably prosaic. Black's virtues—seen in the title poem of that volume, as well as sporadically in *With Decorum* (1967) and elsewhere—are surrealist imagination, intellectual acuteness, rhythmical force, and the ability to combine wit and feeling. His faults are an apparently wilful obscurity, a too great fondness for banging the big drum, and an over-emphatic display of technical virtuosity.

Among those of the younger poets who are only now beginning to be anthologised, the most versatile is Alan Jackson, whose range—in *The Grim Wayfarer* (1969)—encompasses the satirical or the comic miniature, the impassioned assault on arid intellectualism, the blunt assertion of brute fact, the symbolical expression of the struggle between good and evil, the lyrical celebration of rooted earthiness, and the exploration of the mysteries of time and fate in terms of the superstitions of science and science-fiction. But other poems express a raucous violence shrieking in concert with the fashionable taste for what Robert Lowell has called "raw, huge, blood-dripping gobbets of unreasoned experience," and the present writer is not the first critic to feel that Jackson's work has suffered from his membership of a poetry-reading circuit, with a consequent "sacrifice of coherence for superficial impact"[10] and an over-frequent employment of the more obvious rhythms.

The most erratic of the under-thirties is Alan Bold, with five volumes in as many years, all of them oscillating between a too-occasional excellence and remorselessly recurring rant. His personal poems can be both restrained and tender, but the political and philosophical pieces repeat the commonplaces of the radical reviews in a style even less distinguished than that of their sources. Most closely in contact with central human concerns is Giles Gordon, whose *Two Elegies* (1968) are at once moving and controlled, while his landscapes in his more recent uncollected poems are richly evocative not only of the scene itself but also of the emotions of the poet who finds himself while losing himself within them. The work of Douglas Dunn—*Terry Street* (1969)—is also sensitive, but so subdued, on a Larkinesque level, as to make minimal impact.

Of all the most recent arrivals on the poetry scene, the most impressive is Alasdair Maclean, a "late developer" who has found his own voice, a tone of quiet desperation which testifies to personal solitariness, in a largely inimical world, with an unstressed intensity far more moving than any song-and-dance. Combining a spare directness of style with the ability to make metaphors which are at once strikingly unusual and illuminatingly appropriate, Maclean expresses human agony in poem after poem which blow down all the wind-breaks that we raise between ourselves and the chilling gales of chance. Scarcely less impressive—and almost twenty years younger—is Rory Watson, whose work is as striking in the novelty of its technique as in the force of its impact; and Robert Tait and Colin Kirkwood have also written some highly individual pieces. Tom McGrath's verse is still "underground".

Among the writers of fiction, the most outstanding of the pre-war generation is Fred Urquhart, whose collected short stories, *The Dying Stallion* and *The Ploughing Match*, appeared in 1967 and 1968. The best of these are scarcely—if at all—inferior to the few fine examples of the art written by Lewis Grassic Gibbon in the early thirties. Together with Urquhart's first novel on an Edinburgh adolescence, *Time Will Knit*, the tales show him to be the most distinguished of Gibbon's disciples, perhaps the only one whose work will bear comparison with his master's in its comprehension of the Scottish community. Even at that, however, the achievement is notably uneven, oscillating between a near approach to the perfect and a close contact with the absurd. Moreover, this unevenness occurs throughout the whole of Urquhart's career, which spans three decades, from "The Heretic" in 1935 to "Weep No More, My Lady" in 1966. "The Heretic," a study of the religious pressures brought to bear on an individual trapped by his own weakness and by the customs of a closed society, is a masterpiece etched in acid, whereas a story near to it in time, "It Always Rains in Glasgow," written about the Empire Exhibition in 1938, is as cornily "coamic" as a music-hall sketch. In the sixties, again, "Weep No More, My Lady," an attempt to combine the supernatural with the satirical, is too clumsily pedestrian to succeed, but the equally-late "Provide for Your Poor Sisters" paints a picture of the downfall of an Edinburgh spinster in colours which are at once horrifying and hilarious, sympathetic and savage.

In the first of these two volumes, *The Dying Stallion*—which is rather less impressive as a whole than the other—the best piece is probably the title story, in which a sudden disaster falling upon a great horse is presented not only naturalistically but also symbolically, reflecting the powerlessness of the animal's ageing master to resist the views of the young. In the second volume, "The Ploughing Match" is extremely fine in its contrasts between past and present, in its presentation of the lack of understanding between different generations, and in its witness to the way in which the human mind can create a victory of sorts out of almost-total defeat. Some of the best stories are set in the Edinburgh of Urquhart's youth, but during the war he worked on the land, and his tales of rural life are no less piercing in their penetration into the nature of things, no less revealing in the light they throw upon the Scottish character. As far as range of characterisation is concerned, his most striking work is "Once a Schoolmissy," set in a Scottish village and showing a number of schoolma'ms or former schoolma'ms, who have taught for some time in London, trying to deal with an entirely different environment. This story, with its lesbian and other unladylike undertones, is a profound analysis of various kinds of failure and success and equally-various attitudes towards them. Although Urquhart's best work is within the narrow confines of the short story, his emotional scope is wide enough, and deep enough, to make room for an impressive expression of the complexities of human nature. He writes of the realities, the tragedies and triumphs of ordinary life in a local setting, and his sympathetic insight and his unobtrusive skill result in the best of the localised tales becoming works of general relevance.

That last sentence could also be written about George Mackay Brown's two volumes of short stories, *A Calendar of Love* (1967) and *A Time to Keep* (1969). But they also possess the quality which Edwin Muir found in Mackay Brown's first verse collection, *The Storm*—grace. This quality is extremely difficult to describe, but Mackay Brown appears to have no difficulty at all in expressing it. In "Celia," when one of the characters complains to the heroine about his loneliness, she replies—"gently," says the author—"Everyone is lonely. We're all prisoners. We must try to find a way to be pardoned." Yet the girl who speaks those words is no plaster saint but a compulsive alcoholic, drinking with any and every man who will bring her the only anodyne for what she feels to be the agony of existence. These stories are without the slightest trace of sentimentality, but they show the cruelty of life as being everywhere and anytime chastened by a charity of such loveliness as to seem more than mortal. Even in the most terrible of the tales, "Witch," the pitying merciful swiftness of the executioner redeems the legalistic cruelty of the heroine's accusers.

Although a Catholic, Mackay Brown's charity is much too wide for him to give it literary expression only in sectarian terms. In "The Eye of the Hurricane," where an old sea-captain drinks himself to death in despair, the person through whom grace shines is his poorly-educated maidservant, who rattles a tambourine with the Salvation Army; and in the title story of *A Time to Keep*, the hero (who tells the tale in the first person) remains an atheist throughout, and the charity which people show to one another in extremities is illustrated in wholly humanistic ways—through shared work between neighbours and shared sacrifice between man and woman, a sacrifice which becomes a blessing to them and to the community. For in almost all of these stories there is an underlying sense of communal activity, of the interaction of the comic and the tragic and the humdrum in everyday local affairs which at the same time have much more than simply local relevance. The scene is always in or around Orkney—a fact about which some critics have been unwise enough to complain, as if one were to protest that all the best Gauguins are "limited" to Tahiti— and the writer's intimate knowledge of his native place, past and present, gives him the freedom of all human nature, viewed with an unsentimental sympathy which arises from an inner conviction that while "we are poor people ... born to hunger and meikle hardship," we are equally all "princes, potentates, heirs and viceroys of a Kingdom."

While the quality of grace was present in Mackay Brown's work long before he became a Catholic, his religion has added a further dimension to his writing by providing his sympathetic apprecia- tion of his fellow-men with a firm philosophical base. Because of that sympathetic appreciation, there is not a single condemnatory note in either of these books, and scarcely even a suggestion of satire—except perhaps in a sketch of a modernist minister's ser- mon—and that laughter which puritans have denounced as resembling "the crackling of thorns under a pot" is presented with the same steady understanding as the impulse of generosity which makes an otherwise brutal Viking give his finest plunder to a comrade's tattered trull of a widow. In a style of shining simplicity, Mackay Brown provides fundamental insights into our common humanity. His stories are not only admirable, they are—in the highest sense—lovable; and yet they are as keen and sharp as the Orkney wind.

In contradistinction to Mackay Brown, his fellow-poet Iain Crichton Smith, in *Survival Without Error* (1970), his first collection of short stories in English—he had already published two volumes in Gaelic—is concerned less with community than with individual solitariness and the failure of understanding between different personalities. Whether he writes in terms of legend, as in his version of the scriptural story of Joseph, in terms of surrealist fable, as in "The Idiot and the Professor and Some Others," or in terms of the naturalist narrative, his characters are essentially alone, and ultimately they are defeated by the incomprehensible complexity of existence. In "The Exiles," an old Highlandwoman living on her own in a block of flats in the Lowlands finds herself, pitiably, trying to construct a relationship with a Pakistani door-to-door salesman; in "Je t'Aime," the characters who use the phrase are empty of the emotion; in "Murder Without Pain," a solitary schoolmaster nurses an obsessive hatred of a brilliant but unscrupulous pupil; and in "Goodbye John Summers" the narrator confesses his inability to decide upon the essential qualities of a lifelong friend. While Crichton Smith's style is direct and incisive, the ambiguity of experience is an essential theme of his work.

Another solitary is the central character of his first full-length fiction, *Consider the Lilies* (1968), which is less a novel—in the conventional sense—than an embodiment of folk-myth concerning the Highland Clearances. In Crichton Smith's imagination, it would seem, the Clearances happened to people like his grandparents, and it is only by means of assuming those grandparents' vision that he can bear to look upon the great disaster. Regarded in this light, the anachronisms in the work—early nineteenth-century Highlanders drinking tea, playing football, and wearing dungarees, etc., etc.—fall into place, and one can admire without reservation the perceptive portrait of the old woman through whose mind and emotions and memories Crichton Smith builds up his picture of a way of life trembling on the edge of catastrophe.

That indomitable endurance, that close integrity, that limited rectitude—this author knows them in the bone, in the marrow, and he can give them utterance with all the impelling power of inherited energy. He reveals the complexities of a character apparently simple, and he sets that seeming simplicity in scenes of archetypal magnitude—farewell to the son boarding the emigrant ship, defiance of the Duke of Sutherland's agent who seeks to pervert the old woman in her helplessness into becoming an accomplice of Authority. Yet Crichton Smith's method is limiting, for it divides characters into two separate categories, "Us" and "Them," and looks at "Them"—the Enemy, the Great Ones, the High-Heid-Yins—only from the outside. Scotland still awaits the emergence of a novelist with sufficient magnanimity to see the Clearances from the point of view of the clearers as well as the cleared. In Crichton Smith's second full-length prose work, *The Last Summer* (1969), as in his first, scene and action are both viewed through the eyes of the central character, this time a sensitive adolescent in his last year at school on the island of Lewis. The book is most evocatively written, but it is a fictionalised autobiography rather than a novel.

An adolescent hero is featured again in Gordon M. Williams's *From Scenes Like These* (1968), where fifteen-year-old Duncan Logan shows some talent for English and history but has those glimmers of an awakening imagination snuffed out by the ugliness of his environment, which offers him nothing but mean work and even meaner recreation. The book is a flaying indictment of the coarseness and brutality of proletarian life in the West of Scotland with its escapes from the harshness of humdrum toil into the false paradises of fornication, football and whisky. Although the novel's title derives from the Burns line, "From scenes like these old Scotia's grandeur springs"—which features in his most conscious expression of domestic and patriotic piety, "The Cottar's Saturday night"—the present work is neither domestic nor pious, and its patriotism is far too clear-sighted for comfort in its disenchanted view of those Scottish labourers whom Burns once celebrated as "hardy sons of rustic toil." In Williams's presentation of the contemporary scene, nothing remains of Presbyterian piety except individualism of the "I'm all right, Jack" variety, nothing of domesticity except a convenient respectable cloak for sex, and nothing of patriotism except the Rangers supporter's chauvinistic

hatred of Celtic. It may be that Williams's palette contains too
many gloomy blacks and lurid scarlets, but he applies his colours
with considerable vigour. His novel is one of the frankest expressions of the obscenities of lower-class conversation and the inti-
macies of sexual exploration among the young yet to find its way
into print, but its use of obscenities is always functional, always
expressive of the theme, the degraded nature of "scenes like these".
In holding the mirror up to nature, Williams has caught his
fellow-Scots with their trousers down, a human condition which
is more revealing than reprehensible.

Memories of a Scottish adolescence, this time in Edinburgh, also
lie behind Muriel Spark's *The Prime of Miss Jean Brodie* (1961), a
novel which is doubly witty, being both extremely brief and highly
humorous, while at the same time it is a deeply melancholy reflection of the inability of human beings to understand either themselves or others, set in a brilliantly-sketched particular scene and
period, Scotland's capital in the thirties, with unemployment rife
at home and fascism rampant abroad. For the most part of the
book, however, those matters are scarcely more than "noises off"
—as they were for the majority of the British middle-classes during the thirties—but it is one of the work's many ironies that in the
end the foreign political situation provides one of Miss Brodie's
pupils, who has grown up to become her rival in love, with the
opportunity of engineering her downfall. Miss Brodie is one of the
most hilariously comic creations in contemporary fiction, the
"progressive" spinster teacher whose conviction that she represents
"sweetness and light," as she passes on to her pupils her muddled
and shallow notions about the latest (or next-to-latest) views on art
and politics and psychology and religion, sends her blundering on
from fatuity to fatuity, sublimely unconscious of her own fundamental foolishness. But such is the subtle penetration of Mrs
Spark's art that she presents her heroine as a tragic figure too, as a
woman whose maternal instincts have been thwarted and twisted
by the times through which she has had to live, the death of her
lover in the 1914-18 war having doomed her to the spinsterhood
which compels her to find outlets for her feelings in a dominant
relationship with her pupils instead of the children she might have
had herself, and in chasing about after "ideas" as a substitute for a
satisfying love-relationship.

When one of her girls becomes a young woman, and both she

and Miss Brodie are involved with the art-master at their school, the green-eyed monster inevitably rears its ugly head, with the result that the pupil denounces the teacher to the headmistress—not, however, for having practised fornication but for having preached fascism—and thereby provides that dyed-in-the-wool conservative with an excuse for getting rid of the only adult female in the establishment who has been "liberal" in deed as well as word. Having contrived this brilliant irony, Mrs Spark caps it with another, even more telling, when Miss Brodie's denouncer grows up to become a nun and the author of a book on psychology and yet remains supremely unaware of the abominably unchristian nature of her act of betrayal and of her own motives in performing it. While *The Prime of Miss Jean Brodie* provides a remarkable evocation of Edinburgh in the thirties, it is not intended as an exercise in naturalism but as a tragi-comic parable on human folly, in Scotland's capital and everywhere.

Her upbringing north of the Border has also influenced Mrs Spark's *The Ballad of Peckham Rye* (1960), where she looses a Scottish devil-figure—derived from some such ballad as "The Demon Lover"—on an English suburb. Another devil-figure has the leading role in James Kennaway's *Some Gorgeous Accident* (1967), a brilliantly and horrifyingly implacable demonstration of the destructive force of egotism. In this superbly compelling work, the presentation of experience—however narrow—is flawlessly consistent, the plot has the remorseless inevitability of a nightmare where one knows one isn't going to wake up until *after* hitting the bottom of the precipice, and the characters act and talk with the unmistakable accent of life. One way of saying what the book is about—an oversimplification, but perhaps not unhelpful—is to describe it as a kind of Othello tragedy seen mostly from the point of view of Iago. This interpretation is given some authority by the central character's remark, just before committing himself to the decision which brings disaster upon the other man and the girl with whom he is involved, "I never understood this idiot Iago until now. Why didn't someone explain that the man knew he was a loser? Explain that villainy's pessimism, not much else?"

What makes the novel so appalling is that this central character, the all-too-symbolically surnamed Link, who cares only for himself, emerges unscathed while his victims, who have devotedly loved him as well as each other, are ruined by their devotion. But even more horrifying is Kennaway's destruction of the concept of human rationality, of the idea that men and women behave in accordance with the decisions of the intellect and the conscious will. All three of his principal characters are driven into action by emotional urges operating below the level of awareness, impulses of which they themselves remain ignorant but which the reader is made to realise immediately and continuously, through Kennaway's use of a technique which finely combines exposition, narrative, analysis and drama. Savagely witty, needle-sharp, surgeon-incisive, with an impeccable ear for dialogue and a skater's swiftness in zipping through narrative prose, Kennaway has written a study of the corrupting power of active evil which fascinates, cobra-like, from first page to last.

Although the devil-theme of *Some Gorgeous Accident* is quintessentially Scottish, the scene of the novel is London. When Kennaway turns to present-day Glasgow, as in the central chapters of his last novel, *The Cost of Living Like This* (1969), his lack of contact with the contemporary Scottish environment is all too evident, for the Glasgow characters are caricatures and the scenes of student revolt are borrowed (unconvincingly) from the south, where Kennaway resided throughout his all too brief literary career before his death in a car accident in 1968 robbed us of the most talented of all our younger novelists. Almost alone in his ability to present an accurate picture of the social scene in Scotland to-day—as distinct from memories of adolescence—is James Allan Ford. His *A Judge of Men* (1968) is a very nice study in ambiguities, beginning with the title itself—but since this novel is concerned with sex, perhaps it would be more appropriate to refer to its *double entendres*.

While the hero, Lord Falkland, a Senator of the College of Justice, is a judge by profession, and while he is characteristically Scottish in being by habit a somewhat censorious critic of his fellow-men, he is no judge of women—or at least, of the woman who is his wife. Unable to get away from Edinburgh for his usual winter holiday in Spain with his wife, an ex-actress and semi-invalid, Falkland gives vent to his frustration by denouncing sexual permissiveness from the bench while sentencing sexual offenders with all the rigour that the law permits. As a result, he achieves notoriety in the press and receives two lots of scurrilous anonymous letters, which have the effect of deepening his dislike of permissiveness into obsession, and the end is a fatal stroke when he seems to discover that allegations against his wife's behaviour before their marriage are true. But the novel is much more subtle than that brief outline of its plot, for the psychological impulses behind the characters' actions are revealed—or rather, hinted at—only in the course of the story's unfolding. With the judge, at once upright and obsessive, bound by firm standards and yet impelled by drives which are only partly understood, Ford has succeeded, despite formidable difficulty, in presenting a fine portrait in the round. Above all, he has splendidly presented the environment in which his characters are compelled to function, winter Edinburgh.

An attempt at a convincing presentation of life in contemporary Glasgow in Robin Jenkins's *A Very Scotch Affair* (1968) is spoiled by a melodramatic plot which clashes with the meanness of the characters. For his talent to achieve its full stature, Jenkins seems to require a wider stage than his native Scotland, as in *The Holy Tree* (1969), an incisive tragi-comic study of politics and people, faith and betrayal, in colonial Malaya, and in *Dust on the Paw* (1961), where the scene is Afghanistan. Here the atmosphere is highly persuasive—the alpine sunshine, the dust and the dirt, the peasants dignified in their old poverty and the westernised middle-classes desperate in their new, the idealism and the corruption, the blind fanaticism and the wary self-seeking, above all the sheer muddle out of which nevertheless some kind of pattern does seem to emerge as the various characters struggle "between two worlds, one dead, the other powerless to be born." Two characterisations are outstanding—the poet Harold Moffat, whose intellectual assent to the idea of racial equality is undermined by a deep-rooted emotional prejudice which compels him to deny motherhood to his Chinese wife because their children, inevitably, would be of mixed race; and Abdul Wahab, the Afghan whose engagement to an Englishwoman sparks off the action of the book. A patriot divided from his own people by his English university education, Wahab lives on a see-saw of ideas and emotions, one eye on his ideals and the other on the main chance, a man with all his qualities, noble and ignoble, forced into play by the precariousness of his position as a focal point of change in a society undergoing a revolution. No doubt Wahab's situation is one which a Scot, as inheritor of the notorious Caledonian antisyzygy—the conflict of differing qualities in the Scottish psyche—is particularly well-suited to investigate, but the powers of mature imagination revealed in this character-study, and throughout the book as a whole, have created a work which ranks high among western novels on the Asian scene; for it recalls Forster's *A Passage to India* in its unblinking awareness of the wide differences which divide the races of mankind, and also in its profound appreciation of the fundamental sympathies which unite us all.

By far the best of our comic novelists is Clifford Hanley who, after some twenty years in journalism, produced in 1958 his fantasticated autobiography *Dancing in the Streets* and followed it in 1961 with *A Taste of Too Much*, a novel about adolescence in and around Glasgow which is as true in feeling as it is funny. His most hilarious work to date is *The Hot Month* (1967), a deliciously devilish presentation of the wildest and most wicked of all Highland holidays. Fully to enjoy this continuously entertaining book, however, the reader must join the author in making an assumption of the highest improbability—that Scotland might enjoy a whole summer month of unbroken sunshine—and anyone unable to contemplate even the remotest possibility that such a miracle might occur may fail to appreciate the finer flights of Hanley's impish invention. His dead-pan humour is irresistible, and the present writer has laughed longer, and more often, at this one book than at the whole series of Sir Compton Mackenzie's celebrated Highland comedies. *The Hot Month*'s Highland holiday is also a vacation from the Presbyterian view that "sex is no joke," and its laughing liberalism is at the opposite pole from the sexlessness of most of the recent fiction about the Celtic scene. Unlike much of that fiction, again, Hanley deals with the present, and with people who might be ourselves—and that, of course, is dynamite.

Some of the most recent novelists have not yet published sufficient work to enable considered criticism to be made of it. Alan Sharp's best-selling panorama of sexual deviations in the west of Scotland and the south of England, *A Green Tree in Gedde* (1966), is grotesquely overwritten, and the only change in his second, *The Wind Shifts* (1967), is for the worse. William McIlvanney's *Remedy is None* (1966), an interesting variation on the *Hamlet* theme, has much more of the "feel" of the Scottish scene and of Scottish speech than Sharp, but the style of *A Gift from Nessus* (1968) is rather too mannered. In *The Dear Green*

Place (1966), Archie Hind has produced a powerful proletarian version of the autobiographical novel about an apprentice novelist's attempts to write, but he has yet to show himself capable of the inventive talent essential to the craft of fiction. But at least McIlvanney and Hind are still present in the Scottish landscape. Too many of our novelists, after producing studies of childhood and adolescence in their native environment, depart to fresh woods and pastures new and thereby deny themselves the opportunity of looking at the Scottish scene through more mature eyes and with the understanding which only residential experience can produce.

About the future it is hazardous to prophesy, for too much depends on political developments (or their absence). If Scotland remains, as at present, a province of the United Kingdom with slight opportunity for making its own voice heard, one can only anticipate increasing provincialisation, with the concomitant departure of a growing number of writers towards the metropolitan scene where, as they believe, "the action is". Yet the situation, at least in poetry, is not without its hopeful signs. Many of our poets who write in English have succeeded in giving it a Scottish colour, and even those who are in rebellion against Scottish traditions tend to seek their technical models in America and Middle Europe rather than tamely submitting to London styles. There is, too, a "resistance movement" of poets in Scots which continues, against all the odds, to attract disciples, and whatever the ultimate fate of Scots may be, it now seems unlikely that the literary tradition will be extinguished before the end of the century, as once appeared all too probable. The present writer, as a poet who is bilingual in Scots and English and whose themes derive both from Scotland and abroad, naturally would prefer the maintenance of an internationalism which is nevertheless firmly founded on the native rock. In this, he is fortunate enough to find himself in good company.

NOTES

1. David Craig, *Scottish Literature and the Scottish People,* London, Chatto & Windus (1961).
2. Robert Garioch, *Lines Review*, No. 27, p. 47.

3. Under his own name, Glen has recently published an ambitious autobiographical and imaginative sequence, *In Appearances* (1971).
4. *Catalyst*, Vol. 3, No. 1, p. 4.
5. Mr Scott has also recently published an important collection of poetry *Cantrips* (1968) [Editor].
6. John Press, *Rule and Energy* (1963).
7. Lindsay has now published a fine free-verse collection, *Comings and Goings* (1971).
8. *Akros*, Vol. 3, No. 9, p. 66.
9. Norman MacCraig and Alexander Scott, "Introduction", *Contemporary Scottish Verse* (1970).
10. Douglas Gifford, *Lines Review*, No. 31, p. 46.

THE VISUAL ARTS IN SCOTLAND
Cordelia Oliver

VISUAL AWARENESS IS hardly a national characteristic in the Scot. Why this should be so is hard to determine; why our forefathers, living among scenic excitements of a very high order, should have created villages and towns so drab and unlovely that succeeding generations of inhabitants are scarcely to be blamed for growing up blind to the quality, good or bad, of their environment. But on second thoughts, no! Their condoning of squalor— think of the ugly mess of everything from rusty bedsprings to empty gin bottles, that destroys or at least disfigures the natural beauty of so much of the west coast of Scotland and the Highlands—is really unforgiveable, whatever the provocation.

It is noticeable, however, that the less spectacular beauty of the east and south-east of Scotland has tended to give rise to comelier towns and villages, in which, moreover, what you might call the housekeeping leaves less to be desired. Is there perhaps a moral to be drawn? Are we, with our background of awful Calvinist oppression, still so guilt-ridden by beauty and its enjoyment that our misguided consciences drive us to destroy and obliterate it wherever we find it?

Is it to salve the vestigial remains of these once-powerful moral organs that we boast of our overriding concern with things of the mind (as though there were some special superiority in purely mental activity, of whatever quality and to whatever end) and continue to treat with arrogant contempt the pleasures of the senses, most particularly those which come and are communicated through the vision? What a blight Calvin spread over Scotland— from numberless dumb and private miseries of frustration and unfulfilment right down to the blind release of drunkenness (which distinguishes Saturday night in other places than Glasgow) and the hooliganism which makes the holiday Scotsman a byword for unruly behaviour.

For are we not, as a people (though I must admit that only for the purpose of my present argument am I supposing it possible to generalise about a nation so polyglot) far more warm and emotional beneath the crust than is often realised? The ease with which we have assimilated other races—the Italian, for instance, and the Jew, and much more recently the now familiar and rapidly acclimatising Pakistani, who soon become merely more exotic-looking, more decorative kinds of Scot—speaks, does it not, of an attitude of *laissez faire*, if not positive outgoing warmth in the native character.

But trained as we have been to be undemonstrative, to recoil from the casual endearment or public physical contact as though from an indecency, we reach a point, all too often, at which our emotional energy is dammed beyond endurance and must needs burst out in one direction or another. The easiest, most immediate release comes, obviously enough, from drowning all inhibition in alchohol—the quicker the better. And, after all, there may have been sound reasoning behind the old Scottish hour-long sermon with its weekly drama of hell-fire and damnation—a fierce purgation-by-proxy which, if it were powerful enough, might last out the week till the Sabbath drew round again. For that matter perhaps those who run our theatres might consider this possibility of a basic need for verbal scourging when choosing programmes to combat the public apathy which is their constant preoccupation nowadays.

Fortunately there are safety-valves more acceptable than drink, and more self-fulfilling than sitting under the minister. Much Scottish painting in the nineteenth and twentieth centuries has stemmed from such a need for an emotional, proto-sexual, release discovered in this safe area beyond corroding conscience. To be able to drown one's inhibitions in a beaker full of the warm south (or in the far more potent native distillation) allowable up to the eighteenth century when to finish the meal under the table was not inconsistent with the bearing of a gentleman, is unthinkable in polite society today. But to spark off one's banked emotional fires in a rich conflagration of coloured imaginings, controlled only through the painter's craft (and, incidentally, safely enclosed within a handsome frame, itself recognisable as furniture) was, and still is, a very different matter.

The artist in Scotland, provided always that he came part of the way to meet his public, has never been a pariah. The upper professional classes, and the rich merchants, shipowners, ironmasters and so forth, have always patronised him and, affording him a modest fortune in his own right, have tended to accept him more or less as one of themselves. Henry Raeburn was not alone in becoming a man of substance and standing, and Allan Ramsay was only the foremost among the cosmopolitan Scots painters who were as much at home in Rome and Florence as in Edinburgh. Even the "Glasgow Boys", those "young contemporaries" of their day, every bit as much agin the establishment as their counterparts in 1970, eventually succumbed to fame and the fleshpots with hardly a struggle. George Henry, whose "Galloway Landscape" must have appeared revolutionary in 1889 when it dominated its wall at the Glasgow Institute (and even, from this distance in time, seems like a finger pointing to an early Post-Impressionist development in Scotland) descended with unholy speed into the slough of fashionable portrait-painting in Chelsea. And John Lavery and James Guthrie—though the latter, at least, stayed in Scotland, and both retained more of their *panache* to the end—quickly found and "performed for" an audience; in other words discovered and went more than half-way to satisfy the public who were to reward them with a title and a modest fortune apiece.

I wonder sometimes if, for the good of his soul, the Scots artist of real calibre should not choose deliberately to remain as it were below the salt. However tempting it might seem, however pleasurable from a distance, the social round and its attendant political manoeuvring is not merely—as it is at any time for any artist worth the name—a serious waste of precious time and energy; it is a positive obstacle to his full development.

The trouble is that, in Scotland, the good artist's place need never be below the salt unless he himself determines that it shall be. By this same token of acceptance, however, he finds it impossible to be taken seriously as an individual deeply concerned, even obsessed with search and discovery, with pushing out the frontiers of visual knowledge and perception instead of comfortably consolidating his position at base.

Among those who, as our grandmothers might have chorused with Lady Bracknell, "dine with us, or at least come in the evening", the pressures to conform are well-nigh irresistible. The position of the well-respected painter or sculptor is rather like that of the modern constitutional monarch, rock solid so long as no cause for complaint is given. Which, while it may be—indeed must be—acceptable as the only alternative to dethroning, for the monarch, is a pretty tame and toothless state for those artists of real stature who ought to stand out among us like prophets, a constant disturbing element in a society that badly needs disturbing.

"The Eunuchs" was what David Halliwell's "little Malcolm" called those who manipulate the artist. But this, of course, was only a self-indulgent wish-fulfilment dream. It is the artist surely who suffers castration, albeit anaesthetised so thoroughly that he submits quite willingly to the emasculation. What I would like to see is the artist recover some real place in the everyday life of the community; a true grassroots position from which he might function in a less peripheral, less exotic role than at present. Do I hear a querulous chorus demanding how, for heaven's sake, I can equate my prophet of disturbance with this idea of the artist as it might be plumber, or plasterer, or whatever? Without any inconsistency I think I can do so.

In civilisations where the visual arts have flourished the giants have appeared as a matter of course from the fertile soil in which innumerable anonymous practitioners have been at work. And it seems to me that one of the most hopeful signs for the future of art in Scotland is that there are more and more young people who do see themselves fulfilling a function less rarefied, less forced-under-glass, than most of their elders. The difficulty will be to see that they get away with it despite the hidebound ideas and taste of the art-buying public, that minority which is so much more powerful than its size might suggest.

Artists, after all, must live, and short of a return to the barter system (and it may come to that in time) there must be people willing to underwrite their existence—so long as it is, however reluctantly, admitted that that existence is necessary. What is deplorable in influential circles in Scotland is a persistent lack of discrimination which makes a mockery of connoisseurship. Even those with some claim to knowledge and understanding of earlier periods are amazingly resistant on the one hand and gullible on the other when it comes to contemporary art. Indeed some of those very bodies who seem to me to have a duty to help the layman to an understanding of new art concepts; to be bridge-builders (that should appeal to the Scot) between layman and artist, seem instead to be conniving disgracefully at the latter's discomfiture. Glasgow presents some prime examples.

In the Art Club of Glasgow, that sorry shadow of what was once a power for good (it was from there, for instance, that pressure was put on Glasgow Corporation to purchase Whistler's "Carlyle", the first major public purchase of that painter's work; and on the University to confer on him an honorary degree—with the then undreamed-of result that the University of Glasgow would one day inherit the splendid Whistler Collection which makes it a main source for any student of the subject) the minor men-of-affairs, the lawyers, accountants, wealthy tradesmen and so forth, who pass for cognoscenti; who "know what they like" and mistake it for art; find more artists willing to make compromises than to stand their ground, and themselves be arbiters of taste.

The city's art gallery is the repository of one of the finest municipal collections in Britain, which grew, incidentally, by a series of remarkable gifts and bequests rather than through the foresight of its curators who have been, by and large, a race of timid pedants (T. J. Honeyman, the former Director, must be singled out as an exception—a true promotional zealot, and something of a successful gambler—even though one sometimes disagreed with him). The present purchasing policy—if indeed there is a policy—favours the "safe" and second-rate over almost everything vital and genuine in the work even of young Scottish painters and sculptors, whose work could be had for comparatively small sums. Even if only one in ten turned out a winner, the gamble would have been worthwhile. As a patron of significant contemporary art, Glasgow Art Gallery is almost non-existent. True, any body serving a committee of town councillors whose ignorance in art matters has become a byword might be thought more pitiable than blameworthy, were it not for their tell-tale lack of enterprise. Such men should, at the very least, be fighters!

And the Glasgow School of Art, which ought to be above all a dynamo, a very powerhouse of regeneration; how does it stand? As I write, I remember a recent exhibition in the School Museum—a one-man show by a senior student home from a visit to the Continent made on a travelling scholarship; a youth in whose talent and vision the authorities have great faith, to judge by the consequence given to his work. The paintings were clever and knowing, but as art they amounted to no more than a catchpenny amalgam of Impressionism and Seurat, ill-digested and scarcely, if at all, understood. It may be less than fair to blame the student in question (though I think he should realise in time the pitifully low target he has set himself) but those who encourage him in this dreadful misapplication of his talents are culpable beyond description.

In 1969, in the same school, the Diploma work in the Department of Sculpture showed, to any disinterested and exper-ienced visitor, signs of a rennaissance; signs that the students had begun to question, creatively, the value of the stale ideas they had until recently been fed; signs that they were at last rejecting the stereotypes expected of them. The failure rate was unusually high. The final assessment, it is true, was done by an outsider: but I wonder how many on the school staff questioned (do they ever?) the assessor's standards and prejudices on the students' behalf? As it happens, the time may well be ripe for the emer-gence, in Scotland, of a new school of sculpture. This century has produced only isolated figures of any stature—the names of Archibald Dawson, Benno Schotz, Tom Whalen, come to mind. But what Fred Bushe and Tam MacPhail, for example, have been doing with metal, creations rooted in a deep feeling for en-vironment, is very stimulating : and there are others.

Almost, one feels, Glasgow, in the past decade has been visited by a kind of death wish so far as the arts are concerned (music alone, perhaps, excepted). A city of around a million inhabitants—far more if you count the conurbation—which is able to support only one serious commercial art gallery is in a sorry state. There are, in fact, three small galleries—one of which, the Blythswood Gallery, originally intended as an act of private patronage, has always been run with too little discrimin-ation to be taken seriously—but only the Compass Gallery, under Cyril Gerber's direction, makes a continual effort to concern itself with promoting artists of standing and promise from Scotland and beyond. It is significant, I think, that this gallery owes its existence to one of those artists' self-help associations which alone, in Glasgow, seem to yield results. Early in the 'sixties a small group of painters—most notably Bet Low, John Taylor and Tom Macdonald—were so frustrated by the vacuum state in which they were forced to work that, in desperation, they set to and provided themselves and other like-minded artists with a "shop-window" in the New Charing Cross Gallery. This ran success-fully for several years until with the loss of its premises it was forced to close. But from its ashes rose the Compass, in West Regent Street, in a bigger and better gallery and with a more substantial grant from the Scottish Arts Council. The fact speaks for itself that, without too much compromise, the Compass Gallery commands an enthusiastic and gradually widening audience. "The Glasgow Group" is the one respectworthy major exhibiting group in the west of Scotland—one cannot count the massive Royal Glasgow Institute of the Fine Arts, nowadays more a poor man's Royal Academy than anything else; though the Civic Art Show, deplorably amateur in standard in the early days, might yet become a vital force if the present takeover by students and young professionals continues.

Things were not always so in the west. There was that notable flowering in the visual arts towards the end of last century; a movement to some extent sparked off by an impresario, an art pro-moter whose energy and determination made him a match for the great Scottish magnates of this expansive time, men like Burrell and Cargill, with growing fortunes and new, grand walls on which to hang pictures. Alexander Reid was this man of initiative and foresight and his claim to our attention is that instead of selling his clients whatever he thought they would like he set him-self the far more difficult task of educating them to like and to buy the pictures he thought they ought to have. Their descendants at least have been glad that, like the man in the Picasso Exhibi-tion (a hoary tale this, but with the ring of truth) who cried "Get me out of this, I'm beginning to enjoy it!", they succumbed and filled their homes with the work of the Barbizon School, the Maris brothers, Monticelli, and at a slightly later date the Impressionists —and all this during the final quarter of last century when such work was well in advance of British taste as a whole. Alexander

Reid (who will always be remembered, in any case, as the Scottish
art dealer who was painted by Van Gogh) was a phenomenon.
We must jump forward a century, almost, to discover his equal
in Richard Demarco : and fortunately the Demarco story is far
from finished.

For several reasons the "climate" is better in the east, not only in
Edinburgh, the headquarters of the principal exhibiting bodies,
but mainly there. Ten years ago, however, the situation for a
young non-conformist painter or sculptor was much the same in
Edinburgh as it is today in Glasgow. The Royal Scottish Academy,
concerned—as are all such organisations—with matters of prece-
dence and dignity, quite as much as with art, was nonetheless at a
peak moment in its history. A school, based on predominantly
colourist values, grew up around a small group of notable painters—Maxwell, Gillies and Mactaggart—two of whom are still in
full creative vigour. With these painters to dominate the exhibitions, and the younger Robin Philipson displaying every year a
greater and more striking virtuosity, the tone of the R.S.A. was set
for some time to come. It could even risk accepting Charles Pulsford (whom I have heard called the "father of the outsiders") as an
associate member, and hanging his vast, heavily-impastoed ab-
stractions. But Pulsford, like his more brilliant protegees, also
exiled himself, and has never been allowed to graduate to full
membership of the Academy. The "Edinburgh School" apart,
however, a fair cross-section of the better work being done in
Scotland could be found on the walls at the R.S.A. This, alas, is
no longer the case.

The Society of Scottish Artists, in effect a junior academy, was
also more or less dominated by the adherents of this school, and the
younger painters, like John Houston and Elizabeth Blackadder,
who were growing up in its tradition, but, in some ways, it seems to
me, struggling to free themselves. Not at all an easy thing to do
when the one effective commercial gallery, Aitken Dott's, by then
a veteran of over a century, set its face relentlessly against almost
every other kind of work. Aitken Dott, having educated its own
clientele in a colourist tradition, also—possibly without realising
it—encouraged them to resist other kinds of art. This is the way
most galleries work in London, for example, and it is both efficient
and influential in its effect. But for a healthy situation there ought

to exist more than one—preferably half a dozen—such centres of influence.

There is no doubt that this "Edinburgh School", admirable though it is—or was, for its force is almost spent—has been far too readily taken as a Scottish rather than an Edinburgh phenomenon. One has not far to look for contrary proof. Painters from Glasgow and the west—from Colquhoun and McBride in the 'forties, to William Crozier, John Knox, Carole Gibbons, Tom Macdonald, Margot Sandeman, Alan Fletcher (I could treble the list with ease)—could never have come out of the Edinburgh stable. Alan Davie, on the other hand, rebel though he has been, reveals his Edinburgh training with every brush-stroke. In an essay of this length one must generalise for convenience; but to me there is no doubt that the east-west axis which divides Scotland more fundamentally than any arbitrary north-and-south division, is reflected in its art. Edinburgh painters tend to remain essentially romantic in vision and more or less faithful to their traditional values of colourism and surface quality; while in the west draughtsmanship and a strong linear element predominate, along with colours less emotionally charged. No Edinburgh painter would be likely, as does Anda Paterson, to "draw" with paint, more or less disregarding colour as such, almost to the point where the work begins to look towards stylised sculpture.

An Edinburgh-orientation is not difficult to understand. The Scottish capital possesses what has come to be thought of as "charisma"—the kind of star quality which attracts. But Edinburgh sometimes lays claim to artists whose only real connection with her is the occasional exhibition. Joan Eardley was one of the most obvious examples, a painter with some claim to be considered the finest produced in this country in the first half of the century. Eardley (who was born in London) was a product of the Glasgow School of Art in the vintage years of the 'forties when circumstances combined to produce a climate of enlightenment not, I think, regained since. The small scale of an art school in wartime; the rare freedom to work all night (firewatching duties could be "arranged"); the comparative ease with which a rigorous curriculum could be made to accommodate different abilities and attitudes; all these were a bonus of the otherwise "difficult" times, but just as important was the longsighted and perceptive guidance of the head of the painting school, Hugh Adam Crawford, who had the gift—rare in teachers, more's the pity—of taking his best students past the stage of personal influence and remaining open-minded when they rejected his own values for others. (It is worth noting that a much more recent protege of Crawford's, when the latter was Principal of the Duncan of Jordanstoune College of Art at Dundee, was James Howie).

Joan Eardley, too, in her formative years—though fortunately after her own personality as an artist was more or less formed—came into the orbit of another influential teacher, James Cowie, Warden of Hospitalfield School of Art. Cowie sharpened the intellect and widened the vision of more than one of the older student painters and sculptors who spent a summer at Arbroath under his tuition. What he supplied was a sharp, invaluable dose of unaesthetic cerebration, almost of anti-art, to leaven the romantic colourism of Edinburgh, and the Glasgow tradition of draughtsmanship and way of painting that derived partly from Titian, partly from Piero della Francesco and Cezanne.

For a book whose title is *Whither Scotland?*, I may seem to have dwelled overlong on the near past and the dubious present. But the fact is that unless some of those in authority, in the schools of art and elsewhere, prove more willing than they seem at present to do some radical rethinking, the question "whither?" may be answered in a word: London. And that would be a disaster. For there is as great a pool of talent in Scotland now as in any time in the last thirty years, and almost for the first time in the history of Scottish art (not, after all, a very ancient one) there is contact as near continual as makes no difference between all parts of the country. Time was when Aberdeen, for example, seemed very much an outpost, in the intervals of exhibitions like the R.S.A. and the R.S.W., and when Dundee meant McIntosh Patrick and very little else. But the sudden expansion of the new College of Art at Dundee a few years ago put paid to the tendency, familiar in Scotland, to staff inbreeding, with results which are at least promising well. And Aberdeen may take the credit for being the first city in Scotland to appoint as Director of its municipal art gallery (an excellent one, for its size, with a carefully representative collection of the British, not merely Scottish Schools) a practising painter, Ian McKenzie Smith, still in his thirties, whose greatest asset, after his own proved talent, is an open mind.

The real resurgence, however, has been in Edinburgh, and it

has all happened in just over ten years. Since then the Scottish National Gallery of Modern Art has become a firmly established fact, under its discriminating keeper, Douglas Hall (enormously aided by the constant and informed interest of his Director of the National Galleries, David Baxandall). Since then, too, the Scottish Arts Council has become autonomous, with a greatly increased grant and a gallery in both Glasgow and Edinburgh. On the whole, however, its activities tend to be less adventurous than most artists of the younger generation would like to see. (On the other hand, no one who saw it will easily forget "Art and Movement", Bill Buchanan's splendid brainchild in his early days as Art Director, the first major exhibition in Britain of kinetic art, to which Takis, Soto, Camargo, Vasareley, Kramer and many others contributed).

But "official" galleries and organisations are one thing. Indigenous movements are more likely, in the end, to bear fruit. In Edinburgh several creative nuclei have formed in recent years, all having their source, I feel sure, in the annual "troubling of the waters" which comes with the Fringe. It is history now (but none the worse for retelling) that from a meeting in 1959 between Jim Haynes and Richard Demarco came such milestones as the Paperback Bookshop (with its cellar exhibitions as well as late-night poetry readings, philosophical discussions and so forth), the Traverse Theatre, and the Richard Demarco Gallery, which among them attracted, and sustained the spiritual hunger of most of the intellectual and creative non-conformists in town.

The latter has become, as its indefatigable Director has never doubted it would, a gallery which "put Edinburgh on the map as an art centre". For Demarco, as I have said, is of much the same type as Alexander Reid almost a century before him. He is a true impresario, full of initiative and a store of energy that leaves all his colleagues breathless in any attempt to hold him down, let alone keep up with his flights. His aim has been to foster a two-way system with other parts of the world, not excluding England but shortcircuiting London wherever possible. In other words to behave as though Scotland exists in her own right and not merely as a northern province of southern England. Demarco has many enemies among Scottish painters, arrived or hopeful of arriving and above all concerned with preserving the *status quo*: but fortunately his resilient temperament lets him not only recover straightaway from a setback (and he has had his share of those) but as it were twist in falling like a cat, and use the impact for a further leap. The gallery's influence has been incalculable, drawing as it does into its orbit the peripheral art forms of *avant garde* music and theatre, and providing the best chance we have in Scotland of experiencing, at first hand, new concepts in art which, in addition to our knowledge of the masterworks in the National Galleries, we must have if we are to form balanced judgements and extend our sensibilities to their fullest stretch. Edinburgh owes to Richard Demarco its chance—however unwillingly accepted in official quarters—of housing "Strategy—Get Arts" for the 1970 Festival; an extraordinarily stimulating show by contemporary Dusseldorf artists including the legendary Josef Beuys; the most advanced major exhibition for its time held in Scotland since "Art and Movement"; and before that, since 1939, the year of that other memorable show from Germany, held in Glasgow, of the "Decadent German Artists" proscribed by Hitler, including most of the great Expressionists.

The Richard Demarco story, then, is far from finished (it is unlikely that Pat Douthewaite, for example, would have developed as she has done without the R.D.G.), and one can only be glad that the mainspring of his ambition is to make his own country (though Italian by descent he is a third generation Scot) the centre of his activities.

Demarco's increasing success, and the range of his gallery's influence, however, must not blind us to the fact that there are other workings of the soil, less prominent, perhaps, but no less effective, in their way. The Print Workshop in Victoria Street, where anyone may go to work for a daily, weekly or annual fee, is run by experienced printmakers (again with a measure of Scottish Arts Council backing) on the excellent and well-tried master-and-apprentice principle of learning while on the job. Not far away a ceramic workshop, similarly conceived, is in process of being set up, where it is hoped that painters, sculptors and others, as well as trained potters, will bring fresh ideas to the use of the ceramic medium. These recent developments and the growing number of small galleries with their widely different aims and attitudes— even Aitken Dott, to the credit of its present director William Macaulay, is occasionally seen to be pushing out in directions which would not have been countenanced in the 'fifties—seem to me to point to a more hopeful prospect for the young Scottish artist than at any time since the second world war.

I have left to the last the gallery whose creation I always think of, rightly or wrongly, as marking, if it did not actually effect, the turn of the tide. In 1957 a young Edinburgh sculptor, Daphne Dyce Sharp, turned her studio in George Street into a gallery which could be rented for a nominal sum, and in the running of which artists themselves could join. The room was at the top of a steep stair and difficult to find. Nonetheless the need was so desperate that the 57 Gallery quickly became the first effective shop window for many of the most serious and promising, if nonconformist, talents available. Run with discrimination, by and large, by a committee of artists, the 57 Gallery (nowadays housed in more convenient premises at ground level in Rose Street) has continued its original policy of showing good work (or work which its committee believes to be good) in which modishness, that doubtful arbiter of worth, counts little. And as with Demarco, though on a much less ambitious scale, the work of local artists is seen in a context of serious art from England and beyond.

And, in the end, it all comes down to this. Art is something that some of us are driven to make—and more of us, perhaps, ought to recognise and succumb to the need instead of taking it out in bad dreams and violence. But art-makers have no divine right—though some of them would not agree—to subsidy, for no return. What I *am* prepared to defend, however, as a painter and as a critic, is their right to be taken seriously, on their own terms, artistically speaking. Enjoy their work or dislike it; buy or ignore it. But do the artists the simple justice of believing that what they do is done from conviction. And do not forget that time, as a rule, is on their side.

SCOTLAND : FULL CIRCLE
Hugh MacDiarmid

MORE THAN THIRTY years ago, in my autobiographical book *Lucky Poet*,[1] I wrote :

Having regard to the future of Civilization and the intensifying War and Fascism menace of this phase of the imminent collapse of Capitalist Society, and being passionately anxious to "pull our full weight" (as Scotland has hitherto failed to do in the work of world-revolution) in our native country where these issues come closest to us in an immediate practical sense, we are convinced that, just as Connolly said that in Ireland the social revolution would be incomplete without a national revolution too, so in Scotland here it is clear that the objectives of the social revolution can only be fully realised if it is accompanied by autonomy on a Communist basis. In this we are adverting to Keir Hardie's admonition that a much greater impetus would have been given to Socialism if Scottish Socialists had given priority in their programme to Scottish independence concurrently with the Irish Independence issue, and taking up again the great lead given by John Maclean which circumstances have so amply vindicated since, viz. (from his Gorbals Election Address, 1923): "Scotland's wisest policy is to declare for a Republic in Scotland, so that the youths of Scotland will not be forced out to die for England's markets. I accordingly stand out as a Scottish Republican candidate, feeling sure that if Scotland had to elect a Parliament to sit in Scotland it would vote for a Working Class Parliament. Such a Parliament would have to use the might of the workers to force the land and the means of production out of the grasp of the brutal few who control them, and place them at the full disposal of the community. The Social Revolution is possible sooner in Scotland than in

England. The working-class policy ought to be to break up the Empire to avert war and enable the workers to triumph in every country and colony. Scottish separation is part of the process of England's Imperial disintegration and is a help towards the ultimate triumph of the workers of the world. . . . Had the Labour men stayed in Glasgow and started a Scottish Parliament as did the genuine Irish in Dublin in 1918, England would have sat up and made concessions to Scotland just to keep her ramshackle Empire intact to bluff other countries. . . . Ireland will only get her Republic when Scotland gets hers." Further evidence of the correctness and unescapeable necessity of this line lies in the statistics of voting showing the persistent tremendous Radicalism (leading more than once to all-over Socialist majorities) of the Scottish electorate *vis-a-vis* the English, and the extent to which the progressive will of the majority of the Scottish people has been stultified by the English connection. A return now to this separatist and anti-Imperialist line (about which Scottish Socialism has always been so deplorably weak that these considerations have constituted a disastrous blind spot in the entire development of the working-class movement in Scotland) is in incontrovertible keeping with the present historical development in every other country.

Point is given to the closing sentences of that quotation when it is remembered that in the General Election of June 1970 the people of Scotland decided they wanted a Labour Government—they returned only 23 Tory M.Ps out of 71. The people of Scotland have nevertheless got a Tory Government—regardless of how they voted. Is there, as is frequently alleged, no fundamental difference, no absolute incompatibility, between the Scottish people and the English? The evidence is all to the contrary—and the gulf of difference is widening. A recent writer said it isn't surprising that so many people who have got used to this society resist deep analysis of its forms. The forms of accepted analysis, and the judgements that go with them, are part of the deep accommodation to an orthodox consciousness. This doesn't exclude the possibility of local amendment and dissent, which come through as a sort of pragmatic honesty. Superficially we have plenty of controversy, but much of it resembles what passes for controversy in politics. This last case has been particularly in evidence on television since the election was announced.

It can seem extraordinary that at a time like this, and with three available channels, there is virtually no political argument we can turn on and watch. But the absence is overlaid by a surfeit of its substitute: personal display and abuse by projected leaders; selected comparative arguments in a form that looks like but isn't statistics, at the margins of issues. What is not publicly argued is the basic structure of the society, and the possible policies within and beyond it. But then this is not a failure of technique, any more than it is what some people call the necessary vulgarity of the hustings. The limitation of real argument, and the careful production of apparent controversies, are not technical choices, but real ones. Indeed the form of what during this kind of election is called politics needs analysis in much the same way as a literary or dramatic form, which embodies experience in a very particular way, carrying its own values within and beyond the apparent action.

Wilson and Heath and the others are not limiting consciousness, for all the evident calculation of their appearances. On the contrary, they are limited by it, and could not, if they chose, move to real argument without also moving to a kind of political activity which would go so far beyond their accepted roles that not only the techniques but the issues would have changed. This is what I mean by accommodation. A man gets so used to certain limits and their certain emphases that he accepts a particular form of consciousness as natural consciousness, and then, on that conventional basis, develops what can be called a personality, even sometimes an individual position. Seen from outside, these particular differences are quite evidently variations on a common adjustment; but nothing leads to so much anger as trying to point this out. Indeed, when a limited common consciousness is being celebrated, as in this ritual of an election, any absolute dissenter is in at least temporary danger of losing the possibility of being understood at all.

That is one of the reasons why the Scottish National Party has such a record of expulsions and internecine quarrelling. Until now its leading personnel are all just Poujadists and Philistines, any member with an independent reputation, national or international, having been got rid of, and the "mind" of the Party having been purged of ideas until it represents only a revolt of the primitives against intelligence, and operates in a field prescribed by English politics, and with a membership which has had an exclusively English education and consequently little or no knowledge of Scottish literature or Scottish history—and thus with no basis for becoming nationalists in any real sense of the term. I will return to this point later, but first of all, in view of the overwhelming Labour vote of the Scottish electorate, I must point out that the "content" of this conforms to that retreat from socialism by which Social Democratic parties have always betrayed the workers, and directed their venom not so much against the enemies of the working-class as against the Communists. Despite the traditions of Scottish Labour, and the brief flaring of "Red Clydeside" (a term the City Fathers deplore and would fain see disused since, they contend, it is bad for trade and tourism!—a remarkable complaint in a world which is already half-Communist) the case with which I began this essay, taken from a book published over thirty years ago, has nowhere since been argued out.

There have been many books about modern Scottish arts and affairs (most of them utterly unknown to at least 90 per cent of the membership of the S.N.P.) but none of these get to grips with such basic problems. All of them, indeed, are very careful not to. It is worth-while therefore to consider the whole matter of intra-national relationships within the United Kingdom from this Marxist angle and bring up to date what I wrote on the subject thirty years ago. Only so can a book just published be profitably read. I refer to Michael Burn's *The Debatable Land: A Study of the Motives of Spies in Two Ages,* which deals with the English and Scottish agents who planned the *coup d'état* of 1560, which wrenched Scotland out of the hands of the French, and it then uncovers the network of spies and informers which the English Government used to destroy two subversive organisations within its own society, the Puritans and the Roman Catholics. It is important that Scots—especially members of the S.N.P.—should read it, and also another recent book, *The Scottish Insurrection of 1820* by P. Berresford Ellis and Seumas Mac a Ghobhainn, which deals with the frame-up by English agents of a bogus rebellion by Scottish radical groups resulting in judicial murders and the sending of other radicals to

Botany Bay. Can the leopard change his spots? If there is any real development of Scottish Separation, the same perversion of legal processes and the employment of *agents-provocateur* will certainly be employed. Yet even as I write a leading member of the S.N.P., hitherto loud in his denunciation of extremists and his belief that Scotland can get any worth-while measure of autonomy by constitutional means, has suddenly declared that "more serious methods must be used" and suggested that it is now clear that a militant policy should be pursued.

To subject the whole situation to a Marxist analysis, then, we must realise that with the triumph of the English bourgeois revolution in 1649 it became necessary to the English bourgeoisie: 1. To keep the working people in their place. 2. To consolidate the British Isles as a single English entity. An independent Scotland, Wales or Ireland, perhaps in alliance with a continental power, would be a threat to the peaceful growth of capitalism and the development of a British Empire.

To this second end, wars were waged, clearances undertaken, children punished severely for speaking Welsh or Gaelic, and the administration of the British Isles was centred in London.

In 1916, in the middle of an imperialist war, an uprising took place in Dublin. In October 1917, a Socialist revolution took place in Russia. The Dublin uprising and the subsequent war of independence proved that the British Isles were not immune from revolution. The Russian revolution showed that a revolution taking place near the heart of a great empire could be successful and that it could result in the downfall of the whole of that empire.

A certain amount of independence was granted to part of Ireland and the more repressive activities against Welsh and Gaelic were called off. Wales, Scotland and Ireland were left to rot in peace. This simple act of cutting down on repression served to reduce discontent in Ireland, Scotland and Wales to very small proportions. After the second world war came neo-colonialism. Britain discovered how to administer its former colonies in Asia, Africa and the Caribbean on the cheap and, through unequal exchange of commodities as well as the export of capital, to exploit them far more than before. The ruling class of Britain could afford to share some of its enormously increased loot with the rest of the population in order to avoid any form of social upheaval in Britain. For the working class of Britain this meant the "affluent society" and the "welfare state" which effectively destroyed the social base for any sizeable anti-imperialist, revolutionary working-class movement in Britain.

A new approach was adopted to the national question. Scotland, Wales and Cornwall became "development areas" where capitalists received handsome subsidies. Teachers were expected to learn Welsh and Gaelic, instead of being able to punish pupils who spoke these languages. However, the development of imperialism and the previous deliberate neglect of the Celtic areas had ensured that the highly profitable modern industries were centred in England and that commerce and administration were centred in South-East England. No "development area" subsidies could reverse this trend.

Culturally, the language revival came up against the drift from the economically backward Welsh and Gaelic-speaking areas and the growing influence of Anglo-American culture.

Despite the flow of loot, Britain ran into economic difficulties and it became necessary for imperialism to cut back superfluous expenditure. If oil is cheap, why keep mines going? Why run rail services or build roads to places where hardly anybody lives? In the "battle for productivity" between the big monopolies and the smaller local capitalists, the latter were bound to go to the wall. If their position was in an outlying area, they would not even be a good "take-over" prospect for a big monopoly. The net result is that more workers leave Scotland, Wales and Cornwall and the local market shrinks a bit more.

All this has happened, it should be repeated, without any of the loot from the neo-colonies drying up at all, and without England undertaking any repression of Scotland, Wales and Cornwall. The Celtic areas, like all regions with a lot of scenery and few inhabitants, fell back on tourism, the major European "industry". The Government imposed a Selective Employment Tax on non-productive industry, allegedly in order to boost production. Production is limited by the size of the market. So, in an imperialist economy, with increasing productivity and full employment, productive employment is bound to decrease and non-productive employment is bound to increase. S.E.T. cannot affect this general trend. S.E.T., however, helped the growth of

the national parties of Scotland, Wales and Cornwall, by caus-
ing discontent among the local petite-bourgeoisie.

The myth is being spread that the national parties are violent
separatists. (Notably the article by the Glasgow Communist
Movement (part of the Communist Federation of Britain (M-L))
in issue No. 12 of *The Marxist*. How "Glasgow" this body is
when it refers to the S.N.P. as the Scottish *Nationalist* Party
and misinterprets its programme I would leave to readers to
judge.) Nothing could be further from the truth.

No independent customs or foreign policy is envisaged by the
national parties and only tiny armed forces. England is to be
responsible for "defence", i.e. the neo-colonial police force from
which the whole of Britain benefits. The only difference is that
Scotland, Wales and Cornwall will save their share of the taxes
and spend them on making life better at home. National parliaments are envisaged.

Watered-down versions of these programmes are shared by
the Liberal Party and the Communist Party of Great Britain.
The Glasgow Communist Movement also says that "as an
interim measure, the establishment of regional administrative
bodies should be demanded" and "further development of
regional cultures is a necessary step".

There is indeed a remarkable degree of agreement about
separation for Scotland, Wales and Cornwall. The bourgeois
parties may say "economic nonsense", the left may stand for
"proletarian internationalism", but they are all against separatism. The fact that the various trends of bourgeois opinion,
left, right and "national", are against separatism, does not, of
course, mean that it should be supported without further investigation. This further investigation entails an assessment of the
crisis which is likely to lead to revolution in Britain. Are the
contradictions likely to sharpen first at the centre, or first in the
outlying regions?

If the contradictions are likely to sharpen first at the centre,
leading to the dictatorship of the proletariat spreading outwards
into the regions, it would be incorrect to support separatism as
this would provide the justification for establishment of a bourgeois regime in, say, Wales, instead of the dictatorship of the
proletariat for the whole of Britain. If, on the other hand, the
contradictions are likely to sharpen first in Wales, is Wales

meant to wait until the rest of Britain is ready? This is what would be entailed by the phrase "national aspirations for independence can only be satisfied after the replacement of the present system by a socialist one through unified struggle against the common enemy constituting a single class".

We cannot see as far ahead as this, so we are forced to look at the actual situation now. And this situation is that, despite all the futile assistance given to Scotland, Wales and Cornwall, the functioning of imperialism is creating more difficulties for these regions than it is for London and the rest of England.

While this situation continues, it is necessary for Marxist-Leninists in England to counter English sectarian chauvinist opposition to the demands of the national parties and organisations even though, as we have seen, they are in essence merely economic demands. Marxist-Leninists surely cannot oppose economic struggles, whether they involve a workers' strike or con-tracting Wales out of paying its due share of British imperialist taxation.

People in England must face the fact that separate, non-English Marxist-Leninist parties and organisations will be set up in Scotland, Wales and Cornwall because the workers of these areas are facing problems which English self-styled Marxist-Leninists are showing themselves completely unable to appreciate. For example, unemployment, depopulation, low wages, the fight for the Welsh and Gaelic languages, etc.

If, as seems likely on present reckoning, the contradictions continue to sharpen more rapidly in Scotland, Wales and Cornwall these parties and organisations will be able to lead the struggle in those areas in a way which no English-dominated party could do. Mere support for national independence is not sufficient for Marxist-Leninists working in Scotland, Wales and Cornwall since it would entail tailing along behind the radical national elements.

It is essential to speak up for a separatist movement under working-class leadership. It is even more important to raise the question of breaking the imperialist relationship between, say, Wales and Asia, Africa and the Caribbean which at present benefits Wales, including the Welsh working class. They must show how a break with imperialist relationships will bring new life to mining and agriculture by removing cut-price competition from abroad.

The end of imperialism will necessitate a vast expansion of industry, as a few manufactured goods will no longer be able to purchase vast quantities of food and raw materials from abroad. With the establishment of more industries in Wales and Scotland and the lack of opportunity to make an easy living in the parasitic South-East of England, there will be no need for people to leave the Welsh and Gaelic speaking areas. The ending of imperialism is the only way in which the Welsh and Gaelic languages can be saved and developed as part of a general economic and cultural revival of the depopulated areas of the British Isles.

As regards the future, there are two possibilities. One is that the British working class, "the oldest and most advanced working class in the world", to quote the Communist Party of Britain (Marxist-Leninist), will achieve socialism before imperialism has been smashed. This view is also held by trotskyists, revisionists, the S.P.G.B., etc.

The other view is that, before there can be socialism in Britain, imperialism must be smashed in Asia, Africa and Latin America. This is the view of Lin Piao and of people who apply Mao Tse-tung's thought to the concrete situation.

If one agrees with the second viewpoint, one must also see that, at present, the smashing of imperialism is a gradual affair, practically completed in China but hardly commenced in Africa and the Middle East. The drying up of the imperial loot will also be a very gradual affair, facing the British government with the need to cut back on "unnecessary" expenditure every so often. The grants to the under-developed areas of Britain have a high degree of priority for cutting back. One has only to read Enoch Powell to see where the pressure is going to come from.

It is surely the duty of Marxists to ensure that, when the cut-back takes place, it is met with a correctly-led resistance. Such leadership can only be given by Marxist-Leninists who are integrated with the working classes of Scotland, Wales and Cornwall and who are not held back by organisational ties with English-dominated organisations.

The best statement of the position brought about by the recent General Election and the consequent outlook for Scotland appeared not in any of the national newspapers but, as one would expect, in a too little known but very lively and well-informed roneo'd publication, *Sgian Dubh*, in which the editor, the indefatigable Major F.A.C. Boothby, sums up the state of affairs now as follows:

The Liberals were slaughtered. A few survivors linger among the Scottish hills. We are not concerned with whether they can revive in England, but in this country we see them as being effectively dead. In past years they survived on the pretence that the Scottish public preferred their theories to those of the S.N.P. That contention has now been disproved. Therefore they have little or nothing to stand on. George Mackie has been eliminated from a public scene which he did nothing to decorate. Russell Johnston survives, but cannot claim to be a survivor alongside Jo Grimond and David Steel because the two latter are not interested in his sayings, comings and goings. Therefore we have Grimond and Steel as two men who can and must play a major part in politics during the coming parliament.

The Socialists are in an amusing predicament. Dedicated Centralists, they are cornered in Scotland, where they remain with their strength unimpaired, but divested of all power by the English Tories. We understand that their Mr Willie Marshall said recently that he would rather serve under a Tory Government in England than under a Scottish Government in Scotland (or words to that effect). So he at least is happy; but we wonder if the others are. It will be interesting to see how the others react when they come out of their state of shock.

The Tories are merry as pigs in snow. They think that they have got it all their own way. One in Lanark (name of Hume) when questioned about the proposed Scottish Convention, remarked "Oh, we'll never have *THAT*". He won't be the only one. There can be no doubt that many of the stupider and weaker Nationalists swallowed the bait, or used it as an escape from the moral obligation to do a spot of work during the (1970) General Election.

But the fact remains that the proposals are put forward in black and white in the manifesto of the Scottish Tory Party. Whatever the Tories may hope, these specific proposals will not be forgotten.

The Scottish National Party had hoped to win about four seats, and to clock up half a million votes. They got 300,000 votes and what they did achieve in the person of Donald Stewart was the first Nationalist ever to be elected in a General Election. Donald Stewart's name will live in history. The Party did very well in a number of constituencies, and they have nothing whatever to be ashamed of. If you sit down to play poker with a man who you know already has all the aces up his sleeve, you are either a fool or a hero, or perhaps a bit of both.

The election was shamelessly gerrymandered, and even after the election the S.N.P. candidates' names were almost invariably placed at the bottom of the lists of candidates, regardless of the number of votes obtained.

Very many people will have noted with pleasure and relief that the mass support for the Party has shifted from Glasgow to the North. One of the things that has kept many people from supporting the S.N.P. has been the fear of the Dictatorship of the Glasgow Proletariat.

Now there is the possibility of establishing a new centre of power from which may come men and women with whom it is possible to hold a debate, or even have a quarrel, without being bundled out of the Party neck and crop. The Northerners owe it to Scotland to establish themselves in a manner and in an organisation which cannot be tampered with by the keelies.

Other parties will be encouraged by this development to make contact and to discover grounds of common interest, to the great benefit of the National Movement.

It is very probable that the S.N.P. can now look forward to a number of by-election victories. The public has seen their potential, and already people are saying "If only I had realised . . ." This election must have cost the Party much money. It is to be hoped that they can recoup their finances without having to dismiss important personnel without whose dedicated labours the Party would have been stumbling about in the dark.

And finally to Mrs Winifred Ewing; no feelings of friendship for either your Editor (of *Sgian Dubh*) or for the 1320 Club were ever displayed by her. In fact she went out of her way to damage both. We do not know why. Now she has fallen. She fought most gallantly, in 1967 and in the election just past. Her going was dignified, after a most heroic fight. Whatever may come about in the future, her name has its place in Scottish history. We wish her well, and we hope to see her take her due and honoured place in Scotland's parliament.

The presidential election was remarkable only for its squalor and the total lack of distinction of the adversaries. By what may well have been mutual agreement, Scotland and Wales and their problems were kept completely out of the arena and the only subjects mentioned were calculated to appeal to fear and to greed.

Having been summoned to Buckingham Palace by the Queen of England, the mountebank appeared upon the steps of No. 10 Downing Street to make a speech. This was without precedent and was probably calculated to humiliate his opponent. Almost immediately the fellow started to bleat about "one nation".

And who the hell does he think he is? Let him know that, for hundreds of years better men than he have been trying to bring this situation about by force of arms, by bribery and now, in this case, by germanic arrogance and ignorance.

Celts have long memories. The English may forget the carrot dangled before the noses of the Scots, but we never shall, and unless we get that Scottish Convention backed by both Heath and his Secretary of State-designate, the future of the Tories in this country will be desolate indeed and it will be more than electoral eggs that the man will have to look forward to.

I agree with all Major Boothby says in the above article, and it will be clear from that what my answer is to the question: "Whither Scotland?" Briefly, it is still, as it was forty years ago— back to the John Maclean line of Scottish Separatism, Republicanism and anti-Imperialism! I have good cause to know that the bulk of the Scottish Electorate are sick of the London-based parties, and that our ever-increasing Scottish national consciousness goes far beyond the mediocre "ideas" of the S.N.P. and is clearly headed now to make good a prophecy voiced in 1940 and quoted in my *Golden Treasury of Scottish Poetry*:

To find a parallel to present world conditions it is necessary to go back to that great period of the fifteenth to seventeenth centuries commonly known as the Renaissance-Reformation period. The parallels are so close that they can easily be pursued dangerously—history does repeat itself in a measure but never as a whole. Yet the conditions out of which that revolution arose were strikingly similar to the present ones. The Scotland of those centuries participated in those great events and was moved to its core . . . which reversed the whole direction of Scottish purpose. Scotland moved into England's orbit, turned her back on Europe, threw her whole energies into the creation of England's empire. Today we stand at another like point in Scottish history, and it is more than likely that once again Scotland will reverse her course. This time she will return in large measure to her ancient policies. She will become more and more Scotland—but she will also resume her place as a European nation, contributing to and drawing upon the great stream of European thought and action.

The shallowness of the "literature", and of the content of the speeches of its leaders, of the Scottish National Party is incredible. The intellectual traditions of Scotland have evidently gone completely by the board. Nevertheless there have been some excellent books, based on exhaustive first-hand research, but it is questionable whether they have been read by more than a tiny percentage of the membership of the S.N.P. and certainly their findings have not been reflected at all in the deliberations and propaganda of the Party, which, like nearly all the other participants in the Scottish scene, manifest only a hopeless preference for the inferior.

The rectification of long-standing errors in Scottish history, the making-good by thorough research of the gaps purposely left in that chequered story because the truth would never fit in with the official story, and the provision at long last of essential statistics regarding many aspects of Scottish affairs hitherto carefully kept secret by the authorities (though there are still many *lacunae* to be filled)—all these are sufficient proof of a fundamental change in Scottish life. It is a cheap gambit of unthinking people—or stubbornly pro-English Quislings—to sneer at the term "Scottish Renaissance " and deny that anything of the kind has occurred. It is a different story, however, when we turn to those qualified to judge.

In the introduction to *The Penguin Book of Scottish Verse*,[2] Dr Tom Scott—the editor—says:

> The first result of the Union of the Crowns was to associate Scotland with English foreign policy, weakening the ties with Europe, reducing Scotland to a province of England. The story of Scottish literature from here on is largely a story of provincialisation and the struggle against it. The poetry of the European-educated makar is swept away and replaced by the poetry of the provincial petty laird—as amateur as the makars were professional. . . . After Burns, the deluge—of slop and twaddle and couthy kailyairdy rubbish. . . . The position was indeed grim, the efforts to revive the dying tradition seemingly hopeless, when in 1925 . . . the revival of the great tradition of Scottish poetry, dormant since the age of the makars (i.e. of the fifteenth and sixteenth centuries) had begun . . . scouring Scots verse of sentimentality, couthiness, kailyairdism, all manner of petty-mindedness and false-heartedness, above all in re-intellectualizing it, raising it to a height and intensity of sheer thinking unequalled anywhere else in Scots . . .

The problem is whether a like spirit can be kindled in politics and other departments of Scottish life. There are many other testimonies to what has happened in the field of Scottish literature in the past half century. Professors M. L. Rosenthal, John C. Weston and David Daiches, and Messrs Maurice Lindsay, George Bruce, Duncan Glen, David Craig, Kenneth Buthlay and Alexander Scott have in their various books concurred in showing that nothing short of the miraculous has been achieved in this connection. The question is: if in this connection, why not in other connections too. But that may be on the way. Until recently little or no Scottish literature or history was taught in our schools or colleges and then only as inferior sub-departments of English literature and history. A lapse into Scots speech in the schools was punished, and the cultivation of "standard English" insisted on. That situation is rapidly changing today. "Lapses" into the "dialect" are not only tolerated but approved in the class-rooms, and there is a growing accommodation in the curricula for the teaching of Scottish literature and history—albeit the majority of the teachers are themselves too Anglicised to do these subjects justice instead of merely adhering to the official (English) versions. But though there is no Chair of Scottish Literature yet in any of our universities, there are in all of them now (a quite recent development) lecturers on the subject, and in several it is possible to graduate either in the ordinary or honours degree in the subject, and a steadily increasing number of students are doing so. This is a very remarkable development after centuries of neglect and repression, and points unmistakeably to deep currents in Scottish life today which may well in the near future throw up commensurate phenomena, well deserving the adjective "miraculous", in all the other departments of Scottish arts and affairs.

When this process has fully developed, there will indeed have been a Scottish Renaissance. So far the process has only been in the fields of literature and scholarship where such developments almost invariably begin. But it is a poor outlook for the great majority of so-called Nationalists if they cannot take advantage of such beginnings, and imagine that they can truly be Scottish Nationalists without getting rid of the over-influence upon them of an overwhelmingly English education and a consequent inability to think or act except within the scope of English ideas and institutions. It is impossible to be Scottish Nationalist in politics but not in all the other aspects of life. As the great Italian Marxist thinker, Antonio Gramsci, put it :

> Self-knowledge and knowledge of one's historical rights and duties do not come spontaneously, but by intelligent reflection, first by a few and then by the whole class, on why certain conditions exist and how best to convert the facts of vassalage into the signals of rebellion and social reconstruction. In short, every revolution has been preceded by hard critical thinking, the diffusion of culture, and the spread of ideas among men who are at first unwilling to listen, men concerned only with solving their own private economic and political problems, men who feel no solidarity with others in the same condition.

The best thing—indeed, the absolutely indispensable requirement now—is that the leaders of the S.N.P. should do their best to bring some minimal measure of Nationalist sophistication to their members (and indeed acquire that themselves!) and at the same time work, as an absolute priority, to improve their own intellectual foundations. They may then be able to read and profit by such books (at present far over the heads of all but a tiny fraction of the S.N.P. membership) as Professor H. J. Hanham's *Scottish Nationalism, Government and Nationalism in Scotland,* an enquiry by members of the University of Edinburgh edited by Professor J. N. Wolfe, *The Democratic Intellect by* Dr G. E. Davie, *The Future of the Highlands,* edited by Derick S. Thomson and Ian Grimble. They may then be able to put in their proper slot and avoid such books as T. C. Smout's *A History of the Scottish People 1560-1830* and Rosealind Mitchison's *History of Scotland,* which are evidence that the pro-English are sufficiently seized of the reality of the Scottish Movement and are fighting back as well as they can.

The escalation of the S.N.P. is less surprising than that it did not take place much sooner and involve not a hundred thousand or so but the whole of the Scottish people. How set against the alleged intense patriotism of the Scot can this acquiescence in English misgovernment be explained? Lord Boyd Orr of Brechin in his prefatory note to Oliver Brown's pamphlet *Scotland the Satellite* said :

> Mr Oliver Brown has made this collection of extracts from *Hansard* and other sources to show that Parliament has little interest in Scotland. Sufficient time is not allocated for the discussion of Scottish affairs and when they are discussed some English members seem to regard them with ill-concealed contempt and as a subject for jokes.

The Daily Herald, speaking of the "cheap gibes and sniggering of English members", said : "They seemed to regard the discussion of any Scottish topic as essentially funny in itself." The ignorance of English M.P.s is such that it is inevitable that the pages of *Hansard* should be spattered with such ingenuousnesses as Commander Locker-Lampson's query in the Commons, "Is not Scotland English?" and with instances like the following. Asked at a Press Conference at Dalmuir Ordnance Factory why trenching tools made there bear a makers' plate with the inscription "Made in England", Mr J. H. Jones, Joint Parliamentary Secretary to the Minister of Supply, replied magnanimously : "Oh, I don't think we have reached the point where England does not mean Scotland too!"

Similar, and worse, expressions of contempt and even hatred of the Scottish people by English speakers and writers are legion. While I am a confessed Anglophobe in the sense that I wish to free Scotland from any over-influence of England on Scottish affairs and reacquire an entirely separate and sovereign independent Scotland, it would be impossible to parallel these English expressions of contempt by any like expressions of hatred of the English (as distinct from English policy) from the voices or pens of Scots. The English policy has always been one of a determination by hook or more often crook to assimilate Scottish institutions to English standards. There has never been any attempt to assimilate English institutions to Scottish. It would be a great mistake to imagine that the ups-and-downs of voting in either parliamentary or municipal elections mean that there is a like fluctuation in the desire of the vast majority of our people for control of their own affairs and resources through an independent Scottish Parliament. The defeat of Mrs Winifred Ewing at Hamilton in the 1970 election was widely hailed as proof that the Scottish cause had passed its peak. But here as usual the wish was father to the thought, and the success of Mr Donald Stewart in capturing the Western Isles for the S.N.P. more than corrected the balance. Fighting for the first time on a nation-wide scale, with candidates in 65 of the 71 constituencies, the S.N.P. achieved 11.4 per cent of the votes cast in Scotland or 12.2 per cent of the votes in the 65 constituencies contested. At 12.2 per cent, the average poll was slightly down on the 14.3 per cent achieved in the 23 constituencies contested in 1966. Nevertheless, in the 22 constituencies fought on both occasions the vote remained at the same level as before. So the lower average is a consequence of the greater number of contests rather than as a result of declining fortunes in previously contested seats. The S.N.P. candidates saved 22 deposits, as against 13 in 1966. Nine second places were achieved, compared with three last time round. Disappointing as was Mrs Ewing's defeat at Hamilton, the 16,849 votes she secured represented 92 per cent of her winning total in 1967. Altogether the S.N.P. polled well over 300,000 votes, so, as the *Scots Independent* said after the declaration of the results, "the little relevance of the General Election to Scotland was summed up by the *Daily Telegraph* which told us Labour had lost because of their 'traditional policy of bashing the successful and rewarding the parasites and dropouts', and that Mr Heath must 'push ahead with preparing his long-term remedies for the English sickness' ".

The development of Schools of Scottish Studies in Canadian and American universities, and the great amount of research studies into aspects of Scottish Literature and History in these and also in several European countries is beginning to have repercussions here in Scotland itself. It is realised that a new image of Scotland is being projected and that foreigners are increasingly becoming aware that Scotland is not part of England but a separate country, with a voice of its own very different indeed from any that emanates from South of the Border. The whole situation has changed—and will change a great deal further in the near future—as the new-found education in Scottish Literature proceeds apace and engenders an altogether different spirit from England's. This is largely also an inevitable consequence of the decline of England from being the controlling centre of a vast Empire to fifth or sixth-rate status, and in England's decline comes Scotland's opportunity, since Scotland has nothing whatever to thank England for, and the theme song of the new Scotland may well be :

> Me that 'ave been what I've been
> Me that 'ave gone where I've gone
> Me that 'ave seen what I've seen
> 'Ow can I ever take on
> With awful old England again?
>
> I will arise and get 'ence—
> I will trek South and make sure
> If it's only my fancy or not
> That the sunshine of England is pale
> And the breezes of England are stale
> And there's something gone small with the lot !

NOTES

1. Methuen, 1943.
2. Penguin Books, 1970.

NOTES ON CONTRIBUTORS

TOM BONE, Head of the Department of Education in Jordan-hill College, the biggest college of education in Britain, has been involved in teacher training for nine years, in the University of Glasgow Education Department and in Jordanhill College, and previously taught in a Scottish grammar school for five years. He holds the degrees of M.A., M.Ed., and Ph.D., and is the author of one book on the history of Scottish Education and the editor of another. He has contributed extensively to journals of education in Scotland, and has had experience of lecturing and visiting schools, colleges and universities in U.S.A., Canada and Australia.

GEORGE MACKAY BROWN has always lived in Orkney. His publications include *The Storm* (poems) (1954), *Loaves and Fishes* (poems) (1959), *The Year of the Whale* (poems) (1965), *A Calendar of Love* (stories) (1967), *A Time to Keep* (stories) (1969), *An Orkney Tapestry* (essays) (1969), *A Spell for Green Corn* (play) (1970), *Fishermen with Ploughs* (poems) (1971), *Poems New and Selected* (1971). He has recently finished a novel and is working on stories and poems.

NORMAN BUCHAN. Born, 1922, in Sutherlandshire and brought up in Orkney. Educated at Glasgow University (Eng. Lit.). Teacher and lecturer. Contributor to various educational, cultural and political journals—*Tribune, New Statesman*, etc. Editor of *101 Scottish Songs* (Collins). M.P. for West Renfrew since 1964. Under-Secretary of State for Scotland 1967-70. He is now a shadow spokesman on Scottish affairs. At present working with Peter Hall on a book of Scottish folk songs.

DUNCAN GLEN was born in Cambuslang, Lanarkshire, in 1933. He has worked both as a typographic designer and as a publisher's editor and is now director of Akros Publications and editor of the Scottish literary magazine *Akros*. He is the author of *Hugh MacDiarmid and the Scottish Renaissance, A Small Press and Hugh*

MacDiarmid and *The Individual and the Twentieth-Century Scottish Literary Tradition*. He has also published five books of poetry including the recent *In Appearances* and has edited *Poems Addressed to Hugh MacDiarmid, Selected Essays of Hugh Mac-Diarmid, The Arkos Anthology of Scottish Poetry 1965-70* and *Hugh MacDiarmid. A Critical Survey*. He is a Senior Lecturer in the School of Art, Harris College, Preston.

MICHAEL GRIEVE, 38, former Fleet Street journalist, outspoken political commentator and TV performer, has believed in Scottish independence "since the moment of conception". Married, with two sons, he has been in jail and has stood as an S.N.P. Parliamentary candidate in the cause of freedom. A socialist in the I.L.P. tradition he believes, above all, in the preservation of the individual as opposed to the "mass man" of so many religious, political and social movements.

ANDREW HARGRAVE. At present Scottish Correspondent of the *Financial Times*. Has lived and worked in Scotland since 1952, mostly as a political, economic and industrialist journalist and broadcaster : was on the staff of the *Scottish Daily Mail* (now gone); *Daily Record*, the *Bulletin* (also gone) and *Scottish Daily Express*. Also worked for the Scottish Council (Development and Industry). Wrote two Fabian pamphlets on devolution. He represented the West of Scotland on the National Executive Council of the National Union of Journalists.

JOHN HERDMAN was born in Edinburgh in 1941, educated there and at Magdalene College, Cambridge, where he read English, graduating in 1963. He led a peripatetic existence in Scotland and abroad until 1966, then returned to Cambridge to do a year's research work on the Scottish novel; since 1967 he has lived in Edinburgh. He is the author of a short prose work *Descent*, published in 1968, and of two unpublished novels. He edited two numbers of the magazine *Catalyst* in 1970, and has published critical work in *Akros* and elsewhere.

HUGH MACDIARMID (real name Christopher Murray Grieve) was born 1892 at Langholm in Dumfriesshire. Worked as a journalist in Fife, Angus, South Wales, London, and Dunbartonshire.

Served in 1914-18 war in Salonika, Italy and France in Royal Army Medical Corps and Indian Medical Service. Initiated Scottish Renaissance Movement in early twenties. Helped found and took active part in development of Scottish Nationalist movement. Has travelled a great deal in recent years in Russia, China, Hungary, Bulgaria, East Germany, Czechoslovakia, Eire, Sweden, Canada, and United States, and lectured and broadcast in these and other countries. Translations of his poems have been done in French, Magyar, Swedish, Spanish, Italian, Israeli, Chinese and Vietnamese. Hugh MacDiarmid has published over eighty books and pamphlets of poetry and prose, in addition to contributions to many multi-author books and many introductions. Awarded Civil List Pension for his services to Scottish Literature; other awards include Hon. LL.D. (Edinburgh University); member of Speculative Society of Edinburgh; Hon. Fellow of Modern Language Association of America; Fletcher of Saltoun Medal; and Foyle Poetry Prize.

DAVID MURISON has been Editor of the *Scottish National Dictionary* since 1946 and is Senior Lecturer in Scottish Language in the Universities of St Andrews and Aberdeen.

CORDELIA OLIVER. Born Glasgow and educated Hutchesons' Grammar School and Glasgow School of Art, which she was allowed to attend (instead of the more acceptable Glasgow University) only by promising to "be a teacher". Was a wartime student when Art School was small and atmosphere unusually stimulating. Taught briefly and enthusiastically in girls' school and art school evening classes. After a two-year sojourn in London, lived in Edinburgh New Town during the fifties but returned to Glasgow in 1960 and now exists with one foot in each city. As a painter, she has exhibited at the R.S.A., R.A., Glasgow Institute, et al. She writes about Scottish Art and Theatre regularly in the *Guardian* and occasionally elsewhere.

ANTHONY ROSS. A native of Inverness-shire. Read History in Edinburgh University. Later joined the Order of Preachers, otherwise known as Dominicans or Blackfriars. Taught in schools in England for eight years. Roman Catholic Chaplain to students in Edinburgh since 1959. First Editor of the *Innes Review*, described by Professor H. J. Hanham of Harvard University as "one of the best of Scottish learned journals". A director of *Scottish International Review*. Vice-Chairman of the Parole Board for Scotland. For several years Chairman of the Edinburgh Branch of Telephone Samaritans. Member of the National Council of the Cyrenians. Member of the Executive of the Edinburgh Council of Social Service. Appears frequently on television. He is the author of various books and articles on Scottish History, theological questions and social problems.

ALEXANDER SCOTT. Born 1920, Aberdeen. Educated Aberdeen Academy, Aberdeen University. Army service 1941-5, awarded M.C. 1945. Edited *North-East Review*, 1945-6. Assistant Lecturer in English, Edinburgh University, 1947-8. Lecturer and then Senior Lecturer in Scottish Literature, Glasgow University, since 1948. Head of Department of Scottish Literature, Glasgow University, 1971. Co-editor, *Scots Review*, 1950-1, founding editor, *Saltire Review*, 1954-7. Edited *Selected Poems of William Jeffrey*, 1951, the poems of the sixteenth century Alexander Scott, 1952, and William Soutar's diaries in 1954. Author of *Still Life: William Soutar*, 1958. Three plays produced at Glasgow Citizens' Theatre in the fifties, five others published, and many more works performed on radio and television. Alexander Scott is the author of five collections of verse in English and Scots. Received Festival of Britain awards for poetry and verse drama, 1951; Arts Council and S.C.D.A. drama award, 1952; S.C.D.A. one-act play award, 1954; Scottish Arts Council award for *Cantrips* (poems), 1968. Co-editor (with Norman MacCaig) of *Contemporary Scottish Verse 1959-1969*, 1970. Reviews editor, *Knowe*, 1971–. General Editor, "The Scottish Library" (Calder & Boyars), since 1968. Secretary of the Universities Committee on Scottish Literature, 1968-71.

DERICK S. THOMSON. Born Stornoway 1921. Educated Nicolson Institute; Aberdeen University; Cambridge University; University College, Bangor. Taught in Universities of Edinburgh, Aberdeen and Glasgow. Professor of Celtic at Glasgow since 1964. Author of numerous books and articles on literary, linguistic, and historical topics in the Celtic field, e.g. *The Gaelic Sources of Macpherson's "Ossian", Branwen Verch Lyr, The Future of the Highlands* (ed. with Ian Grimble). Author of three books of Gaelic verse. Broadcaster. Editor of *Gairm*, the Gaelic quarterly, and of *Scottish Gaelic Studies*. Chairman of the Gaelic Books Council.

ESMOND WRIGHT. Educated Universities of Durham and Virginia. War service 1940-6 in Middle East, demobilised as Lt. Colonel. Lecturer (1946-51), Senior Lecturer (1951-7), and Professor (1957-67) of Modern History, University of Glasgow. M.P. (C) for Glasgow Pollok, 1967-70. Visiting Professor, University of Strathclyde. Director, Institute of United States Studies, and Professor of American History, University of London, from October 1971. He is the author of *Fabric of Freedom* (1961), *The World Today* (3rd edition 1971) and other books.